To
JAMES.

Best Wishes

My Story: The Rough and the Smooth

My Story: The Rough and the Smooth

ALAN ROUGH

with Neil Drysdale

headline

First published in 2006
by HEADLINE PUBLISHING GROUP

1

Cataloguing in Publication Data is available from
the British Library

ISBN-10 0 7553 1564 2
ISBN-13 978 0 7553 1564 2

Typeset in Stone Serif by Palimpsest Book Production Limited,
Grangemouth, Stirlingshire
Printed and bound in Great Britain by
Mackays of Chatham PLC, Chatham, Kent

Headline's policy is to use papers that are natural, renewable
and recyclable products and made from wood grown in
sustainable forests. The logging and manufacturing processes are
expected to conform to the environmental regulations of the
country of origin.

HEADLINE PUBLISHING GROUP
A division of Hachette Livre UK Ltd
338 Euston Road
London NW1 3BH

www.headline.co.uk
www.hodderheadline.com

For my mum, Jean, who was always there and for
Maggie who believed in me

Contents

Acknowledgements   ix

1 A Narrow Escape   1
2 Thrashing the 'Tic   17
3 In with the Auld   33
4 Scotland Dreams – and Nightmares   49
5 The Cocks of the North   67
6 Please Cry for Us, Argentina!   91
7 Picking up the Pieces   123
8 More Pain in Spain   143
9 Sunshine and Shadows   161
10 A World Cup Farewell   183
11 No time for Miller   205
12 Paradise and a Reality Check   219
13 The Cup that Boileth Over   237
14 Really Saying Something   253

Career Statistics   273
Index   289

Acknowledgements

I would like to thank the following people, all of whom were and have been inspirational to my career, both on and off the pitch.

Ally MacLeod; Jock Stein; Jimmy Dickie; Eddie McCulloch; Jackie Husband; Davie McParland; Pat Stanton; Bertie Auld; Donald McCorquodale; Davie Campbell; Jock Timpaney; Jay Crawford; Graeme Hunter; Randolph Caughie; Sunday Mail Picture Desk.

A Narrow Escape

I woke up slowly with only a vague sense of where I was. As I came to my senses, I gradually became aware of a group of people standing around my bed engaged in earnest discussions, apparently oblivious to the fact that I could make out only one or two words in every sentence they spoke. My arm felt incredibly sore. I couldn't move my limbs and a sick feeling engulfed me. Nurses and medical attendants sped in and out. I was in the emergency ward of Glasgow's Oakbank Hospital, and a stern-looking doctor was approaching me.

'How do you feel?' he asked.

'I don't know, mister, not too great, I suppose. What's happening?'

He gazed rather sorrowfully at me, his expression unchanged, and said in a 'there-is-no-alternative' monotone, which made me gasp: 'I'm sorry, but it is just too far gone. I am afraid that we are going to have to amputate your arm.' Not exactly what you want to hear.

I was ten years old. Numb with worry, already shocked and scared, and here I was being told that all my football dreams were being dashed even before they had really begun. My father and my grandfather both sought to re-assure me, but, as you can probably understand, I was inconsolable. In retrospect, I never considered that if I had lost my arm it would have affected a lot more than my football career and would have had a massive impact on the

1

rest of my life. All I could think about was that a one-armed goalkeeper is about as much use as a three-legged horse.

Only a few hours earlier, on that winter's day in 1962, I had been playing with my mates around Maryhill, in Glasgow. As usual, we had dumped our school books and our satchels and headed off to our secret world, a football park, our own private field of dreams (even if the majority of adults rightly regarded it as a midden). At that time I was a member of a little gang; we called ourselves the Tartan Army. I am not pretending we were angels, but we didn't go around vandalising phone boxes or smoking behind bicycle sheds: no, we were so obsessed with football that if we had been offered the slimmest chance of escaping from mundane reality to become soccer heroes, we would have grabbed it with both hands. Our mothers had kitted us out with wee tartan patches and, I guess, in some respects we were the forerunners of the Bay City Rollers (with more singing talent obviously – you've heard *I Have a Dream*, haven't you?). Thinking about it now, the words 'gang' and 'tartan patches' don't really go together, do they? In reality we were simply a rag-tag collection of youngsters with a collective passion for one sport and that was the game of Denis Law and Jim Baxter and Jimmy Johnstone.

One of my pals had once remarked to me: 'Alan, can you ever imagine playing for Scotland at Hampden Park in front of 100,000 supporters?' and they would tease me about how I used to get this faraway look in my eyes, as if I actually believed that I could go on to achieve that. But, almost from the time that I could walk football was my all-consuming passion, and why *shouldn't* I be starry-eyed?

But now, suddenly, in that hospital bed, I felt as vulnerable as you can imagine. On our way to our hidden pitch we had to climb up and down this slatted door, which was covered with sharp hinges. Normally we hardly even noticed these, let alone worried about them, but this time I slipped and lost my footing and crashed into one of them. I remember this searing jolt of agony as it ripped through my arm. I was screaming and yelling out: 'Help me, for God's sake, it hurts like hell.' And then, when I glanced down I saw the flesh had been pierced clean through to the bone . . .

Until something like that occurs, you never truly know how you will react, and it all happened so quickly. Unconscious, there was no time to reflect on what might become of me if the amputation went ahead. (Even forty-five years later, the prospect still induces a shudder.) All I do know is that if the original diagnosis had been acted upon, I would have missed out on being involved in three World Cups, and the chance to participate in one of the biggest Cup final upsets in footballing history. Nor would I have gone to Wembley to best the English in their own backyard, quite apart from meeting some of the greatest football performers across the planet and being privileged to share in some tremendous adventures from Maryhill to Mexico City.

Yet, for a few hours, there was the genuine possibility that I would be denied all these things, that I would lose my arm, and find myself consigned to a future without any expectations whatsoever. And that isn't some melo-dramatic analysis. It might come as a surprise to many – okay, maybe not – but my report cards from the local schools at Oakbank and Knightswood would testify that, while I was pretty quick with the banter, I was never likely to win many 'Brain of Britain' contests. But I have always been a practical, level-headed individual.

Besides, by that time in my life, the die was already cast. Every Saturday and Sunday, wherever we could find pitches, the only thought in our minds was to organise matches of six-a-side, or twenty-two-a-side, and the weather, the state of the facilities, or the prospect of looming exams, were irrelevant. It was another world, to be honest, and although I am certain there will be many youngsters who simply can't envisage existing without their mobile phones, or PlayStations, iPods or the Internet, the 1950s and 1960s in the west of Scotland offered equivalent, if more rudimentary pleasures. If it snowed and then froze, as it frequently did, we would use mounds of sand to mark out impromptu pitches; if it rained (as it even more frequently did), we would clamber over walls and sneak into car parks and school grounds and kick lumps out of one another on concrete. Luxuries extended to the occasional present of a new strip or a leather ball. You were considered pretty posh, in most parts of Glasgow, if you owned a telephone and television when I was born in 1951. As for fridges, washing machines and all the other electrical appliances which are nowadays taken for granted, let alone video recorders, microwave ovens, curling tongs (didn't need them!) and compact disc players, they were either beyond our ken or hadn't yet been invented.

Basically, we had football, and our mates, and from the moment the bell rang at school, and the two best players assembled everybody else together, picked their best pal, and then gradually moved down the line until there were two kids left, who invariably wound up as the goalies, nothing else entered our hearts or minds.

It really was that unpremeditated, and I had no particular inclination to be a goalie at the outset, considering it was hardly the most flamboyant or charismatic of roles, but I just had to get on with it. Within a matter of weeks I had grown hooked on the thought of being the man who stands between the striker and his objective, the last line of defence. There was something about the challenge which appealed to me, impervious to the abuse which used to be dished out at me whenever I conceded a goal, even if it was not remotely my fault. That's one piece of advice which I would recommend to anybody contemplating a career in keeping: don't do it unless you are prepared to bear the brunt of serious and sustained criticism and don't touch the job with a bargepole if you are a sensitive soul.

But, as I lay in Oakbank Hospital, and my family strove to console me, while a variety of doctors continued to discuss my fate, all I could think was that it was goodbye to the game I loved. I don't exaggerate: in the early 1960s, football was my life, I was completely enthralled by it, and my attention never strayed to anything else. Youngsters in Scotland nowadays have grass surfaces, Astroturf, and community centres, but we had none of these things and we didn't care. Our matches were fought out on red ash or on a selection of gravel and blaes surfaces and we competed on that stuff, week in, week out. I can remember many afternoons when I would be sitting in a spartan dressing room, picking bits of grit out of my legs, but we still considered ourselves fortunate. After all, we weren't living in the Gorbals and I never regarded myself as a victim of poverty.

On the contrary, I stayed in a new development in Lincoln Avenue and, because they reckoned there was precious little for us to do, the local parents, including my dad, Robert, and his friends, Archie Scoular and John Gilfinnan, rather than permit us to loiter around the flats and stumble into trouble, decided to establish a football club. We were no world-beaters, it's true, but we were passionate and committed and as hard as nails, and it kept us occupied. I am the last person to try and air-brush the depressing aspects of Glasgow life out of history – the Lincoln boys *were* high-spirited – but we managed to avoid crossing the line into hooliganism. Elsewhere the city was hardly a haven of tranquillity, and gangs were rife from the Drumchapel Cumbie to the Calton Tongs – they would convene on football parks on Sunday mornings and the ensuing mayhem was straight out of a spaghetti western. Without justifying their actions, they tended to keep their conflicts private, which, is a lot different from the current climate in which youths mug old women and worse. The bottom line is that I avoided becoming part of that scene because my parents, and their neighbours, had the good sense to find an outlet for their children's energy.

In addition, we were growing up in an environment where football was king. Neither myself nor my friends were interested in pursuing academic qualifications; the sole preoccupation we had was soccer. When people asked us what we wanted to do when we grew up, we hadn't an earthly beyond some blurry notion of scoring the winning goal in the eighty-ninth minute of the World Cup final or, in my case, saving the last-gasp penalty, which ensured that Scotland lifted the Jules Rimet Trophy. In reality, the probability was that, out of all those hundreds of kids who flocked to the pitches, come rain or shine at weekends, the vast majority were going to end up as coal miners, or road sweepers, or council employees, or pursue an apprenticeship. Yet most of us had this sprinkling of ambition, which sprang from the knowledge that Glasgow might have been viewed as the second city of the Empire, but I have always considered it the first city of football.

Okay, that may sound bumptious but I'm proud of my roots. Even though the Lincoln Avenue team quickly became the whipping boys in our catchment area, it was a hellishly competitive circuit. There were schools around us who were producing future internationalists of the calibre of Kenny Dalglish and Asa Hartford. Every kid who could master keepie-uppie worked his socks off to develop his own tricks, and if that meant escaping the possibility of a lifetime down the pit, could you blame them? Let's not forget that at school, I received ten sessions of PE a week (a figure which had fallen to four by the time I left). Although I may not have been the brightest lad in the classroom, I was tremendously fit and so were nearly all my peers.

In short, we were a carefree, harum-scarum crowd. When I wound up in hospital my parents, Robert and Jean, and the rest of my family were as dumbfounded as I was; we considered ourselves to be immortal. My father obviously was as shocked as anybody, but while it was clear that my injury was serious, he remained resolutely upbeat throughout the ordeal and he visited me as often as he could. His message was always the same – chin up, son, this will get sorted! From my perspective, I was just gone; I was in the depths of despair, and convinced that I would need the amputation. When you are ten and an authority figure such as a doctor comes along and uses fancy language to a child, you can hardly tell him he is talking rubbish, can you! (Probably still wouldn't today – if I understood him that is.) And yet, as the discussions continued over what was the best treatment for me, and yet more senior medical staff became involved, I recall wondering whether I was perhaps in with a chance after all.

I didn't build my hopes up – after they came and took X-rays, the hospital people weren't exactly dancing jigs of joy – but shortly afterwards, I noticed this doctor, wearing a green turban, standing over me and heard him telling me: 'Alan, I am sure we can fix this and we can sort it out, as long as you understand that you will have to show patience if it is to heal properly.' I was overwhelmed. It was as if a dozen Christmases had arrived at once, and despite my never discovering the name of that doctor who saved me, he commands my undying gratitude. He sewed me up, and subsequently talked to my parents, warning them that my recovery might take upwards of nine months, a forecast which proved unerringly correct. None of that mattered to me; I had been spared, I could start counting down the days and weeks until I was one hundred per cent fit again, and thank my lucky stars.

Perhaps it was a portent, because I have been blessed throughout my career in football. Frequently, at low points, the telephone has rung with a new challenge or an unexpected offer and that is why I always remind youngsters to remain optimistic and to be persistent; something will often turn up when you least anticipate it. If that makes me sound akin to a sporting Mr Micawber, so be it. I'm sure that by staying positive I've found myself in the right place at the right time. And sometimes, for whatever reason, the gods have chosen to hand a poisoned chalice to a rival.

I had decided to leave Knightswood Secondary as soon as possible and, as it transpired, just in time. A few weeks before my abrupt exit we were introduced to our new head of physical education, a chap wearing a large cravat, called Mr Dunlop, who announced that the new curriculum was going to revolve around hockey. You can imagine how well that little gem was greeted in the corridors and playground. I was out of there as quickly as Bart Simpson on his skateboard. I had already decided I was going to aim to become a full-time footballer and, if that didn't work, an electrician.

At that point, I was playing for Lincoln Avenue every weekend, and representing the Boys' Brigade whenever I was required. My dad's pal, the redoubtable Archie Scoular, an inveterate enthusiast, was also involved with an under-21 team, Avon Glen, who played down at Old Anniesland on Crow Road. Despite knowing that I was just fifteen, he heard that I had impressed several of our opposing clubs, even if I'd let in a hatful (remember, it is never the keeper's fault – it's those bloody defenders!), and phoned me one Saturday panic-stricken: could I step into the breach for his second side at the last moment, because his goalkeeper hadn't turned up?

This was clearly an opportunity to savour – Anniesland was a veritable sea of football on Saturdays and it was common knowledge that scouts from the professional scene would often cast their eye over half-an-hour of this or that game. Anyway, regardless of my callow years, I didn't disgrace Archie and kept a clean sheet with a series of decent saves. It just so happened that Jimmy Dickie, one of the senior Partick Thistle scouts, who had been despatched by his club to watch Glasgow University tackle Queens Park Strollers, only for the fixture to be postponed at short notice, caught sight of my display. He was sufficiently impressed to ask Archie if he could speak to my father. He requested some basic information and was initially under the impression that I was seventeen or eighteen. When he learned I was only fifteen he invited me, on the spot, to come along to training at Firhill with the Thistle squad the following week. I was gobsmacked, as you might understand, and yes, Lady Luck was smiling on me. Right place, right time, but there again, you have to capitalise on these situations. Suddenly I was in the frame, irrespective of how unfair my rapid elevation must have appeared to many of the equally talented lads who flocked to those packed Anniesland pitches.

When I eventually advanced into the Thistle reserve team,

I was seventeen. The then-manager, Willie Thornton, was forced to make a choice between me and another teenager, Billy Vance, for the keeper's jersey in an important tie against Celtic, who needed to win by a barrowload to displace Rangers in the section. I recollect the gaffer calling us together and saying: 'Look lads, I don't really think there is that much to choose between the two of you, but I am going to plump for Billy, because he boasts slightly more experience than you, Alan.' Given the circumstances in which I had been fast-tracked into the whole Firhill set-up, I wasn't especially disappointed at the news, and most emphatically not after the game itself. I'd avoided the poisoned chalice. Celtic won 12-0, and poor Billy was so crushed that he went away and became a plumber or something. It was the last time he featured in Partick's colours.

Naturally, it could have been me. I would probably have fared just as miserably. Yet, in a perverse fashion, the regular trials which I suffered amidst a heavy run of defeats, both at Knightswood Secondary and Lincoln Avenue, toughened me up mentally, and I was a pretty difficult customer to unnerve or ruffle. Prior to that trouncing at the hands of Celtic, I had been between the sticks the previous week for the Thistle reserve side against Rangers, which included another callow youth called Alex Ferguson. I conceded five goals during a dispiriting opening half, and was privately wondering how many they might stack up by the death. Instead, and to nearly everybody's amazement, we staged an astonishing recovery and finished with a creditable 5-5 draw. That was one of the first occasions when I recognised that life with the Maryhill Magyars was likely to prove one hell of a roller-coaster ride.

But what an adventure it was! On the first Monday night I was invited along to training I discovered there was nobody there and all the gates were locked. I instantly assumed I had been the victim of a wind-up, and then realised that Jimmy Dickie had actually said Tuesday. I was twenty-four hours too early. I should have known immediately I was ideally suited to the Jags! My introduction to Thistle was a crash course in moving from the sublime to the ridiculous. It often reached Olympian heights and plumbed Stygian depths (and sometimes in the same match).

I started out with their under-16 side, then advanced to a regular berth with Sighthill Amateurs which was a feeder team for Thistle's youngsters, who were looked after brilliantly by Eddie McCulloch. He was one of those wise, behind-the-scenes mentors whose influence is never recorded in banner headlines, but who was instrumental in developing people such as myself. He made us not simply better footballers, but better human beings as well. Nowadays, any volunteer has to grapple with an absurd amount of form-filling and red tape before being allowed to coach youngsters across the sporting spectrum, and if we aren't careful, we will drive away scores of talented people because of a few rotten apples.

Eddie was a joy to work with, and I have no hesitation in declaring that he was one of the biggest, most positive influences, on my career. Occasionally, if the weather was warm and sunny in July or August, he would drive six or seven of us to Saltcoats or Irvine, and buy us ice cream and bottles of Irn-Bru. Given that we had grown up in the grim, industrial behemoth which constitutes Glasgow, these excursions to the seaside were as close as we came to believing we were something special. This, remember, was in a distant past where going on a mystery tour to Burntisland and making ourselves sick on toffee apples and candyfloss was considered the height of sophistication.

The beetle-browed Eddie was devoted to football, but he appreciated that you can't earn respect by being a tyrant, particularly when dealing with young kids: a lesson which should be rammed down the throats of some of the hatchet-faced characters who have steered Scottish football down a spectacularly unsuccessful cul-de-sac in recent years. At Sighthill we grasped the reality that a club such as Partick could never equal the Old Firm in terms of spending power or fan base numbers, and that we had to thrive on other qualities: building camaraderie, instilling a never-say-die spirit amongst the troops, sweating blood for the man next to you, and never forgetting your roots and the people who ultimately paid your wages by shelling out their ticket money every week.

Surprisingly, I was rarely among that number as a ten- or eleven-year-old, although I would sometimes sneak into Firhill at the interval and collect the empty lemonade bottles for the redemption money. But once I was a teenager, I began to show a greater enthusiasm towards Thistle. They had a good side, including players of the calibre of George Niven, Neil Duffy and Sandy Brown, and by then the soccer bug had really infected me with a vengeance.

Scotland and Africa. Not immediately similar I'll grant you. But I detect parallels between my days as a keen youngster hoping to make it and the way so many of the African countries and former Eastern Bloc nations have sprinted up the global rankings on the back of a conveyor belt of ambitious, hard-working young men, who appreciate that the only means of rising above their background is to excel at sport in general and football in particular. The same phenomenon used to be present in Scotland, but something has gone awry. Our competitive edge isn't what it used to be; the majority of our youngsters have fallen out of the habit of getting their hands dirty, and while there is nothing wrong with texting your mates or e-mailing your friends – my programme on Real Radio would be in pretty poor shape if everybody was out on the football pitch rather than listening to our scintillating and erudite banter! (I think that's what the press release said anyway) – a proper balance has to be struck between sitting in front of computers and pulling on sports shirt and shorts.

Don't get me wrong, there were plenty of days where I thought to myself: 'No more. I'm chucking in this crap' when I was involved in matches, on full-sized pitches, at the age of nine, ten and eleven. It was crazy. I couldn't even reach anywhere near the crossbar, and all these wee strikers, they cottoned on to the situation quickly, and would just keep chipping the ball over my head. Goalies at that age were reduced to jumping up and down, like some demented kangaroo, with no chance of touching the ball, let alone stopping it hitting the net. Indeed, I recollect being involved in a BB final, and we were losing 10-0 at the interval, and I refused to go out for the second half, because I felt so embarrassed and humiliated. I was greetin' my eyes out and telling anybody who would listen: 'It's not fair', and, with hindsight, it wasn't. But, as I've said, these experiences toughened you up, and when people phone me nowadays and ask how I think a keeper should react after committing a howler, I always respond that: 1. what's he doing in goal if he's committing howlers, I never did . . . and 2. he has to dust himself down, ignore the taunts of rival fans, and practise as much as possible to prevent the scenario from recurring. Blaming others is not an option once you pull on the keeper's jersey. (Well, perhaps occasionally it is an option, and okay, maybe once or twice I shouted at my central defenders, but you know what I mean.) Right from the start there would be matches in the park where the spectators immediately looked accusingly at the goalie, whatever the circumstances, and regardless of whether the defence had stood flat-footed. It was the automatic reaction to fling pelters at the boy marooned between the posts. And that knowledge can make or break an individual.

Occasionally it bothered me as well, but I tried hard to prevent anybody from noticing that I might be struggling with any pressure. On the contrary, as I climbed up the ladder and developed an increasing affinity with the Thistle squad, I was determined that I would never be accused of shirking my responsibilities. After picking up the rubbish which accumulated on match days, the next step up was asking the Partick players if I could wash their cars. Then I would wait outside the dressing room and collect their autographs, and gradually, I forged relationships with some of the senior personnel. I believed that these people were as big as anybody at Rangers or Celtic. Why not? Partick may never have enjoyed the same worldwide fame and European success as the Old Firm, but those of us in that Sighthill squad in the late 1960s were as proud of our origins as any of the stars at Parkhead or Ibrox. Considering the disparity between the different organisations in Glasgow, I think that we were a credit to the city. We punched above our weight, we attracted a significant amount of families and students to Firhill, and there was none of the sectarian baggage which plagued the Old Firm, and which continues to be carried by their less enlightened, so-called fans.

Predictably, my father was always spurring me on and he would travel to every match, until it reached the stage where he was there at my shoulder at training nights, reserve fixtures, and whenever he felt he could encourage me. In my heart, I was grateful for his loyalty and faith in me and I knew that he only wanted the best for me and was acting out of familial affection. But when you are a teenager that constant parental presence can sometimes give you a bit of a red neck, and it reached the stage where I would say to him I wasn't playing on a particular day, so he wouldn't come along and cramp my style. Maybe that sounds mean, but he was desperate to be involved in every part of my development and was actually beginning to smother me. I had to be economical with the truth, without hurting him, because he was one hundred per cent in my corner from day one. And, if truth be told, I was thankful for his support.

Meanwhile, my career was progressing at a rate of knots. Two days after bringing me to Thistle, Willie Thornton left to be succeeded by Scot Symon. All I received was £8 a week in expenses at the outset, but I was on cloud nine and would have turned out for nothing, which was just as well, considering my subsequent experiences at Partick. I filled in the relevant forms, and I remember walking home from the ground to my home with this broad, beaming smile on my face, because I felt on top of the world. It didn't concern me that I hadn't scanned the fine print of my contract, but then I have never been obsessed with money. As the years rolled by, perhaps I should have been more careful in my financial dealings with football. These were the days however, long before the Bosman era, when you were tied in to ridiculously prolonged deals and a club could effectively do what they liked with you once they had your signature.

But all that was blissfully immaterial to me at the time. I was as blithe as a lark when I turned up for my first session as a full-time player, fresh-faced, keen as mustard and agog with anticipation. I was met by Davie McParland, one of Partick's stalwart performers. 'The guys are out on the pitch already, son, just go and join them,' he told me. So I hurriedly got changed, walked out onto the Firhill pitch and there they were, the men I had long viewed as my heroes – Sammy Kean, Neil Duffy and Frank Coulston – all lined up against a wall, having a fag, and generating enough smoke to leave that part of the park resembling a sauna. From which point, I realised that plying my trade at Partick was never going to be a drag.

2   THRASHING THE 'TIC

For my money, Partick Thistle have always been one of the more cherishable institutions in Scottish football. Whether being lampooned in *Taggart*, habitually linked with the scoreline 'Nil', or denigrated as the club of choice for that sizeable band of Glaswegians who prefer to keep their Old Firm affiliation hidden behind the Jags' cosy façade, those of us who have grown up in the bosom of the Maryhill brigade have heard all the gags in the joke book. You know what I am talking about: there was one wag who remarked that Thistle had been organising their annual reunion, but had to cancel it, because somebody had vandalised their phone box. And another who launched into disparaging references to Firhill, culminating in the punch line that Glasgow City Council had refused to have the stadium condemned until it was given a fresh coat of paint. Hah, bloody, hah!

But, as somebody who spent thirteen years as a professional at Partick, I can genuinely tell you that what we may have lacked in lavish facilities, we compensated for with lashings of hard graft and a collective joy in our work. Nobody did us any favours; the Firhill board was constantly having to struggle to balance the books, which invariably necessitated the sale of their most talented players. Whereas Celtic had entered the record books with their hallowed victory over Inter Milan in the 1967 European Cup final, and Rangers had gone close a few days later to emulating their achievement when they lost to Bayern Munich in the Cup-Winners' Cup final, Thistle seemed condemned to dwell on scraps of condescension.

Until, that is, the afternoon of 23 October, 1971, when we achieved what I still believe to be the most remarkable result in the history of Scottish football, by beating Celtic 4-1 in the League Cup final at Hampden. Since that momentous occasion I have seen our victory compared to Berwick's defeat of Rangers four years earlier or the more recent Inverness success over Celtic, which prompted the celebrated headline 'Super Caley Go Ballistic, Celtic Are Atrocious'. Yet personally, I rank Partick's win as being a far greater achievement, considering we were in a final, scrapping for silverware, not merely in an early round of a competition where surprises are always possible.

Even now I often bump into people who ask for my reminiscences of that autumn day, and there is occasionally an undercurrent of scepticism in their voices, almost as if they subconsciously believe that Celtic didn't turn up in spirit, or were so complacent that they handed us victory on a plate. They just can't seem to comprehend that Partick might have been a decent side, bolstered by a group of youngsters who would later wear Scotland jerseys. We were motivated, we were an ambitious bunch, we had nothing to lose against Celtic, and we had the shared philosophy that the worst thing we could do was to be diffident at Hampden and try to keep matters respectable.

For starters, a lot of us had risen through the ranks together via the Sighthill Amateurs, and all we desired was the opportunity to gain a first-team place as quickly as possible. I was one of those pitched in at the deep end, and although Thistle had already been relegated from the First Division when I made my debut in April 1970, I was still only eighteen, so it was time to soak up the lessons from those around me and demonstrate that I could handle the strain. I was absolved from any blame after we lost 2-1 against Morton at Firhill, but soon discovered the steepness of the learning curve I was on the following week, when we ventured to Somerset Park and I landed myself in a battle with the Ayr United striker, Dixie Ingram. Basically, he kicked lumps out of me, and at every corner clattered into my ribs. As there was no protection for keepers in those days, I was covered in bruises by the conclusion and as sore as hell the next day.

As it transpired, there was a postscript to that tussle, because we returned to the same stadium two years later having bounced straight back up after one season in Division Two, and Ingram was still up to his old tricks. At every corner and every free kick he launched himself at me and splattered me, until I was a bit dazed and confused. At the interval, Partick's senior players gathered round me, en masse, and spelt out the message: 'You'll need to do something about this guy, so sort him out.' They were all shouting and bawling at me, and I was so pumped up by the time I returned to the pitch, that I had probably convinced myself that I was stepping into the ring with Ken Buchanan. Thus, right at the beginning of the second half, Ayr attacked and there was a cross heading in my direction, with Ingram sprinting towards me, and I thought: 'Right, here's my chance.' So, I rushed out of my area and, instead of hitting the ball, smashed Ingram in the face and he crashed to the ground, pole-axed. Initially, I was feeling quite happy with myself, until my team mates dashed up to me and bellowed: 'What the f*** are you playing at, you headcase!' I was puzzled and replied: 'But that's what you told me to do.' To which Dave McParland said: 'Aye, but look at the f***ing ball.' And then I glanced behind me and saw, to my horror, it was nestled in the Partick net. I was hardly the flavour of the month on the bus home that night.

All the same, that incident should help serve as proof that we were hardly a group of shrinking violets. Throughout our promotion run in the 1970–71 season we had established the mindset that the team that kicks together sticks together and we were afraid of nobody. We had the right ingredients to flourish, with a clutch of youngsters such as myself, John Hansen, Ronnie Glavin and Denis McQuade bolstered by a string of more experienced characters. Marshalled by the formidable McParland, who was now the manager, we climbed straight back up to the top echelon with the minimum of difficulty. It was at that stage that we began to realise we could give any opponents a decent tussle – on our day. There still remained, however, a quixotic quality to our performances which ensured that our supporters continued to refine their gallows humour, but certainly, as the League Cup campaign progressed, we served notice that we were no slouches.

We also required stamina in those days, disposing of Arbroath, Raith Rovers, East Fife and Alloa en route to the last eight, and we had stacked up twenty-three goals from these tussles before we lost 2-0 in the first leg of our quarter-final meeting at St Johnstone. But it was a measure of our side that season that we never believed any cause was beyond salvation. When we entertained the Perth side in Glasgow, we dominated the contest from start to finish, and secured an emphatic 5-1 victory at which our supporters perked up, even if nobody was precipitate enough to suggest that Thistle's name would be on the Cup. After all, we had appeared in three previous finals of this tournament, and slumped in the lot, suffering defeats against East Fife, Celtic and Hearts. So we had no reason to be complacent as we entered into a semi-final joust with Falkirk, who had already disposed of Aberdeen, Dundee and Hibernian. But, with hindsight, I was quietly confident: we possessed a good blend to prosper in the knock-out competitions, with pace up front, solidity in the midfield and experience at the back (apart from the teenager in the goalie's gear!). And we duly advanced to the final with two goals from McQuade at Hampden, guaranteeing that the Bairns were in full teddies-out-of-prams mode on the short journey home.

Thistle, in contrast, were jubilant, but I still never bumped into a single person in the run-up to the final itself who genuinely believed that we could trouble Celtic, let alone beat them. You have to bear in mind that Jock Stein's team were feared and admired the length and breadth of Europe. They were racking up domestic titles with a mixture of clinical efficiency and aesthetic beauty from the likes of the immaculate Bobby Lennox, the tough-as-teak Tommy Gemmell, and the late, lamented Jimmy Johnstone. Although one or two of the Lisbon Lions had slipped into retirement, they had been replaced by such individuals as Kenny Dalglish and Lou Macari, so it wasn't as if there was the slightest hint that they might be vulnerable to Partick's menace.

Nor, in the early 70s, was there anything resembling the level of media coverage which has become an increasing feature of the sport on its advance into the twenty-first century. If anything, my preparations for meeting Celtic could hardly have been more prosaic, given that I spent the morning taking my BB team to a game – which they won 3-2. And no, I wasn't playing – I was young, but not *that* young. I helped coach the boys in my spare time. Meanwhile, at home, my mother Jean had ironed my kit and packed by bag in readiness for me heading off to join the rest of the Partick squad at Esquire House for a pre-match meal. If it sounds unglamorous, then the positive aspect of being low-key is that there is no pressure. Yet there was something simply surreal about what happened when I jumped on to the No 11A bus at Knightswood.

I remember sitting in the top deck, and all around me were Celtic supporters, festooned in their scarves and strips and singing their anthems. They didn't have a clue who I was, and the general tone of their conversations ranged from 'We'll murder this lot' to 'How did Partick Thistle get this far anyway?' Or words to that effect – the language might have been a tad more colourful. Eventually, they cottoned on to me, possibly sparked by the fact I was staying silent and attempting not to attract their attention. It hardly helped that I was wearing my lucky, multi-coloured jacket, which was about as inconspicuous as an explosion in a fireworks factory. I remember a couple of their more middle-aged aficionados asking me: 'Well, are you are going to Hampden to watch the Bhoys collect another trophy?' But I just smiled, and mentioned that I had to meet my family for a meal, and hoped they enjoyed a pleasant afternoon.

Frankly, it wasn't the time or the place to be shooting my mouth off. By and large, this was the kind of response we had grown used to at Partick: the Old Firm had bigger fish to fry than worrying over dear old Thistle, and I definitely reckon that attitude helped me to stay pretty relaxed as the kick-off beckoned.

Obviously, anyone who tells you that they don't feel a few nerves when they are poised to walk out in front of 60,000-plus supporters, is lying. But I was so thrilled to be involved in an occasion of this magnitude that I revelled in the atmosphere. Frankly, I have never been afraid of failure in football – ultimately, we are not heart surgeons or nuclear technicians. For a nineteen-year-old to be granted the opportunity to walk in the footsteps of legends was mind-blowing. Yes, there was a terrific din and clamour from the sidelines, but it didn't affect me adversely, and I guess that you don't worry unduly about a few boos emanating from strangers in the crowd when you have had a couple of hundred parents hurling abuse at you for letting in a soft goal on a red ash pitch. My approach was to say to my colleagues: 'Let's go out there and do ourselves justice, because nobody expects us to win this match.'

And that was the general vibe in the dressing room. Dave McParland had advised us that it would be crucial to keep the elusive Johnstone on a tight leash (we could have guessed that, boss), and Ronnie Glavin was assigned the task of marking the diminutive winger, while we could derive some comfort from the fact Celtic were missing their talismanic skipper, Billy McNeill, who was unfit. Looking at the team sheets, it would have been easy to grow apprehensive, if not downright terrified; but, on that particular afternoon, I don't recall any frisson of anxiety amongst our personnel. Rather, there was a shared acceptance that these kind of high-profile encounters don't materialise very often for Partick Thistle, so it was time to step up to the plate and do our club proud.

I think you could say we did that in the opening half-an-hour of the contest. First, Alex Rae, a coiled spring, confounded Evan Williams with a twenty-yard lob for the first goal in the tenth minute; then Bobby Lawrie, a pacy, dangerous presence at his best, cut inside Davie Hay and slotted the second in the fifteenth; almost immediately thereafter, Johnstone had to leave the field with an ankle injury, which ended his involvement in the proceedings. As the swaggering self-confidence began to disappear from the favourites, Thistle cranked up the momentum and on the half-hour mark, a corner from the ubiquitous Lawrie was headed on by Rae. The ball went off Frank Coulston to Denis McQuade, and his deflection finished up in the net. Six minutes later, Jimmy Bone added a fourth and the hush from the Celtic faithful suggested that they were as dumbfounded as their heroes by the fashion in which we had seized the initiative and so clinically, emphatically, rammed home our advantage.

Amidst this fantastic tale of the unexpected – even Frank Capra might have balked at such a script – I was standing up the other end, but I could have been sitting in a deck-chair reading the *Daily Record* for all that I was asked to do. When Rae established our lead, I was like: 'Hang on, we've scored', and as I craned my neck and surveyed our onslaught, I had to battle hard to keep my emotions in check. 'Jeez, there's another one,' involuntarily spilled from my lips as Lawrie doubled our lead, and by the stage of McQuade and Bone's efforts, I was rubbing my eyes and exclaiming: 'Oh my God, Oh my God, what on earth is happening here?' In fairness, it wasn't all one-way traffic. Celtic created a couple of chances, but the disbelief on their faces was only surpassed by the funereal reception from the vast majority of their fans inside the national stadium, and the hollering and whoops of delight from the Partick patrons, most of whom probably wouldn't have been surprised with a 4-0 half-time scoreline . . . but not in their favour.

As we walked into the dressing room at the interval, I have to admit I have never witnessed so many stunned expressions and, honestly, there was no singing or prema-ture celebration from us during that period. If anything, the mood was more bemused and bewildered than anything else – had we *really* gone out there and stuck four past Celtic? Inwardly, the lot of us were perfectly aware that, given our reputation, we could still end up losing 6-4 or 7-4. But credit to McParland, he didn't attempt any Churchillian speeches or try discussing tactics, but allowed us to collect our thoughts and catch our breaths, before telling us quietly as we steeled ourselves for the resumption: 'You have done half the job, lads. I am proud of you. Now finish it.'

In other surroundings, on another afternoon, caution might have been advisable, but one suspected there was something special in the air that Saturday for those whose allegiance lay with the Thistle. I was fairly confident that we could weather the anticipated storm awaiting us upon the resumption. We knew enough about Jock Stein to appreciate that he must have been incandescent at the break. Yet we all felt we boasted the requisite reserves of resilience, tenacity and courage to hold them at bay.

Sure enough, they hammered away at us, and carved out a number of opportunities, but the lads refused to buckle, they kept their shape and retained their composure, and we certainly didn't spend forty-five minutes being forced to cling on for dear life. I produced one good save to repel Lou Macari and followed that with another to deny Kenny Dalglish, but this was no Siege of Mafeking, and as Stein's team streamed forward, we could actually have increased our tally. The bottom line is that anybody who still clings to the idea that our victory was a fluke should face reality. Yes, eventually, after seventy minutes, Dalglish broke Celtic's duck, but there was to be no miraculous recovery, and it is doing a disservice to Partick to pretend that this was anything other than a magnificent performance, full of guts and chutzpah and derring-do from the underdogs. And the majority of the Celtic fans – or at least those who waited for the final whistle – acknowledged we were entitled to bask in a rare glow of triumphalism.

It was only later we discovered that a BBC sports announcer had refused to believe the interval score, and tartly informed viewers that the network would 'check it out'. And I have since heard ample anecdotal evidence of similar incredulity across the world's media, as the news filtered down a hundred phone lines from Hampden. Yet, as we marched up to collect the League Cup, and I gazed at the players within touching distance, there was no reason for us to feel we had been the recipients of a charitable donation from our opponents. Admittedly, Celtic made us pay a heavy price whenever we locked horns in the years ahead under Stein, but I was thrilled at the displays of such stalwarts as Alex Rae and Hugh Strachan and Jackie Campbell. It is impossible to convey adequately the excitement and exhilaration which we felt at the climax.

None the less, it was evident as we waltzed towards our supporters with the trophy that the outcome was a shock to everybody: our fans, the bookies, the sporting press, and even Partick's own committee. In the circumstances, we were entitled to celebrate with a traditional open-top bus parade, but our officials were caught short. Nobody had booked such a vehicle, maybe unsurprisingly, so we had to commission a single-decker bus (it could only happen at Thistle), and attempted to clamber through the skylight. However, we couldn't fit through the hole, so there was more than a semblance of farce as the news filtered across Glasgow that Thistle had whipped the mighty Celts. Eventually, a few of us managed to clamber on to the top of the bus, but it was a wee bit embarrassing – we were driving along and people in the street were watching and wondering who the hell we were. It struck home then that most Glaswegians were probably drowning their sorrows (the Celtic ones) or celebrating in Govan (the Rangers fans) or still around Hampden (the Thistle supporters), and we were waving a trophy to complete strangers. When we returned to Firhill, we found the place locked and we were baffled as to where the crowds might be. Then we began to notice a few stragglers wending their way, somewhat unsteadily, back towards Maryhill, and they informed us that there were indeed scores of Jags aficionados still supping merrily in the pubs around the scene of our triumph.

So yes, it was chaotic, and later that evening the players went out with their wives and girlfriends and we toasted our triumph in Royal Exchange Square and wished that we would have bottled these memories forever. Yet, amidst the hysteria and the festivities, we soon realised that our Cup success would be a double-edged sword. Dave McParland and the cream of his squad would now be household names. This meant that there was little doubt the bigger Scottish and English clubs would come calling with their chequebooks and that the squad was likely to break up in a matter of months.

Late on that Saturday I had a chat with a couple of the younger lads, and we all agreed that we might not defeat Celtic too often, but there was more exhilaration and optimisim on that particular October afternoon than in any number of humdrum league fixtures. Basically, we were a collection of ambitious youngsters, in search of stardom. None of us had appeared in a senior Cup final before, so we were precocious, and we weren't intimidated by the opposition, the setting or the atmosphere, because we had nothing to measure it against. And, without tooting my horn too vociferously, quite a few of us, myself, Ronnie Glavin, Jimmy Bone, Alex Forsyth, John Hansen and Denis McQuade, went on to represent Scotland. So it wasn't as if we were a bunch of no-hopers, content for one solitary shot at glory before slipping back into the shadows. This was a Partick team who refused to be bracketed as one-hit wonders. The only sad thing was that I alone stayed at Thistle, although even that part of the story could have been transformed within the next seventy-two hours. I still wonder from time to time what might have happened if I had moved on from Firhill.

Once the celebrations had concluded, and the Alka-Seltzer had done the trick the next morning, we were quickly forced to accept that we were transient heroes, and that it was business as usual on Tuesday, prior to tackling Dundee on the Wednesday night. At this stage, I didn't drive, but preferred to travel by public transport. As I headed along for training, I saw this car pull up outside the ground and recognised the gentleman who climbed out of it – it was Terry Neill. He was at Hull City and, I subsequently discovered, had come to Glasgow for the express purpose of signing me. After I had burnt up some of the calories amassed since the canapé-munching commenced on the previous Saturday, McParland called me into his office. 'Hello Alan, sit yourself down, I have just had a chat with Terry Neill,' he said. 'He was doing his best to persuade us to sell you to Hull, but we didn't think £50,000 was a good enough offer, so we have turned it down.'

That was it, no further discussion, end of story, and yet it was a decision which would have ramifications for the rest of my life. After all, I was sufficiently confident in my abilities to believe that if I had gone down to England, I would have made a favourable impression and who knows what trajectory my career might have taken? But, on the other hand, I had to bear in mind that Partick Thistle had shown the vision to sign me up in the first place, on the sole recommendation of Jimmy Dickie, and that, if I persevered, kept working on my fitness and sharpened up my game, there would surely be other clubs, better offers and bigger transfer bids in the years ahead.

Apart from which, it wasn't as if I was desperate to extricate myself from Firhill. OK, so we were consistent only in our inconsistency and we did have a tendency to flirt wildly from one extreme to the other (a week after thrilling the nation with our giant-killing exploits, we were demolished 7-2 by Aberdeen at Pittodrie – terrible defending of course; I was just unlucky to let the odd seven sneak past me . . .), but we had gained an inkling of celebrity. Everybody wanted us, and the following summer we found ourselves being invited on a pre-season tour abroad to Malaysia and Indonesia. This was obviously a massive stride into the unknown for players whose concept of world travel extended only as far as a fortnight in Bute at the Glasgow Fair.

The flight seemed to last forever, and once we had touched down, we discovered that we had been booked into a luxury hotel complex. Despite a stern warning from McParland that we should strive to grab some sleep and stay in the shade – the temperature was 105 degrees – we were like a group of kiddies on a trip to Disneyland and his plea was as futile as if he had told us not to call room service, or open the mini bar. As usual Dave was right. Irrespective of the fact that we knew we had a match lined up the following day against the Malaysian national XI, we swanned around the pool, sun-bathing as if we had never glimpsed the sun before (well, hailing from Maryhill . . .). Result? We were collectively burnt to a cinder. We had no lotions or creams to protect us from the baking heat, and while the fact that most of the locals chose to stay indoors should have alerted us to the threat, we were as naïve as we were carefree, as devil-may-care as we were daft. Nowadays, I would never dream of travelling abroad without a suitcase-load of every substance designed to prevent skin cancer, but how many of us in our forties and fifties can honestly proclaim that we didn't feel immortal at twenty?

But my God, we suffered that evening and the next morning. I recall us turning up at the stadium and when we took off our clothes to get changed, we were the colour of lobsters; the pain was unrelenting. McParland had no sympathy, and offered a fairly decent impersonation of a raging bull once he had surveyed the evidence that we had ignored his advice. But how he must have secretly laughed at the nature of our punishment. We had to perform in front of 80,000 spectators and couldn't touch the ball without feeling as if we were treading on hot coals. It was worst for the outfield players – whenever one of our lads had to chest the ball or make a tackle, and their limbs came into contact with the grass, all you heard was 'Ya bas, ya bas, ouch, ouch, ouch,' or a series of variations on that theme, with language unsuitable for pre-watershed audiences. To our credit, we clung on, and secured a 1-1 draw, and the Malaysian fans were tremendous and treated us as if we were Manchester United or Celtic or Rangers, pursuing us for autographs and cheering us all the way from the ground back to our hotel. All in all we felt as if we had enhanced Partick's name.

Our reward arrived the next morning when one of the Thistle directors, Colonel Jimmy Graham, called the team together, praised us for our exertions in stifling conditions, before adding that he thought we all looked exhausted, and therefore deserved a spoonful of sugar to act as a balm. This bluff old cove had noticed, among an extensive range of amenities within our five-star accommodation, a 'Massage Parlour', and informed us that he was treating us all to a free session, where we could relax and shed our tension and inhibitions. And who were we to spurn the gentleman's generous offer? Possibly, he imagined that everything in this parlour was above board, but, of course, it was a knocking shop with a range of 'extra services' provided on request. I can assure you that we all emerged with beatific smiles on our faces, and it was nothing to do with inner calm!

That excursion was one of the fringe benefits of our League Cup success. Another was the fact that Partick duly qualified to compete in the second UEFA Cup (it had hitherto been known as the Fairs Cup). We were drawn against

Honved, the famous Hungarian Army collective of the mid-1950s, whose ranks had once been graced by the little Galloping Major himself, Ferenc Puskás. It seemed a formidable proposition – and so it transpired – but what was really striking about these experiences was the manner in which Thistle had grown accustomed to being known in parts of the globe which we couldn't even have pinpointed on a map. As for the players, it was mind-blowing: we were used to walking into airports, we had passports and visas, and this was the gateway to an entirely new world for people such as myself. I remember telling my father that I was popping over to Hungary, and he simply looked up from his newspaper, remarked 'That's nice, son,' and continued reading. It was incredible how quickly what had once been exotic became almost routine and yet that was one of the definite pluses of the period. Low-cost air travel meant that, suddenly, the globe shrunk and it certainly broadened my mind to new cultures and backgrounds.

As for Honved, that was an anti-climax, both on and off the pitch. They were a decent side, but the country was grim, the Iron Curtain was securely drawn, and while we were only there for a few days, we all reached the same verdict: the place was a dump, a drab, featureless void. We just felt sorry for the people who had to live there and cope with the realities of nothing on the supermarket shelves, the misery of endless queuing, and their quiet desperation. We were mere interlopers and could escape, but there was no release for the locals and that saddened me, as much as it did to witness the one-armed children forced to beg for scraps in Kuala Lumpur. We tried to help them, and their eyes lit up at receiving what they regarded as fortunes and what we considered to be nothing but a few pounds, but you were invariably left with the impression that football was used to mask a morass of social problems and appalling poverty in many parts of the globe, and that assuredly applied to Hungary.

The stadium summed up the nation: it was poor, it was lacking in any kind of character – Firhill was akin to the Maracana, by comparison – and it ponged, it really, seriously stank. There was no indication the place had been cleaned in months, and it smelled like a sewer. When I walked into our dressing room, which was stripped bare of anything but the most Spartan amenities, I wrote my name in indelible ink above my coat hook, and, do you know, it was still there when I returned to the ground sixteen years later with Celtic in 1988. Indeed, it was one of the quirks of my career that I only appeared in European matches twice, and both were against Honved, a coincidence that would, I suppose, make a decent pub trivia question.

As for the match itself, we acquitted ourselves fairly well in the first leg and we left Hungary trailing by a solitary goal. But revolution was in the air at Partick and, as some of us had feared, the nucleus of the 1971 team was vanishing elsewhere. We simply had to grit our teeth and keep playing, but Honved won comfortably in Glasgow and, in truth, there was nothing romantic about that short-lived Cup experience. On the contrary, it was a portent of what lay ahead for me at Firhill as my pals left me behind.

IN WITH THE AULD

The League Cup success might have put Partick Thistle on the map, but, as I've said, it proved to be the catalyst for a gradual exodus of our leading youngsters. Ronnie Glavin joined Celtic, Alex Forsyth went to Manchester United, and almost every week that I headed into Firhill, gossip was circulating about another farewell on the horizon. It was a strange feeling, because while I had received a string of complimentary reviews for my goalkeeping prowess both from my peers and the media, I seemed stuck in a perpetual groove with Partick, although that wasn't necessarily a bad thing. The club invariably survived rather than thrived, operating on a hand-to-mouth basis which guaranteed there were plenty of Monday mornings when I awoke, unsure of whether I was on the verge of a windfall or a catastrophe.

Our inspirational manager, Dave McParland, also made his exit en route to the backroom at Parkhead, and that heralded the arrival at Thistle of one of the more charis-matic characters in the club's history, albeit an individual with whom I shared a tempestuous relationship. Bertie Auld, late of the Lisbon Lions, an aficionado of cigars, quips and cracking the whip when the mood took him – which was often – certainly livened up the Firhill dressing room. In the intervening years, I have met him regularly at football dinners and other functions, and we have since forged a relationship which is rather different to the one we enjoyed when we were hurling abuse at each other during his tenure in Maryhill.

As soon as he swaggered through the Firhill portals at the start of 1974, it was spelt out, Sinatra-style, that he would do things his way and dissenting voices could go in search of a new employer. From the outset I knew he would probably regard me as being a bit laid-back and confuse that with a lackadaisical mindset, but I hadn't prepared myself for the fashion in which he would rule by fear and induce trepidation amongst nearly everybody who worked with him. He had absorbed a lot from Jock Stein, which was understandable, but, while he had mastered the Big Man's impersonation of Vesuvius in full spate when annoyed, there was little trace of the humanity and essential warmth which were vital components in Stein's psyche. Instead, he was the sort of manager who simply inspires fear. On one occasion he drove one of our players, Bobby Houston, into such a state of nervous agitation that he locked himself in the toilet at half-time and refused to come out from behind the bowl. He simply couldn't abide any more abuse from the gaffer. Bertie thrived on adrenaline and testosterone and expected his charges to follow suit.

Personally, I rolled with the punches and refused to be intimidated, which only irritated Bertie all the more, and if there was a love-hate association going on, it was his creation, because I simply couldn't bring myself to view football as a matter of life and death. Every day, on the road from my home to Firhill, I would pass ambulances and fire engines speeding to emergencies, or watch some poor bugger risk his life on a rickety piece of scaffolding at a construction site, and reflect to myself: 'That could be me, and yet a football club is actually paying me decent money to stand in front of an empty net.' (Well, empty as long as the opposition ball wasn't nestled in the corner.) Don't misunderstand me, once

I was in the heat of the action, I was as committed to the cause as anybody, but this notion that you could only offer your best by cursing and swearing and scaring the daylights out of anybody at a hundred paces was absurd.

At times, to be blunt, I was curious as to why he didn't sell me and be done with it, given the friction and frisson between us. It was only later in my career that I discovered that there had been inquiries about me from the likes of Coventry City, Sunderland and Sheffield Wednesday, but Auld had told them all to piss off in his usual tactful manner. Against Bertie you needed the hide of a rhinoceros, because he took his criticisms to the extreme. Some of the things he said were downright unacceptable and wouldn't be tolerated in the modern age. From the moment he stepped into the manager's office I had constant run-ins with him. I was always getting punishment, whether it was to turn up for training, morning, afternoon and evening, five days a week (for a princely £35) or a spell in the reserves for three months, on some spurious grounds that I wasn't displaying the requisite application. I recall asking him one day, after we had exchanged a deluge of unpleasantries: 'What the f*** is your problem?' And he just glanced back at me, shrugged his shoulders, and retorted: 'Son, I've made you a better keeper and you should be grateful for that.'

The jury has to remain out on that contention. I suppose, with hindsight, that Bertie did command respect, but it was only as a consequence of him employing the hair-dryer technique at half-time. More than one Saturday when I was trying to engage in a discussion his response was to fling a hot pie in my face. Try maintaining your dignity when you are covered in bits of pastry and gristle and grease (not that I'm saying Firhill pies weren't of the highest quality you understand) – believe me, it is immensely difficult. Neither did it help that the Partick Thistle dressing room was a huge place. When Bertie was finished haranguing one corner, he would move along and start tearing the next group to shreds. Often, I used to piss myself laughing, but if you had made a mistake or if the team was performing badly – which wasn't an irregular occurrence – you never wanted to be the first to go through the door at the interval, because you knew you were going to be walking into a torrent of bile, flak, spittle (and sometimes gristle!). It was basically tyranny.

We had one lad, Denis McQuade, a hero of the League Cup triumph, and nicknamed by some as the Enigma of Firhill, who had been studying for the priesthood and he was as bright as a button. He would confront Bertie head-on, not with expletives, but intelligent, reasoned debate, which provoked even greater fury. The trouble with Denis was that he would embark on those lovely, mazy runs and weave past four or five adversaries, only to surrender possession, from which the opposition would often score. This drove Bertie, a defensive-minded fellow, to utter distraction. So whenever he cornered McQuade later and bawled at him: 'What the f***ing f*** were you f***ing trying to do there, you c***?', Denis would look at him, almost sympathetically, and reply: 'Well, Mr Auld, I thought my *raison d'être* was to be the catalyst for our attacking forays, so what do you think is wrong with my modus operandi?' The rest of us just cracked up. It left Bertie rampaging around the room, muttering about how Denis had swallowed a dictionary and how he would have been better employed in a seminary. At least if he was spitting the dummy at McQuade it guaranteed the rest of us a brief reprieve.

Yet, more commonly, the Auld approach to man-management cast a pall over the whole dressing room, and grown men would be frightened of airing their grievances or retaliating when Bertie was on hyper drive. He always wore his European Cup winners' medal around his neck on a chain – the king of bling before the term was even coined – and when he was involved in a verbal dispute and was losing the argument, he would whip out his medal and pronounce: 'Have you got one of these, son, have you?' It was his party piece. One Saturday, when we were playing Rangers, one of our youngsters, Tony Higgins – now the highly respected head of the players' association in Scotland – was suffering a pretty miserable game, and everything he tried seemed to come to naught. What wasn't in doubt was the fact he was giving one hundred per cent. Nevertheless Tony, as conscientious and decent an individual as you will encounter in the sport, was predictably chewed to pieces by Bertie, ruthlessly and efficiently. He sat there for what seemed like an eternity, being the butt of Auld's diatribe. 'Jeez son, you are having a nightmare, aren't you. What the f*** were you thinking about with that pass? Why the f*** didn't you do this?' And so it continued, the master of invective destroying his prey. Eventually, Tony mumbled: 'Well sorry, Mr Auld, but I am doing my best, and I will strive to do better.' At which point, his tormentor exploded once more, until Higgins could tolerate the barrage of abuse no longer and spoke up: 'What the f*** are you doing here at Partick, anyway?' It was a brave act of defiance, but we all knew what Bertie's reaction would be and, sure enough, he produced his medal, and bawled in Tony's face: 'I've got this, look at it, just look at it! Have you got one of these, have you, have you!!'

By this stage, Higgins, who was normally as quiet as a church mouse at these half-time briefings, stood erect and screeched back: 'Naw. And as long as you are the manager here and running this club like a madman, there is not a f***ing chance in the world that I will ever get one.' Some of us felt ready to burst into applause. Others looked down at their boots and tried to remove imaginary specks of dirt. You could have cut the tension with a knife, but, to his credit, Tony played a blinder throughout the second period and there was a grudging nod of approval from the manager at the death, which said more than a thousand words.

In these circumstances, it was inevitable that Thistle failed to capitalise on their 1971 success, beyond remaining financially afloat, an achievement in itself. They went through a veritable conveyor belt of personnel, and, in fairness, Bertie's belligerence drove us upwards in adversity. When we won the re-constituted First Division title in 1976, much of it was due to his sheer bloody-mindedness. He knew the biscuit tin was full of crumbs and the only means of remaining in existence was to sell a couple of his prime assets every season. In that light, I could be accused of having a dearth of ambition by staying at Firhill. But the contract situation in those days was incredibly biased in favour of the club and not the individual player. You would sign a three-year deal, with perhaps an eight-year option on it, and once your signature was on that paper, that was you stymied. In retrospect, I could have agitated for a transfer if I had really desired one, but, given my connections with Partick and the manner in which the supporters had started to regard me as some kind of folk hero, why would I want to desert them? Let's face it, my lifestyle, for somebody in their early twenties, was pretty enviable. I would turn up at 9.30am, train until 12.30pm, have an ice cream or an Irn-Bru, then saunter off to play snooker or golf, and grab a bag of chips. To me that was luxury, especially in comparison to most of my mates, who were slogging their guts out, on construction sites or digging drains. Remember, this was a turbulent period in British society, when the trade unions and the government were at each other's throats, when the country had endured a three-day week and industrial action was rife. It was a time when the highlights of the television schedules were *Billy Smart's Circus*, *On the Buses*, and *The Black and White Minstrel Show*. More entertainment could be found on a wet and cold Saturday afternoon at Firhill – and that's saying something. Compared to all that, an occasional spat with Bertie Auld was a stroll in the park.

As the years passed, it developed into a game of cat and mouse between Bertie and me. I loved going out and enjoying a social evening, but as soon as Thistle travelled anywhere and Auld announced, in stentorian tones: 'There is a curfew tonight', it was a challenge which I couldn't ignore. I reckon that he did it deliberately with me, because we would regularly go up to the Highlands, to tackle Brora or Inverness or whoever, and he would issue dire warnings as to what would happen if he caught any of us sneaking out of the premises. One time my hotel room was three storeys up, and I discovered it had a tiny veranda, at which point I spotted this set of ladders and tip-toed downstairs and moved them discreetly under my window. Then, when we were all supposed to be tucked up snugly in our beds, I crept down the rungs and was out until 2am.

The trouble was that Bertie, like Jock Stein, was a smart man, with a keen insight into human nature, an expert at rumbling where his players were and when they might be wandering off the straight and narrow. That time, for instance, he had nipped out himself for a modest libation. The trick was to get back to the hotel before him, and I reckoned I had managed to pull the wool over his eyes. Once I had climbed back up to the veranda, however, I suddenly heard Bertie laughing below me on the ground. He had discovered that I had gone AWOL and locked the veranda door, so I was stuck outside my room on that narrow perch until 10am, in the middle of winter, and I was frozen to the marrow. Nor could I raise any objections, as he fully appreciated. I had chanced my arm and been rumbled.

It didn't stop me, however. In my opinion – and it was shared by several of my contemporaries – curfews were for war-ravaged cities, not footballers. Hand on heart, I was sufficiently professional to understand that you had to be conscious of your health and that no player could survive unscathed if he yielded to temptation and knocked back a dozen pints on the night before a match. These nocturnal escapades centred less on alcohol, and more on demonstrating to Bertie that I wasn't going to be confined to quarters and treated like a naughty child. On several occasions he latched on to my plans, and there were other times when I gained the upper hand and enjoyed a quiet pint and a chat with the locals, while he was back at base, parked around the hotel entrance, spying for miscreants.

One fight the players were never going to win, though, was in trying to dictate financial terms with the manager. Every year at the start of a new season we held signing talks with the gaffer, when we had to enter his lair and discuss the possibility of a salary rise. Prior to one of these meetings the fee we decided to settle for was £50 a week. Charlie Smith drew the short straw and had to go in first. The rest of us were sitting outside the office and we overheard Bertie being remarkably amiable: 'Hi there, Charles, sit yourself down and let's have a chat – what are you looking for in your wage packet this year?' To which Smith replied: 'Well, I am actually asking for fifty quid a week.' Then, suddenly, we heard one of those laughing machines being switched on – the kind you still find inside those talking Santas – and the room was filled with the sound of 'Ho, Ho, Ho'. Wee Bertie had opened a drawer and pressed a button. Charlie could go and whistle. Of course we were all deflated and yet, looking back, I guess at least he had made his point without having to open his mouth.

Bertie was an absolute expert when it came to money. I was on a weekly wage of £40 for about six years, and although we were always striving to up the ante, we would probably have enjoyed more luck with Scrooge. Early in Bertie's reign I remember Thistle going on a pre-season tour to Inverness, where Jackie Campbell and Hugh Strachan, and a few of the other experienced players, convened us together. 'Right lads, this is it, there is a lot of cash coming into the club through various sponsorships, and we are entitled to a share of it – what we'll do is draw up a list of fourteen or fifteen demands and that way, if we end up getting four or five of them, it will be a positive step forward.'

We reckoned this was a pretty cunning wheeze, and prepared the agenda, with various suggestions. Towards the end of our discussions, Bertie appeared and asked what the hell was going on. Undeterred, Jackie told him: 'We would like you to take a look at this, gaffer, and give these proposals to the board.' He acquiesced, or so it appeared, accepted the list and shut the door behind him, leaving us all feeling fairly happy with the situation. Two minutes later, the door opened again, and a hand came in, and hundreds of little shreds of paper descended around us like confetti, together with four words: 'Get that up ye!'

Jackie just sat with this incredibly demoralised expression on his face, muttering: 'What can you do with that guy? He's a f***ing nightmare.' Then we burst out laughing, because it seemed the only appropriate response in the circumstances. What else were we going to do? Go on strike? Call a secret ballot? The fact of the matter was that this was a million miles removed from the days of David Beckham and Wayne Rooney, or even Paul Gascoigne and Andy Goram. Nobody ever joined Partick if they harboured dreams of becoming a millionaire.

But, if it was never a lucrative pastime, it was similar to being on a permanent holiday in a big playground, and I was blessed to ply my trade on the swings and the roundabouts. I was allowed twenty years at the highest level, whereas many others only lasted a few months. Away from Firhill, I was also being noticed at international level, and starting to gain under-23 caps as part of a very talented Scotland line-up – with players such as Graeme Souness, Kenny Dalglish, Gordon McQueen, Joe Jordan and Asa Hartford. Being a part of that exalted company was another reason why I never yearned to leave Partick.

I realised pretty quickly that the only way to escape being forever bracketed as the goalie with the curly perm who played in the 4-1 victory over Celtic was to move elsewhere – which given my contract situation was unlikely – or to be 100 per cent professional, regardless of what was happening around me, and do my best to force my way into Scotland contention. It helped that life was never quiet in the Partick goal – I was always in the thick of the action, and the press noticed I was doing okay, even if I had to grow used to the dreadful puns in the papers week in, week out. If I'd had a good game, it was all 'Rough and Ready' or 'Rough is Smooth'; a bad game would produce 'Tough for Rough' or 'Rough on Thistle'. If I had a pound for every occasion that 'Rough Justice' was trotted out, I'd have been in the Millionaire's Club!

It also helped that compared to the present time, we had a fantastic bunch of players rising through the ranks. We were all groomed at youth level, grew up with one another, and came to appreciate each other's quirks and idiosyncrasies. It was a bit like a club environment, which helped explain why we qualified for so many World Cups, even if we never fully realised our potential.

I am totally convinced that I should have been at the 1974 tournament in West Germany, and I blame Bertie Auld for the fact I wasn't there. I was suffering a horrendous time with him at that stage, and it was as close as I ever came to quitting Thistle. He kept dropping me and accusing me of not being focused on the job (which was absurd). We argued continually, and basically, I should probably have moved to another club, but I was determined not to let him win the battle and, once again, I couldn't have gone on my own terms. Until then, we had always maintained an uneasy relationship, and I was accustomed to his mood swings, which meant I would be a hero one minute and a 'f***ing poof' the next. But there was open hostility between us for a sustained period in 1974 and I was stuck in the reserves for three months, until John Arrol had the misfortune to break his leg. Only then was I dragged back, though not without Bertie warning me that I had to improve my attitude.

As it was, I was pipped for Scotland's campaign in Germany by Jim Stewart of Kilmarnock, who was the third keeper in the squad alongside David Harvey of Leeds and Dundee's Thomson Allan. I was disappointed, of course, and it was the one that got away in my career, but I watched the tournament doubly committed to making sure that nobody, least of all Auld, would prevent me from participating in future World Cups. A small part of me wondered whether it was because I was a Partick player that I hadn't been selected. Eventually I decided there was no point in growing paranoid; I just had to maintain my standards and demonstrate my professionalism, and my opportunity would materialise.

Watching from the sidelines back in Glasgow, the tournament panned out with what can now be seen as a certain inevitability from a Scottish perspective. From '74 onwards, regardless of the meticulousness of our preparations, and the strength of our squad, we have seemed pre-programmed to fail at the final hurdle and to do so in a manner which leaves our supporters weeping into their beer at what might have been. If they handed out trophies for hard-luck stories, Scotland would be world champions. Something always happened to dampen the spirits, whether it was goal difference, a controversial refereeing decision, a player falling out with the manager, or normally unflappable guys perpetrating schoolboy howlers.

First up in '74, Zaire should have been lambs to the slaughter, especially after Peter Lorimer had broken the deadlock with an unstoppable shot. But 2-0 ensured that we were staring down the barrel and Brazil and Yugoslavia weren't so careless in disposing of the Africans. I remember almost hitting the ceiling when Billy Bremner came within inches of helping us beat the Brazilians, but, not for the last time, a feisty, gutsy performance yielded nothing better than a 0-0 draw. This meant we were required to win our last match, and we pounded the Yugoslavians into near-submission, only to concede a late goal. Of course we then equalised with two minutes to go – never ones not to heighten the tension and expectations – but couldn't find the killer blow. I was as crushed as anybody at the side's elimination. Willie Ormond's team had not lost a single game, but it was an ominous template for what lay ahead on our subsequent World Cup forays, even though we didn't appreciate it at the time.

Back home, I was still engaged in a mental joust with Bertie, but my form was so consistent over the next couple of years that, despite Partick's characteristically erratic displays which forced him to hide his eyes under his bunnet at regular intervals, even he couldn't complain. When he took us to Celtic Park, his old stomping ground, it was the b-all and end-all for him – a legend returning to his roots and he placed special emphasis on these occasions. Not that you would have guessed it from the results, which were invariably dire. They had gained almost instant revenge for their

Hampden defeat by demolishing us 5-1 at Firhill and thereafter they posted a series of individual and club records at
our expense. Bobby Murdoch scored their six thousandth
league goal to save a point against us in the following
season, and then, in November 1973, I was left clutching
at fresh air as Dixie Deans established a post-war milestone
for the Parkhead side with a personal contribution of half-
a-dozen goals, in a 7-0 thrashing. Indeed, I can still hear
Bobby Lennox asking sarcastically, a couple of seconds
before a corner: 'How many is that now, Dixie?' And the
striker replying: 'Five . . . no, hang on, make that six', as
the ball whizzed past me again, and the Thistle troops did
everything but raise a white flag of surrender.

On a positive note, you could never complain about
being inactive in the keeper's jersey at Partick. Constant
attack sharpened you up, refined your instincts, and you
were rarely standing around, twiddling your thumbs. I
relished being under pressure, with people relying on me
to stem the tide. And if I didn't always succeed – who
does? – even Bertie, who was almost as sparing in his distri-
bution of praise as Simon Cowell, once remarked that I
was worth fourteen to sixteen points a season to Thistle.
Certainly, there could have been few keepers on the Scottish
circuit who were pressed into service as much as me, which
meant firstly, that I was under sustained scrutiny and,
second, that I sometimes used to collect the man-of-the-
match award even when we were beaten.

All of which ensured I was a Thistle stalwart by 1976,
and the only thing which hadn't changed was my pay,
which remained on the £40-a-week it had been in 1970.
For a spell, Alan Hansen and I were the only full-timers at
the club, so you had this bizarre situation where the two
of us would train during the day, and then join the rest
of the lads for a couple of evening sessions. It wasn't an

ideal scenario, but we simply had to be professional and pretend that the system made sense. We also had to justify our salaries – such as they were – so this rigmarole continued for months. Eventually the Partick board recognised that other clubs were sniffing around me and Alan Hansen, and, let joy be unconfined, I was offered a new contract.

When the talks commenced, I was in a strong bargaining position, but I didn't have an agent or an adviser, and that wasn't overly clever. I was so delighted to be gaining a wage rise that I didn't pause to contemplate the consequences or consider my options. Thus it was they informed me: 'We are going to offer you £170 a week, and top that up with a signing-on fee, as long as you sign a new contract.' I asked: 'For how long?' And they responded: 'Six years, at an additional fee of £1,000 a year.' This, of course, added up to £6,000 between 1976 and 1982, but I had no reservations. I remember strolling out of the office, punching the air, whistling a merry tune and thinking I was a millionaire.

But, of course, you were naïve in those days and thrilled that your employers were so keen to hang on to you. Since then the pendulum has swung, sparked by the Bosman ruling, to the stage where the best players, flanked by rafts of advisers, can dictate their cash demands. The best are now rewarded almost as well as Hollywood stars, on £80,000 to £100,000 a week, which means that they don't have to worry about life after retirement. Personally, I don't have a gripe with that, considering they have to endure stalking by the paparazzi, endless tabloid intrusion into their activities, and are denied any kind of private life. Ultimately, for people of my generation and background, we were simply glad that somebody thought highly enough of our abilities to offer us a wage. As for what we might do at forty, we were totally in the dark.

Not that that mattered then. We were on the telly, we

were the cocks of the north, we were the heroes of the terraces, and there were other perks to the job. For instance, there was one night where I met Miss United Kingdom, Madeleine Stringer, at a restaurant in Glasgow, and she happened to ask if I was going along to the 1978 Miss Scotland competition. I told her I had been invited and she said 'Fine, I'll meet up with you there – and do you mind if I bring a friend?' I said 'Who is it?' And she replied 'Oh, it's Mary Stavin', who just happened to be Miss World at the time. But I hadn't passed my driving test and I had this old Ford Fiesta banger with an L-plate on it, and I thought 'F***, I'm going to show myself up here if I have to give them a lift.' So when the pair of them appeared, I blurted out that I had left my Mercedes at the stadium, and, because it was a nice night, we could walk round to the contest. So I came with my dinner suit on, and there we were, the three of us, walking to the Albany Hotel, with me flanked by these stunners. As we strolled along the road, all the punters were shouting 'Aye, great, Alan, no bad for a wee Thistle player.' I felt like George Best!

SCOTLAND DREAMS –
AND NIGHTMARES

When I was growing up in the 1960s, Scottish football may not have been the best in the world, but there was a widespread feeling that we could offer most opponents a decent contest. As we revelled in the mastery which Celtic displayed in becoming the first British club to lift the European Cup, or gloried in the trickery of individuals with stardust on their boots such as Jim Baxter, Denis Law and Jimmy Johnstone, it never occurred to me – and thousands of other pint-sized wannabe internationalists on a hundred parks across Glasgow – that there might come a time when Scotland would struggle to beat the Faroe Islands, Iceland, or any small nation with a reasonable defence and a couple of English Premiership players. Yet that, of course, is exactly what has happened during the last decade as our ambitions have diminished to the stage where we regard victory over Slovenia as something approaching a minor miracle.

I have heard many reasons cited for Scotland's decline at international level. Some football authorities still persist in blaming the teachers' strikes of the 1980s for a multitude of woes, as if criticising a group of volunteers excuses their own failings and lack of foresight. For me, one of the most significant factors behind Scotland's plummeting fortunes was the mass arrival of foreign players at the start of the 1990s, as too many clubs, asked to choose between creating youth academies and investing in state-of-the-art facilities, or opting for the quick fix of flinging cash at overseas recruits, opted for the latter. Whether by accident or design it established a situation where a whole generation of Scots have been ignored and our football has suffered accordingly.

Don't get me wrong, I am certainly not claiming that all the imports have been to the detriment of the Caledonian game. Henrik Larsson was a consummate professional, a valuable addition to Celtic and the SPL. The discipline and skill which he exhibited throughout his prolific stay in Scotland were rightly applauded by anybody with the capacity to see beyond the parochial abuse habitually dished out by one half of the Old Firm to the other. Brian Laudrup was another craftsman, a priceless asset to Rangers. His rapier-style destruction of multiple defenders during his spell at Ibrox provided fresh evidence that ability, application and artistry invariably offer a potent mix.

Regrettably, though, that quality of foreign recruits has been the exception. More commonly, and ever since Graeme Souness was the catalyst for the revolution by bringing the likes of Terry Butcher, Chris Woods and Trevor Steven to Rangers in 1986, Scotland's leading organisations have ploughed down a cul-de-sac of spendthrift excess. It has seen scores of second-rate non-Scots earn a king's ransom in a country to which they have no allegiance. Fair enough, these individuals shouldn't be held responsible: the genuine culprits are those who ignored the raw material on their own doorsteps and packed the Scottish league with mediocre journeymen, apparently convinced that a foreign name was a guarantee of class.

In the process, we have witnessed Spanish and South American enclaves at Dundee, prior to the club being placed into receivership, a similar situation at Livingston, who suffered the same fate; and even at Airdrie, who subsequently crashed out of existence. By now it should be evident that the effects of this trend have been calamitous. Only in the last couple of years has common sense finally returned at the likes of Hibernian and Motherwell – even if I suspect that the transformation has been largely dictated by cold financial reality. Heaven alone knows how many Scottish youngsters have in the meantime been reduced to frustration and resignation, floundering in the reserves, or driven away from the sport altogether.

Back in the late 1960s and early 1970s, there was none of the despair and cynicism which currently pervades Scottish football, and I speak as somebody who benefited from the general optimism of the period. Harold Macmillan might be lampooned nowadays for uttering the words: 'You've never had it so good' but even if the sixties didn't exactly swing for me, anything seemed possible, at least as far as football was concerned. Straight from the moment I was snapped up by Jimmy Dickie and nurtured by the ever-willing Eddie McCulloch at Sighthill Amateurs, prior to joining Partick Thistle, I began to attract the interest of the SFA's representatives. Nevertheless, I had to wait a long time to achieve my dream of pulling on a Scottish jersey at full international level as there was sufficient talent around in those days to ensure that competition was ferocious.

Bluntly speaking, I never considered myself a world-class footballer, and I have always been honest enough to recognise there were plenty of lads better than me who were denied similar opportunities to graduate into the full-time ranks. But I grabbed my chance, embraced it with both hands, and I suppose I was assisted by the fact that precious few youngsters were itching to be stuck between the posts – they were far more keen to emulate the likes of Johnstone or Baxter than risk suffering the ignominy of Frank Haffey.

He will always be linked with that 9-3 drubbing dished out by England, even though few people can recall the defenders in front of him who were equally culpable in the humiliation.

From the outset it helped that I was surrounded by players of the calibre of Souness, Kenny Dalglish, Willie Young, Derek Parlane, Alfie Conn, Joe Jordan, Ian Munro and Asa Hartford, and we rose together through the SFA's age-group structure. As I've mentioned before, we were comfortable in each other's company, and formed a mutual bond which never wavered throughout the following decade, whatever fate held for us.

I recall being part of the Scotland under-18s, who were involved in a UEFA youth tournament in our homeland, and we all stayed together at Inverclyde, and took our first fledgling footsteps on the international circuit. We weren't afraid of any of the other teams – what was there to fear? – but we did have to come to terms with our manager, a stern disciplinarian called Roy Small, who was really strict with the up-and-coming lads, and spelled out the message that he would tolerate no dissent.

We had tackled Italy, and beaten them at Fir Park, and Roy gave us the night off, which allowed Souness, Hartford and myself to travel down to Seamill. Despite the fact we didn't drink then, we popped into this tavern and bought ourselves a pint of lager shandy each. You can imagine the scenario: we were young, we considered ourselves the bee's knees, and had convinced ourselves that we were roaring boys, who could handle the drink and nobody was going to stop us enjoying ourselves. Small had imposed a 10pm curfew, but we were careless in our time-keeping, and we decided that we would walk from the centre of Largs back to Inverclyde, which wasn't exactly two hundred yards down the road. Still, who cared! At 10.20pm, as we were strolling along the promenade, oblivious to anything but our own freedom, Roy suddenly turned up in his car and gave us a serious reprimand. When he noticed that we were hardly quaking in our boots, he uttered the immortal words: 'I'll make sure that you three never play for Scotland again.' Maybe he believed it. But we just shrugged.

That attitude both worked for and against us in the future. Few of my Scottish contemporaries could ever be accused of harbouring an inferiority complex, which was one of the reasons why our results in Europe at that time were pretty impressive. But, on the debit sheet, many of the hairier incidents which blotted a variety of players' copybooks had a direct correlation to alcohol consumption and I can understand why so many managers, from Jock Stein through to Alex Ferguson, were desperate to prevent us from getting our hands on the stuff.

It was, nevertheless, a thorny issue and one which was never properly resolved. After all, the stark fact is that we were young working-class men, whose specialist subject was football. We were hardly likely to spend our free hours on away trips, perusing *War and Peace* or *Finnegan's Wake*. On the contrary, particularly under somebody such as Stein, who was as wily as he was suspicious of what party plans his players might be hatching, we would be stir crazy in our hotel rooms. Whenever we sought a release from the tedium of gazing at drab hotel-room walls or gave up trying to understand foreign television, the solution invariably turned out to lie at the bottom of a beer glass. Sure, there were high jinks, and practical jokes, which would occasionally develop into what the tabloid newspapers were so fond of calling 'nights of shame'. But there was a lot of hypocrisy in the media's attempts to stir up controversy; they were forever themselves searching out the nearest flesh-pots.

However, I would prefer to forget one episode in 1973, when Stein was in charge of the under-23s, and we were in Romania. I was team mates with the likes of Souness, Jordan, Young, Pat McCluskey and Derek Johnstone, and we had worked hard the night before the senior team were involved in a match in Bucharest, and secured a 2-1 success. Jock was remarkably upbeat about our display and must have reckoned that we would find it difficult to misbehave in such a country, so he decided, surprisingly, to give us an evening off. Little did he appreciate that Pat and Willie had already carried out a reconnaissance of the city, and discovered that the British Legion club were happy to invite us along for a few beverages. There were all kinds of embassy staff there that evening and, considering that we thought we had already finished with football for that trip, we relaxed, played some darts and dominoes, and enjoyed a long night's journey into oblivion. It was a festive occasion – there were cans of beer and lager being carried in and out of the place for hours – and we shared a laugh and a carry-on. It was 3.30am by the time we returned to the hotel.

Well, who was sitting at the front door but Stein. Everybody was vainly striving to sober up and string a coherent sentence together, but we were all absolutely plastered and spouting gibberish. Jock said, mildly in the circumstances: 'Okay, I can see you have had a good swally, so you can all go to your beds and sleep it off, but, you, son, hang on.' And he was pointing at me! I was near shitting myself. He asked: 'Have you had a lot to drink?' which, given my condition, was like inquiring if Casanova enjoyed sex.

Eventually, after a few attempts at linking two words which might bear any relation to the other, I replied: 'I'm sorry, there is no point in denying that I am totally guttered.'

He glanced at me, unmoved. 'Precisely how much have you had? Do you think you will still be drunk in the morning?' I was terrified of him, and couldn't conceal it. 'Erm, er, well isht's twenty to four, isht's going to be four by the time I get to shleep, so I am absholutely shure (the less I tried to slur, the worse it grew), I'll shtill have alcohol in me by the morning.' Then he delivered the killer punch. 'That's tough, son, because you are in the full squad. You won't be playing, but you'll be on the bench. I am not happy about it, but Stewart Kennedy has pulled out, we need cover for David Harvey, so you had better get your act together and do what you can to dig me out of a hole.'

He didn't present me with any option. Here I was on the cusp of what could become my international debut and I was lurching around like Barney from *The Simpsons*. I tossed and turned and fretted and fussed and it was one of the worst nights that I have ever experienced, but I recognised I simply had to make the best of a bad job, otherwise Jock would never forgive me for letting down my country. So I made an effort to sober up, but I was still all over the place the next morning, and when I read a note, which had been shoved under my door, informing me that the senior team were holding a meeting at noon – the match was a 3pm kick-off – I didn't know whether to laugh or cry. I felt sick, I was shivery, my head was throbbing, and, from the moment I awoke, I was throwing up all over the place.

Breakfast was a non-starter, but I showered, got dressed and went off to meet Willie Ormond, who was in charge of the senior squad. He was one of the nicest wee lads I have ever bumped into in my life, but I couldn't stop wishing that I didn't feel as though I was poised to spew my load any second. Willie was civility personified, and he joked and jested with us, but, in retrospect, it is utterly beyond my comprehension how he became the Scotland manager, considering that his remit seemed to stretch to nothing more than handing out bottles of juice.

But I digress. As midday approached, I walked into a room packed with all these luminaries of the Scottish scene – amongst them Charlie Cooke, Jim Holton and Kenny Dalglish – and parked myself down on a little seat at the end of the table. Then Ormond appeared and you could have sworn he was a waiter, because he walked in with a big case of Coca Cola and Fanta, and advised us that it was 'going to be warm out there' – the temperature was 105 degrees Fahrenheit. He then spent the next ten minutes opening all these bottles of fizz and passing them round. I sat in disbelief, but he continued with a tactical discussion, which was fairly rudimentary stuff, as the precursor to reading out the team.

Ormond was terrible with names, and after he announced that the substitutes would be x, y and z, and 'that boy over there' (which was me), he added 'and the boy McDonald'. We all looked around at one another in puzzlement. There was nobody called McDonald in the room. But eventually, Willie spluttered a sort of explanation: 'Och, sorry, I was thinking of a boy I signed for St Johnstone. He would never have made this side, he was murder.' With which he wished us all the best and, shortly afterwards, we drove to the stadium in Bucharest.

As the temperature rose to 110 degrees, I was still feeling like death warmed up. In fact, I'm just glad that there were no TV cameras there, given that I was sitting on this bench, with a towel over my head, and a bucket perched in front of me into which every five or ten minutes I was throwing up. It was a miserable day and Dalglish didn't help me. He was also a substitute and, at regular intervals, would nudge me in the back and say: 'Oh f***, that's our goalie knackered. He's writhing in agony. You better get ready to go on, Alan.' Naturally, it was a wind-up, but I was in no state to split my sides and I was simply glad when the final whistle sounded and I never had to take the field, thank God!

Yet that was as nothing compared to my next assignment abroad, in Denmark, where I was fortunate to escape without my international career being finished before it had even properly begun. Having kept a clean sheet against our rivals in Fredrikshavn, where we recorded a 1-0 victory, courtesy of a goal from Des Bremner, the under-23s were once more in fine fettle, and we celebrated at a jazz club, mercifully without any of the outbreaks of bampottery which frequently break out when footballers and bar tabs collide on either side of the midnight hour.

Sadly, however, although we avoided controversy that evening, there wasn't too long to wait for the eruption of one of the most notorious episodes in the oft-sullied chronicles of Scottish soccer. Next morning, we drove to Copenhagen to join up with the first team for their European Nations Cup match with the Danes, and emerged with another victory, Joe Harper proving a thorn in the Scandinavian's side. Unsurprisingly, the whole squad was in jubilant mood as we prepared to visit the night club attached to our hotel. I was on friendly terms with Harper, who was a smashing bloke and a terrific player, but nobody's idea of a monk, and Joe informed me that he had been invited to a party with Billy Bremner, Willie Young, Arthur Graham and Pat McCluskey, and they were intent on painting the town red.

I asked if I could accompany them, and we agreed to book two taxis at 11pm. The rain was coming down in sheets, bouncing off the streets and pavements, and the thought flashed through my mind: 'I can't go out, dressed like this, in a wee T-shirt, I'll catch pneumonia.' So while we were waiting for the cabs to arrive, and even as the first vehicle picked up a trio of the guys, I told Harper: 'Hang on Joey, there is no way that I am going anywhere in this without a coat, so I'm just popping up to my room to collect a jacket. Don't go away without me. I really want to come to this thing.'

With which, I rushed back into the lobby, and destiny and disgrace veered off in separate directions. Luckily for me the lift was a bit creaky and dilapidated and what felt like an eternity elapsed before I reached my room on the third floor and grabbed the coat which would save me from death by drowning. On the route back down in the elevator I also bumped into a couple of Scottish supporters, who were in high spirits, and we chatted for a few minutes, which – praise be! – halted my progress. By the time I had extricated myself and gone outside, Joe and Willie had vanished and I was left on my lonesome, kicking my heels in disappointment and bemoaning the whole situation.

Blessings in disguise don't come any bigger. I've subsequently heard what happened from one of the lads who was there. Denmark's bar prices have always been exorbitant, and my colleagues had decided to take their own duty-free supplies of alcohol into the club, which caused immediate tension with the management. Then one of the waiters confiscated Billy Bremner's bottle of whisky from below the table and placed it high up on a shelf. The wee lad wasn't happy about that – he wanted his amber nectar, created a scene, and logic and clear thinking vanished. Bremner was so small he couldn't reach his Scotch, but he persuaded Willie, six foot four inches of sinewy muscle, to step into the fray, and all hell broke loose. There was a ruckus, a scuffle – call it what you will, by the time the tabloids rushed into print, it had become 'Carnage in Copenhagen' – the police were summoned, and several players' careers ended abruptly in a whirl of flashbulbs, mass newspaper exposure and relentlessly negative coverage.

To my mind, the story was blown out all proportion. Of course, it should never have happened. But the subsequent post-mortems and life bans dished out by the SFA to 'The Copenhagen Five' were a gross overreaction to the kind of messy incident which occurs routinely on most weekends in every major city in Britain.

All the same, I was thanking my lucky stars and counting my blessings all at the same time (not easy) when the news reached me. Truth be told, if the weather had been dry that evening, I would have felt duty-bound to stick with my mates, whatever the consequences. It hardly seems relevant now to observe that the suspensions were lifted in 1977 and both Harper and Graham went on to represent Scotland, but the Danish debacle highlighted the absurdity of asking young athletes to behave like the Angel Gabriel. It also showed that, wherever in sport you have a group of exuberant, physically fit people, you will inevitably find a few who are addicted to sailing close to the wind, possessed with a self-destructive streak.

Personally, I think that is no bad thing – ultimately, you can't expect spontaneity from robots, so if you are searching for individuals with the ability to express themselves, you have to balance their chutzpah and cheek against their transgressions. I have heard plenty of comments to the effect that Scotland has produced more of these flawed characters than any other nation, but I disagree. Okay, Jimmy Johnstone plunged into scrapes, and Jim Baxter's off-field penchant for alcohol is well-documented, but neither of these guys were hooligans or genuine trouble-makers. Indeed, they were probably more dangerous to themselves than to strangers. They also contributed hugely to the gaiety of Scottish football and the tributes paid to both, following their untimely deaths, are an accurate reflection of how they were loved by the fans. The slaps on the wrist they received from over-officious little men in blazers will be forgotten.

Still, as my career advanced, I started to recognise how easy it was to be dragged into disrepute, particularly when Willie Ormond brought me into the full squad and I graduated from turning out for Partick in front of four or five thousand supporters every weekend, into the maelstrom of the international circuit. As kind as he was vague, as well-intentioned as he was ineffable, he used to meet us at Seamill, and while these squad gatherings were probably considered something of an imposition by the Anglos – the likes of Dalglish and Souness, who were used to parading their talent, in front of huge crowds and accustomed to jousting with the giants of European soccer – I never stopped counting my blessings and uttering a silent prayer of thanks for being involved with Scotland.

Perhaps I was star-struck. I was definitely just glad to be a part of the furniture, even though Ormond regularly had trouble remembering my name. Once or twice we would be sitting in some hotel foyer with our bags – the only people in the hotel – and Willie would pair everybody off. It would be Asa Hartford and Archie Gemmill in room 103, Dalglish and Souness in 104, and so on, until everybody had been billeted. Eventually, as the others departed with their luggage, he would notice me there, twiddling my thumbs. On more than one occasion I recall him turning to me and saying: 'Oh hello, what are you up to, son?' Unsurprisingly, I tended to be a bit flustered, but told him: 'Well, I'm actually a part of the squad.' He would then glance at me for a few seconds, and you could almost spot the cogs turning in his brain, before he smiled, declaring: 'Och aye, so you are, you're, erm, the keeper from Thistle, aren't you?' Then he would find me somewhere to sleep and I was content.

Basically, Willie was a lovely wee chap, who had been a tremendous player in his prime, but he was hardly the most disciplined or organised person in the world and a million miles removed from the autocratic, imperial figure that was Jock Stein. Ormond would have his tea with us, exchange a few football anecdotes, then retreat to his room with his bottle of Gordon's gin and that would be the last we would see of him for the night.

Ormond would often switch our training schedules at short notice, and, in one instance, trotted down the stairs and proclaimed: 'Right lads, we are not going to bother travelling to Inverclyde, we'll just convene on the beach.' We obeyed his instructions and sat on the sea wall, waiting for him. When he appeared and saw us doing nothing, he barked out: 'What the f*** is happening here?' We tried to interrupt him in mid-flow, but he continued. 'You are all seasoned professionals, you don't need to be molly-coddled, c'mon, get your fingers out and let's get on to the beach.' Finally, Charlie Cooke piped up: 'I'll tell you what, boss, you go first.' Accepting the invitation, he walked towards us, vaulted over the wall, and the water surged around his knees. The tide was in!

The atmosphere overall in the camp was robustly optimistic and there was a collective feeling that Scotland boasted a group of performers who could prove tough adversaries for anybody. If that statement makes me sound like some dewy-eyed old romanticist, then I make no apologies. In the 1970s we had no fear of the Scandinavians or of anybody else in Europe: our league circuit was dominated by Scots, with a conveyor belt of individuals migrating to England; and one merely has to check the team's results from that period to appreciate the deterioration in the intervening decades. The Tartan Army, too, was accustomed to embarking on foreign forays. There was none of this relish of basking in a self-deprecating glow. Although nobody pretended we were world-beaters, there was a definite confidence, a strut in the step of the squad and their followers. Unlike today, the build-up to every match was surrounded by keen anticipation.

On a personal level, every squad call-up was an adventure, and while I suppose I was a pauper in paradise compared to the majority of my international colleagues, who would have turned up their noses at the notion of being paid £40 a week, prima donna-ism was conspicuously absent. To his credit, Ormond was determined that the younger players were made to feel as valued as the seasoned stalwarts. For my part, I reckoned that if I persevered, I would gain my reward, even if I couldn't have predicted the circumstances which brought about my Scotland debut in April, 1976.

For the previous eighteen months I had been the regular stand-in for David Harvey, and while it can be frustrating sitting on the bench, I was honestly just delighted to be mixing with all those superstars. I was always confident my time would come, and without wishing to sound arrogant, reckoned that I deserved my place in the squad, so it was merely a question of when, not if, Willie would elevate me to the Number One berth. Thus it was that we were preparing for a friendly tussle against Switzerland – a fixture which earned call-ups for John Blackley, Tommy Craig, Willie Pettigrew, Alex MacDonald and Frank Gray – and I was enjoying a few frames of snooker at Seamill when Gordon McQueen, one of Harvey's team mates at Leeds United, called me aside and whispered: 'Hey, big man, I think you will be playing against the Swiss on Wednesday.' I was a bit perplexed by Gordan's slightly clandestine behaviour and also by the fact that Harvey hadn't made an appearance, as expected, on the previous day. However, I still suspected that Gordon was just winding me up, so I asked him what he was blethering on about. From that moment, he was pretty tight-lipped, and I was none the wiser, but on Tuesday, the gaffer asked if he could have a quick chat with me and I began to wonder what on earth was going on.

Ormond was less affable than normal, but the message he conveyed was wondrous. 'Alan, you are going to have to take over the goalkeeping duties tomorrow, because David isn't available. Unfortunately, a couple of his pigs aren't feeling well, so he can't make it up to Scotland this week, which means I am flinging you in at the deep end.' It was a slightly surreal conversation, given the talk of sick animals. But Harvey was a farmer, nearing the end of his career and striving to settle into a new livelihood. McQueen had joked in the past about him turning up at Elland Road in dirty big wellies. So that was how I was handed my Scotland debut and I was delirious.

Yet, despite the nature of my induction, there was nothing haphazard in the process by which no less than eight of us, who had advanced from the under-23 ranks, were involved in the meeting with Switzerland. It was a logical progression, and people were growing excited at the depth of talent which existed within the Scottish system, not least with the emergence of such figures as Dalglish, Alan Hansen, Souness, and Gray, all of whom were prominent players with the leading clubs in England. It was the dawn of a new era; you could detect a buzz around the whole country, and although my nerves were jangling for a few minutes following my chat with Willie, I certainly wasn't overawed or worried at the prospect. On the contrary, I remember phoning all my family members and we were whooping and hollering down the line, probably as much from relief as anything else.

Later, a sizeable contingent of Roughs was at Hampden Park to watch me launch my Scotland career with a fairly comfortable 1-0 victory, after Willie Pettigrew latched onto an early opportunity and got the Hampden roar going as early as the second minute. The visitors rarely put me under pressure. I barely had to touch the ball, let alone make anything which could be described as a 'Save of the Season', but one of the newspapers reported that my display had been 'calm and assured' and that was a balanced assessment, as far as I was concerned. I knew when I merited praise or vilification, so I wasn't inclined to let one cap transform my attitude. The fact was that I had finished my apprenticeship. Now I had to earn my rewards.

Many people ask me what I consider to be my strengths and weaknesses. Obviously, I was a pretty tough cookie, rarely fazed by anything which might be happening around my goalmouth. I was also good at instinctive, reflexive saves, and, for the most part, backed myself in one-to-one situations. Perhaps I could have learnt how to deal with set pieces more effectively, but although the English media seemed fixated with accentuating any errors committed by Scotland keepers, I refuse to believe there was any huge gulf between me and Ray Clemence or Peter Shilton.

The reality is that in the 1970s there was nothing like the emphasis placed on free kicks which exists nowadays, where craftsmen in the mould of David Beckham, Roberto Carlos, Thierry Henry and Zinedine Zidane are capable of bending the ball past any wall with a simplicity that betrays the hours of practice they have expended on perfecting the art. Thirty years ago, whether at Firhill or with Scotland, whenever an opposing team were awarded a free kick within striking distance there were three possible outcomes. They amounted to concussion and a sore head for one of my defenders; the ball landing in Row Z of the terraces; or, very rarely, a snorter of a shot crashing into the back of my net. But it wasn't scientific and, while the South Americans, and especially Brazil and Argentina, had latched on to the attacking potential of these dead-ball situations, they weren't a problem in a typical Scottish league game.

As for the challenge of defending corners, I maintain that any keeper, irrespective of quality, athleticism or bravery, is in trouble if the ball is whipped into his area with sufficient pace and accuracy. In that scenario, if the striker times his jump precisely, in the middle of a crowded penalty box, the goalie will have to rely on those players in front of him to do their job correctly. But there is invariably a degree of luck, good or bad, which enters the equation. Sometimes it smiles on you, on other occasions, you will be left looking foolish and the analysts will assess the pictures in slow motion, and reach their damning verdicts. But any goalkeeper worth his salt knows the score.

THE COCKS OF THE NORTH

When I was growing up in Maryhill, my parents taught me some important lessons. I was encouraged never to forget my roots and reminded that having a big mouth is pointless if you can't justify your words with actions. As befitting the manner in which Scots have punched above their weight across the globe for centuries, I had the message rammed home that if you feel inferior at anything, you'll always finish second best.

These words were to assume an increasing significance as my Scottish football career took off with a vengeance in 1976. Just a month after my debut, I was pitched into the Home International Championship, and once we had comfortably beaten both Wales and Ireland, I found myself contemplating a tussle with England and their litany of household names, in front of a typically passionate, nationalistic crowd at Hampden Park. It was a very different world from my normal weekends on duty with Partick Thistle, and there were several queasy questions which flashed briefly through my mind as I prepared for one of the most eagerly awaited clashes on the soccer calendar. What would the atmosphere be like? Would my nerves buckle under the strain? And what *was* with all the coverage of how England had reduced a variety of hapless Caledonian goalkeepers to quivering jellyfish and how I was, supposedly, destined to be the latest in a queue of patsies, waiting to be exposed by the fancy-dan Auld Enemy brigade?

Actually, even if performing in packed stadiums was a novel experience, it was amazing how swiftly I adapted to the transformation from my usual routine. Clearly I had absorbed my parents' teaching. Whereas in the course of my career I met a number of Scottish players who visibly shrunk in confidence prior to tackling the English, I was exactly the opposite. After all, these occasions were electric; they constituted a terrific opportunity for us to bruise the egos of our Southern neighbours, and, especially in the cauldron of Hampden, we enjoyed a massive numerical advantage in terms of fans.

What wasn't there to savour for somebody such as myself, soaking up all the adulation, and storing so many memories in my head? There was no reason to be apprehensive ahead of meeting England, particularly considering the fashion in which our revitalised team was stacking up victories, increasing momentum, and preparing to set off on an incredible roller-coaster ride of highs and lows during the next two years.

At that time there was some serious anti-Englishness amongst our supporters, partially fuelled by the perception – since substantiated – that our neighbours were siphoning off Scotland's oil, in league with an arrogant cabal of Westminster-based politicians and London civil servants. Nor did it help that the World Cup triumph for Bobby Moore's team a decade earlier was still continually being replayed as if it was the most momentous event in global history. But, as I kept reminding my soccer companions, it was overdue for us to throw off the shackles of 1966 and begin making positive headlines of our own. We had the requisite commitment, the camaraderie and collective will, but there remained a question mark: did we honestly, truly believe we were better than England? After all, they had thrashed us 5-1 at Wembley in 1975, which maybe explains why the mood around Glasgow on the morning of 15 May 1976, was a curious combination. From the sunny side of the street, some reckoned the Scots were due sweet revenge, while those from the army of Private Fraser thought we were doomed!

I had few reservations, nor did anybody else in the team as we steeled ourselves to the task at hand. The expressions on the faces of such redoubtable warriors as Danny McGrain, Tam Forsyth, Bruce Rioch, Joe Jordan, Archie Gemmill and Kenny Dalglish exhibited an emphatic declaration of intent. Willie Ormond ambled into the dressing room, but this was one of those afternoons when Harpo Marx could have delivered the pre-match oration and it wouldn't have made a bit of difference. We stared at one another, gazed into our colleagues' eyes, and it was all there: a blue tide of determination that this contest would be dictated on our terms and that we would yield to nobody.

At that time in the old Hampden ground you waited at the top of the stairs for the pre-match pageantry to cease, then walked down into a veritable sea of tartan, and Saltires, and people in kilts, many of them with bagpipes, all making an incredible racket. For a plebeian lad from Maryhill who, less than six weeks earlier, hadn't even played for Scotland, it was mind-blowing. I had never witnessed anything like it in my life.

Despite these scenes sending a shiver up your spine, you had to be tough. You couldn't allow yourself to be sucked into an emotional vortex. What I do recall vividly is standing next to white-shirted players such as Mick Channon, Kevin Keegan and Ray Clemence and thinking:

'I wonder what these guys' response would be if I mentioned that I earned £40 a week at Thistle.' Probably 'Where about in Scotland is "Thistle"?' But, there again, that kind of reflection only stiffened my resolve. Nothing, neither the crowd, nor the opposition, nor the fact that the championship was at stake – and we hadn't won it since 1967 – was going to damage my concentration.

Ormond had warned me beforehand about his suspicion that I might be a bit casual. 'You know, Alan, you frighten the life out of me whenever you go for the ball one-handed,' the little fellow had cautioned. He was so fretful about this that he was trembling in vexation. But I just patted him on the shoulder and promised that I would not be anything less than completely focused on the task in hand, and that a Scotland–England international was no place for party tricks.

If anything, the contest carried even more importance to the Anglos in our side. As the immensely patriotic Bruce Rioch remarked in the hours leading up to the kick-off: 'It's fine for you guys. If England triumph, you can stay here in Scotland and switch off your radios and televisions. But we have to venture down there again tomorrow and listen to the bastards crowing about it for the next twelve months.'

With individuals such as Rioch and Gemmill prowling around the dressing room, it hardly needs adding that we were all so pumped up by 2.45pm that we would have charged through a brick wall if ordered. Not that I needed to, as things turned out. The truth was, I had so little to do, for one simple reason: we were far better than them. We received an early fright when Mick Channon put the visitors ahead, but although that briefly induced a mild panic among the fans, Don Masson soon levelled matters and the ubiquitous, ever-menacing Dalglish, who had been rested in the Wales fixture, nimbly nut-megged Clemence for a second goal early in the second half, which was a true measure of our supremacy. In fact, we squandered several other chances, and perhaps there is some validity to the statement that when the English win these affairs they really rub it in, while Scotland prefer to drive their supporters to distraction with otherwise overwhelming 2-1 or 3-2 successes.

Certainly, having studied the video of that game, I can't comprehend how we didn't annihilate them, considering our dominance in every department. But there was still an opportunity for me to induce panic amongst the Tartan Army, and my concerned gaffer, Ormond, in the second period. Bolstered by our 2-1 advantage, we were pressing for a third, clinching goal. Everybody had pushed forward, so Keegan tried to spring the offside trap, and broke away from the halfway line. I noticed that the linesman had stuck his flag up, so I sauntered from my area to collect the ball, and it was only once I was miles outside the box that I saw Keegan charging towards me and thought: 'What the f*** is happening?' So I put the ball through his legs, and, to my horror, I heard the Hungarian referee shout 'Play on', at which point I was suddenly in no-man's land. It was a pretty scary moment, and I am convinced that you will still discover a brown stain on the Hampden turf to this day which no amount of super-strength detergent will cleanse. Nevertheless, that was as close as I came to feeling disconcerted throughout the proceedings, notwithstanding the redoubtable Tam Forsyth having to produce a famous tackle on Channon near the end to prevent the English snatching what would have been an entirely undeserved draw.

By the end of the match we had reinforced the impression that we could achieve our aim of qualifying for the

World Cup in Argentina in 1978. Although from the benefit of hindsight there will be plenty of cynics who believe it would have been better if we had failed in that objective, I have never subscribed to the theory that Scotland, as a small nation, should be content to seek respectability and not aim too high, for fear of vertigo. Across the sporting sphere there are sufficient examples to inspire us, from the All Blacks' excellence in rugby, to wee Ken Buchanan scrapping his way to world boxing glory, to Denmark winning the 1992 European Football Championship. We should cease this Scottish cringing, which afflicts so many of my countrymen.

Back in 1976, for instance, when we opened our qualifying bid with a treacherous away trip to Prague, and a meeting with the powerful Czechoslovakians, it was remarkable how one defeat, sparked by goals from Antonin Panenka and Ladislav Petras, attracted a plethora of 'Here We Go Again' headlines from the tabloids. The encounter was marred by a series of unsavoury confrontations between Andy Gray and Anton Ondrus, which led to both men being sent off and collecting three-match bans. It was almost as if there were sections of Scottish society who were happier with the notion of brave, but futile endeavour, than the philosophy that we should be proud of our ability and sing from the rooftops.

Equally galling, from a personal perspective, was how from the moment we touched down on Czech soil the build-up to the match was dominated by our hosts' conviction that I must be the weak link in the chain. Ormond was interrogated repeatedly: 'How can a player at a part-time club be of the same standard as the rest of the high-earning members of the squad?' It was an insulting and ignorant question. Whatever the status of Partick's other players, I was being squeezed through the wringer by Bertie

Auld and probably working harder than most of my peers. I was affronted too by the slightly scornful air with which the Czech journalists pestered Willie, as if I was some second-rate impostor, who had been selected by mistake.

For example, when we were training in the stadium on the night before the game, a camera crew hired by our opponents set up their equipment beside my goal and concentrated on me for the entire session. Meanwhile our rivals' assistant manager, [Dr] Josef Venglos, whose name will be familiar to all Celtic fans, was spotted undercover, checking out our tactics. I suppose that this was designed to prey on my inexperience and knock me off my stride. As it transpired, I had a pretty decent game; I wasn't at fault for either of the goals (of course!), and while we were clearly disappointed with the result, we also recognised that they were a quality team on their own turf, albeit one that would probably struggle to replicate that form on trips abroad. None of this prevented parts of the media from predicting a rocky road for us. But if we were to achieve our ambition of reaching a second successive World Cup, we were fully aware that these qualifying competitions were marathons, not sprints. As the next ten years were to show, Scotland were nothing if not stayers.

We needed, however, to prosper in our home fixtures and, if anything, our next display, against Wales at Hampden, was much less convincing than our showing in Prague. We only scraped a victory, with an own goal from Ian Evans who did his best to shrug off the close-range attention of Kenny Dalglish, but merely succeeded in diverting the ball into his net. I had other concerns to grapple with, not least the constant threat posed by the incisive Welsh striker, John Toshack, with whom I enjoyed several gritty contests over the years. Despite Gordon McQueen being assigned to mark the Liverpool man, it was one of those evenings where you are never certain what is happening in front of you, which was far from ideal. Allied to which, the crowd's anxiety swelled up the longer the tussle progressed; there was scant sign of the free-flowing football which had been a feature of the Home Internationals. A worried pall settled over the stadium which simply served to heighten the tension on the pitch. In the modern era, they call it 'winning ugly' and tomes have been penned on the subject. But in the 1970s Scots demanded flair and flamboyance and there was little sign of either that day.

As we left the field at the death, our countenances reflected both relief and anxiety. Willie Ormond, an honest, industrious gaffer with nary a malicious bone in his body, had other worries. It was bad enough copping flak from the journalists at regular intervals, but much worse to be the subject of constant rumours and behind the scenes criticism from his own employers. Just over five months after our stuttering victory over the Welsh, Willie had endured enough and promptly announced he was quitting to join Hearts. It was a bizarre scenario – remember, this was one of Hibernian's illustrious 'Famous Five', a Scotland boss, with a record of just one defeat in his last twelve matches in charge of his country, including a 3-1 swansong win over Sweden, with goals from Dalglish, Asa Hartford and Tommy Craig. Okay, he may have suffered difficulties in settling into the role, but nowadays a Scotland manager with his success rate would surely deserve a knighthood. Furthermore, today's SFA executive committee would cut off their right arms to find somebody with the potential to replicate Ormond's unbeaten sequence at the 1974 World Cup. But, in the final analysis, Willie was too decent, too unassuming, too nice for his own good, and he vacated his post in April 1977 with a wry comment or two on what he might have achieved if he had commanded the support of several of his senior administrators.

Exit the quiet man. Enter the King of Comedy, the master of the feel-good factor in the shape of Ally MacLeod, who was to lead his compatriots on an odyssey from elation to despair throughout the next fifteen months. Evidently, from this distance, it is easy to indulge in condemnatory post-mortems and reach the verdict that the architect of Scotland's ill-fated 1978 World Cup campaign was, at best, an optimist, at worst a deluded soul who crashed to earth like Icarus. Personally, I considered Ally a breath of fresh air. He invited his people to embark on a magical mystery tour, and everybody jumped on the bus. It was fun, it brought the nation together in a common purpose, and, albeit briefly, Scotland appeared a better place to live in.

This was no small feat, considering how the country had endured years of conflict between successive governments and the trade unions, the catalyst for bread rationing, mounds of refuse lying uncollected in the streets and all manner of industrial disputes and wildcat strikes. In that climate, was there anything wrong with MacLeod swaggering into the limelight and proclaiming that his team were on the verge of a glorious new dawn? Nobody got killed, nobody suffered anything more serious than a damaged ego, and yet Ally is still depicted in some quarters as the character whose hubris sparked a terrible apocalypse. Indeed, I have even read high-flown political analyses blaming him for Scotland's failure to embrace devolution in the 1979 referendum. That is garbage, pure and simple. Ally wasn't some tartan-clad Pied Piper. If the majority of Scots chose to follow him and wander off into Tinsel Town, they did so willingly.

Certainly there were few dissenters when, less than two months in the job, he guided his men, accompanied by battalions of fans, down to Wembley for the annual meeting with England and orchestrated another triumph over the Auld Enemy. His tenure had started falteringly, with a drab 0-0 draw against the Welsh in Wrexham. But MacLeod, an effervescent individual, blessed with an apparently endless stream of pithy one-liners and positive messages – he was a motivational guru, before the term had been invented – then began to weave his magic. The Irish were demolished 3-0 at Hampden, with a brace of goals from Kenny Dalglish and one from Gordon McQueen. When pressed afterwards for his thoughts on how the trip to London might pan out, he boldly predicted that 'his boys' possessed the talent, not merely to be the best in Britain, but to be a match for anybody.

I know that some of our English-based players never genuinely appreciated the impact which MacLeod had on his home-based audience, but he was terrific for me. He couldn't have done more to bolster my confidence. There's no doubt that he occasionally strayed into hyperbole, but as we approached our Wembley assignation, Ally instructed us to ignore the rantings of the London-based tabloids, and made a special effort to support and encourage me, amidst the now-traditional attempts of the media to remind visiting Scottish keepers of how Wembley was tradition-ally their graveyard.

It was irritating enough to be confronted with endless tele-vision replays of the five goals conceded by Stewart Kennedy at the stadium in 1975, never mind the refer-ences to how Frank Haffey and Fred Martin had let in sixteen between them at the same venue. But that was as nothing compared to my annoyance when I bumped into Bob Wilson on the eve of the 1977 contest. The English-born, former Scotland goalie actually discussed the possibility of history repeating itself. How did he expect me to react? I let him know that past events were no concern of mine, that I had confidence in my own ability, and that I was fed up with hearing talk of 'jinxes' and 'hoodoos'. He seemed surprised at the depth of my angry response, but the truth was that the papers were full of little else except how the 'part-time' Partick Thistle keeper was in the firing line for abject humiliation and I was sick to death of it. Mind you, I didn't sleep well that night and went in search of some advice from Graeme Souness and Kenny Dalglish, a couple of seasoned performers for whom Wembley was simply another large soccer arena.

They told me that, although it was obviously an unforgettable experience to walk on to the pitch and shake hands with the dignitaries – a feature of the afternoon which seemed to last forever – the pivotal thing was to keep composed in the tunnel, And they were absolutely correct.

The next day, as soon as we had completed the formalities, and the bold Ally had given a typically barn-storming speech, reminding us of our history and heritage and how privileged we were to be representing Scotland, the sides marched out together and we stood in that tunnel for what felt like an eternity. Once again, I stared around me – as I had done a year earlier – and inwardly gasped at the calibre of the company I was sharing. There was Clemence, Trevor Brooking, Emlyn Hughes, Mick Channon and Kevin Keegan, rubbing shoulders with Dalglish, and Souness, and Don Masson, Gordon McQueen and Joe Jordan. As the minutes ticked by I just had to say to myself repeatedly: 'I am as good as these lads and I have as much right as anybody else to be here this afternoon.' Then, once we had entered the arena and it was plain that Wembley had been transformed into a Scottish theatre of dreams, all my inhibitions faded away.

As far I was concerned, the jinx merchants were an irrelevance and when I looked around the ground and heard the reverberation of 'Scotland, Scotland' echoing across the stands, I recall having this giant smile on my face. I mean, if you couldn't enjoy yourself in that environment, then you were in the bloody wrong profession.

It was also an amazing demonstration of the bond which had been established between the players and the people on the terraces. They honestly believed in us, and us in them. The symbiosis was summed up at Jimmy Johnstone's funeral when Billy McNeill declared that if Jinky hadn't been a maestro with a ball at his feet, he would have been screaming his lungs out on the sidelines, such was his passion for the game and his loyalty to anybody who wore Scotland's colours.

Given that degree of dedication it was scarcely surprising that we were quickly into our stride. I had absolute faith in my defence – I was also helped by receiving an early touch – and once more we seized the initiative and imposed a stranglehold on our rivals. Not even John Bull – or Jimmy Hill – could have complained when we surged into a two-goal lead with the damage perpetrated by McQueen and, perhaps inevitably, Dalglish. It staggers me that I still bump into people who criticise his alleged 'under-achievement' in a Scotland jersey, considering both his immeasurable contribution on the pitch and his consummate professionalism off it, but there you go. I reckon Kenny has been one of the most gifted individuals to turn out for his country in the last fifty years. His credentials scream out at you, so much so that I can't take seriously those who are inclined to damn him with faint praise. The fact is that if Scotland had enjoyed the luxury of being able to select ten more guys with the same amount of ability and application as

Dalglish, then Ally MacLeod might have achieved his dream of winning the 1978 World Cup.

Kenny's ingenuity was too much for the harassed English defence at Wembley on that afternoon in June, and despite Channon narrowing matters with a late penalty, I was in my element by the final whistle. Thousands of Saltire-carrying fans then swarmed on to the hallowed turf and proceeded to gather souvenirs and mementoes, impervious to the police and security staff whose efforts to stem the tide resembled nothing so much as King Canute trying to turn back the tide. As pandemonium reigned around me, and the rampage continued apace, I saw quite clearly that there was no malice in the Scottish supporters: they were simply thrilled to pieces with gaining success at Wembley – for the first time in a decade – and their laughter was infectious, even if I do remember thinking that there would be hell to pay when I saw them breaking the goalposts.

Their orgy of celebration was unstinting and, although the game had finished as usual at around 4.45pm, I didn't reach the dressing room until 5.15, so embroiled was I in that stampede of my compatriots. For a while I imagined that I might end up getting lost amidst their chaotic ecstasy of delight. Eventually, albeit only after a torrent of handshaking, hugging, high fives and howls of 'Well done, big man!', I managed to retrace my steps back to the dressing room to be with my team mates. We were pretty drained, physically and emotionally, and we simply looked at one another. Nothing of any significance was uttered, yet you could detect a slight sense of unreality. It was as if we had collectively been pummelled into accepting that things had changed and I went away with this nagging sense that MacLeod had transformed the whole picture. 'Good God, these supporters out there really think that we are world-beaters,' I told a couple of the players. 'We'd better not let them down in the future.'

By then the English security people had given up the ghost and handed Wembley over to the kilted hordes. I know that, because we had at least a dozen Scottish fans, dressed in tartan, carrying cans of lager and feeling no pain, sitting in the baths with us and nobody was batting an eyelid. It was extraordinary. When Ally walked along and saluted the fans at the final whistle, he could have been the Messiah. In retrospect, perhaps we should have recognised that this highway of great expectations wasn't the wisest road to follow. And I will always maintain that neither Scotland nor their adherents had anything to be ashamed about that afternoon. There were no stabbings, no murders, nor were scores of innocent victims being rushed to accident and emergency departments across London. Instead an invading army with its tongue firmly in its cheek were determined to party as if there was no tomorrow. Appropriate really, in a summer when the film, *Saturday Night Fever*, was shattering records at the box office.

Mind you, we were offered scant opportunity to catch a movie, or enjoy a breather. On the contrary, we had no sooner beaten England than we were flying to South America for a three-match, pre-season tour of Chile, Argentina and Brazil: three fixtures between 15 and 23 June. On the face of it, this was hardly ideal, but MacLeod was already spreading his gospel that the only preparation for beating the best was meeting the best. Oblivious to such piffling concerns such as the fact that we still had plenty of work to do to secure our passage to the 1978 World Cup, he was beginning to sprinkle stardust over the entire Scottish nation. Hence it was that a group of ever-so-slightly knackered players touched down in Santiago on 12 June.

* * *

By anybody's standards, this was a controversial visit. Months before we had even departed Scotland, Amnesty International and other human rights organisations had sent us literature highlighting a catalogue of abuse against ordinary Chileans. Allied to this was the systematic murder of thousands of dissidents, as part of the dismantling of democracy and the installation of an unelected military regime. This information was sent to us individually and we should have been mature enough to reach a collective decision, namely that it was obscene even to consider participating in any sporting encounter in a stadium where human beings had been shot, en masse. Predictably, however, as mostly young footballers, we stuck our heads in the sand, fuelled by the thought that if we refused the chance to play for our country, there were scores of others who would have fewer moral scruples, and were ready to fill our boots. At that stage, I was still a believer in the traditional maxim that sport and politics shouldn't mix. Now that I am older and wiser, I appreciate that this was no excuse for us playing in Santiago.

From the moment we arrived in Chile, it was clear that everything we had been warned about was true. Heaven knows why the SFA agreed to a game in these circumstances. It was a horrendous experience. There was a 10pm curfew across the city and we could hear the sound of gunfire from our hotel rooms. The army brooked no dissent. If you were caught on the streets after that time, you were dead. The military were everywhere, and the local citizens working in our hotel told us how people had been rounded up, bundled into the backs of lorries, driven to sports stadiums throughout Santiago, and summarily executed without trial – and there we were, a bunch of daft Scottish laddies over here in the summer for a trivial football match.

None of us was in the mood for banter or socialising:

the general feeling was that we should get to blazes out of there as quickly as possible and be thankful that we had an opportunity for escape. On the afternoon of the 'friendly' – I hesitate to use that term in the circumstances – we reached the ground at 5pm, and the atmosphere was stomach-churning. Even the normally garrulous, high-spirited MacLeod seemed stunned by what we saw. As I walked through the arena I spotted bullet holes all along a wall which the Chilean authorities had tried – and failed – to conceal with plaster. It was a reminder that, in the grand scheme of things, football was hardly a priority for those unfortunate enough to be regarded as the enemy by the government. For the first time in my life I had to confront the question: 'Where do you draw the line?'

It was an eerie experience. The whole episode was a wake-up call to us and the SFA's officials who had surely witnessed enough of the world and its iniquities to have avoided the whole farrago in the first place.

And it continues to this day. Who can forget the dithering and procrastination which surrounded the staging of the Olympic Games in Moscow in 1980, or more recently when Nasser Hussain and his England cricket team were passed the buck by their governing body in relation to similar human rights outrages being committed in Zimbabwe. Too often it seems sports administrators fail to appreciate they are living in the real world. Chile was a defining moment for me in that regard, and the details of how we won 4-2, with goals from Lou Macari – he bagged a couple – Dalglish and Hartford are insignificant. I only participated for the first forty-five minutes, prior to being replaced by Jim Stewart at the interval, but it was a sombre three quarters of an hour. I was under so little pressure that I had plenty of time to reflect on the slaughters and the assassinations which were everyday occurrences in that benighted place. I wonder if the Park Gardens bureaucrats harboured any regrets afterwards. Certainly I never felt less like celebrating a victory in my life and went straight to bed.

Our next port of call was to be Argentina and, twelve months before we headed there in earnest, it would give us a chance to test our mettle against a side, who, unlike the Chileans, were capable of mounting a sustained challenge for the World Cup, in their own country. It was a fiercely competitive tussle, and one with ramifications for Willie Johnston, who was sent off in farcical circumstances by a referee who was clearly determined to appease the noisy crowd at the Boca Juniors ground. The Rangers star, who had been on the receiving end of some disgusting treatment from the Argentine, Vicente Pernia, who spat at him, and kicked him on several occasions, finally raised his arms in frustration. There was no physical contact, and the rest of us reckoned that justice had been done, however belatedly, when the Argentinian full back was handed his marching orders, only for Johnston to suffer the same fate. It was a dreadful piece of refereeing, but perhaps we should have anticipated it, considering that the same whistler, having awarded a penalty to Scotland, which Don Masson converted, subsequently squared things up, in the softest possible circumstances, by permitting Daniel Passarella to level matters at 1-1.

Understandably we were frustrated at the finish, a reflection of how swiftly Scotland's aspirations had risen beyond acquiescing in respectability. But I have to pay tribute to Passarella who was a majestic presence in his team's otherwise faltering display. Time and again he was instrumental in serving up little glimpses of magic, and one could sense he possessed the inspirational qualities which were duly emphasised at the World Cup. As for both managers, Ally, already a media darling, expressed modest satisfaction, while the chain-smoking Cesar Menotti did football a service by ensuring the wretched Pernia was ditched from his squad.

Later that night, we had a few drinks and a couple of us were chatting with one of the Lufthansa air stewards who accompanied us throughout the South American trip. Wolfgang was gay and made no effort to conceal it, nor did he believe that there wasn't at least one member of the twenty-two-strong Scottish contingent who was concealing his homosexuality. 'Come on, I have noticed all these attractive members of your squad (my jaw dropped at this remark, but we'll let it pass), and I can't believe that a group of your size can all be heterosexual, so what's the dope?' he remarked, insistently.

As the evening progressed Gordon McQueen and I reckoned we might as well offer Wolfgang the thrill of the chase. So I whispered to him: 'OK, you see that wee guy over there with the hairy arms and the shorts, well, his name is Archie Gemmill, and he's gay.' We wished him good luck, and thought nothing more about the matter. Suddenly, ten or fifteen minutes later, we heard this massive explosion of rage from the corner. 'Ya f***ing bastard, what the f*** do you think that you are playing at! Who telt you that I was a poof? I'll f***ing flatten them.' Mercifully, Wolfgang emerged unscathed, but ever since surveying the fall-out from that deception (from a safe distance), I have occasionally wondered about this residual anomaly of the football circuit. You can be accused of almost anything – alcoholism, theft, wife-beating, accepting bungs, racism or sectarianism – and it's like water off a duck's back. But if you even suggest that somebody might not be interested in the ladies, it festers the kind of resentment and fury which you associate with a Mike Tyson fight.

But there were more pressing problems on my mind as we travelled to Rio de Janeiro and the glittering fixture of the summer, a meeting with the resplendent Brazilians at the Maracana Stadium. During the Argentine match I had clashed with Passarella while dealing with a corner and the pain in my hand intensified so much during the next twenty-four hours that I was forced to go to hospital in Rio for an X-ray, prompting worries that I might miss the main event. Fortunately, it was only bruised, but I suffered a fresh scare as the game beckoned, which felt daft at the time and sounds even crazier now, but since I have vowed to be as candid as possible, there is no point in drawing a veil over anything.

In a nutshell, I had been finding it difficult to get to sleep so on the night before the Brazil tussle I asked the team doctor for a sleeping pill. It was purely a precaution, and I didn't take it, but woke with a sore head which forced me into another consultation with the medics. Eventually, I went for a lie-down, swallowed a tablet, and was out for the count. When an alarm call woke me half-an-hour before our pre-match meal at 5pm, I felt utterly dreadful and thought I had contracted some bug. Suddenly, it struck me: I had taken the sleeping pill by mistake. I felt about as lively as Rip van Winkle. There was nothing for it but to order a constant supply of black coffee and hope that it would stir me from my lethargy. Gradually, swallowing cup after cup, I began to come round while we were sitting in the dressing room. Nobody had to tell me that it was scarcely the perfect preparation for a meeting with some of the globe's finest artistes, and I endured some predictable ribbing and a few quizzical glances from Ally MacLeod.

However I had only to walk into the Maracana to realise that I wouldn't have missed this for the world. Quite simply, it was fabulous. Many football connoisseurs speak about the grandeur of the San Siro or the Bernebau, but for me that place was something special. It wasn't simply the carnival atmosphere, or the singing, dancing and glorious rhythms which resonated through the arena for the whole of the ninety minutes, but also the joyous expression on the little children's faces, enraptured with soccer. To them this was as much a cathedral as it was a sports ground. In the first few minutes I couldn't help looking round this spectacular auditorium and thinking to myself: 'Here is football's spiritual home and it is as far removed from the red ash parks of my childhood as the Earth is from Mercury.' The word 'Wow' was continually on my lips and I made some decent saves, leaping into the fray with an energy which no one who had seen me a couple of hours earlier would have believed.

That match was my introduction to Zico who scored from a sumptuous, bewildering free kick. Perhaps I should have written his name down in a notebook for future reference, because I was to suffer from his brilliance in the future. Brazil also had Rivelino, who crashed a shot at me from thirty-five metres out with such ferocity that my hands were still stinging twenty minutes later – we didn't wear gloves in those days. If truth be told, Scotland never threatened to spoil the crowd's evening by doing anything so rude as winning. Yet, despite Cerezo adding to the hosts' advantage, there were some skilful touches from Dalglish and Gemmill, which the audience applauded, and it was no disgrace to lose 2-0 in that environment. Indeed, if we expunge the Chilean visit from memory that excursion to South America was far more enjoyable than anything which lay in store. The sportswriters on the tour voted me the Best Scotland Player and presented me with an inscribed tankard.

Back home, however, the nation wasn't just expecting us to qualify for the World Cup, but taking it for granted. I didn't share that complacency, nor did my team mates. We acknowledged that we would probably need a minimum of a win and a draw from our remaining games against the Czechs at home and Wales away, and that wasn't a cinch in anybody's language. So I was cautious, and whatever optimism and triumphalism might be brewing elsewhere in the country, I stuck simply to the team view that our profile was rising, our squad was working together like an extended club, and we weren't afraid of meeting any opponents. Sure, we had seen enough of the likes of Passarella and Zico, and grown cognisant with the speed of thought and movement of the South Americans, to understand that launching a challenge at the World Cup – if we got there – would be incredibly tough, but we had lit the touch paper at Wembley. Regardless of the fact that not a single Scottish player ever stated we would lift the Jules Rimet Trophy, MacLeod oozed such impish confidence that I am not surprised the massed ranks of the Tartan Army sang: 'We're On the March with Ally's Army', long before the record had been recorded, let alone entered the charts.

Yet it was pretty presumptuous to think we were merely required to turn up at Hampden to swat away the threat of Czechoslovakia. They were, after all, the reigning European champions and the last thing we needed was to view them lightly and concede any soft goals. Aye, right! I am the first person to accept responsibility when I have screwed up – and my readiness to do so used to reduce Bertie Auld to apoplexy – but luckily, by the time I allowed a long-range shot from Miroslav Gajdusek to evade my grasp, we had already secured revenge for their win in Prague with goals from Joe Jordan, Asa Hartford and Kenny Dalglish. Judging by the tidal roar which engulfed the national stadium, the fans sounded convinced we had secured our slot in Argentina.

We hadn't, of course. Far from it. The Welsh had served notice of their threat with a 3-0 success over the Eastern Europeans, and so we still required a point when we ventured to Anfield to meet them on 12 October. There may well have remained not a single nervy twitch among the support and the press, but certainly the down-to-earth characters who populated our dressing room were not taking anything for granted.

Nowadays, such a high-octane fixture would be staged at the imposing Millennium Stadium in Cardiff and the likes of Charlotte Church and Katherine Jenkins would lead the massed ranks of communal singing. But, back in the 1970s there was a dearth of flexibility between the different governing bodies and I honestly believe that the Welsh FA missed a trick by moving the game to England. They had originally intended to meet us in Cardiff, until a crowd restriction of 10,000 was slapped on Ninian Park for safety reasons. As soon as the tie was switched to Liverpool it was inevitable that the Scots would flock south in their thousands, and any home advantage which might have bolstered Wales would evaporate.

That's exactly what happened and the clamour from the Tartan Army was all-pervasive as Ally indulged in his pre-match oration. His eyes were sparkling as he spoke and the pride in his face was unquenchable. 'Look, look,' he counselled us, 'at all the people who are depending on us to clinch World Cup qualification. Listen, listen, to them chanting their hearts out and clutching their Scotland scarves as if they were their most treasured possessions.' To an outsider, this may sound clichéd or obvious, but when MacLeod was in full spate, he could tug at the hairs on the back of your neck. On this occasion he was plucking at our heartstrings, and playing them like Eric Clapton.

It was an evening to be brave and aim for the stars and

it soon developed into one of my most memorable experiences on international duty. The score was locked at 0-0, with the outcome perched on a knife-edge, when John Toshack, as dangerous as ever, spotted that I had advanced from my line, and essayed a lob, which seemed destined to finish in the net, until I darted backwards, stretched to my limit, pushed the ball on to the top of the crossbar and over for a corner. In an instant, I was besieged by my colleagues, patting me on the back and screaming 'Well done'. To his immense credit, Toshack, who must have been gutted by the end result, hung around to pay me the compliment of declaring it was the best save anybody had ever made at his expense.

Perhaps it was. Deep down, I knew that I had produced many similar efforts at Firhill but without gaining a single column inch of recognition, such was the disparity between my 'day job' and these fantastic, incident-packed, emotion-charged Scotland appearances. There was still ample work to be done, and, maybe predictably, when we broke the deadlock in the seventy-ninth minute, Anfield was awash with controversy and recriminations. Joe Jordan had jumped with David Jones in pursuit of a cross from Willie Johnston and the French referee, Robert Wurtz, immediately awarded us a penalty for handball, a decision greeted with fury by our opponents, who claimed that Joe was the offending party.

The debate raged on, but to what effect? I suppose these type of marginal decisions excite supporters, especially now that we have twenty different angles from which to scrutinise every incident, but I have always been amazed at the number of players who pick up bookings for arguing with officials. It is utterly futile, a waste of breath, and yet one of the safest predictions you can make ahead of any major tournament is that we will witness senior players, experienced enough to know better, flinging vitriol at referees as if they expected them to reverse their original verdicts.

In any case, Wurtz was as cool as Antarctica and Don Masson displayed equal sangfroid, flighting his penalty inside the right-hand post, to Scotland's rejoicing. Our adversaries who, to be fair, had posed us difficulties all night, were justifiably deflated, and a few minutes later Martin Buchan, who had replaced Sandy Jardine, sprinted down the wing and delivered a magnificent cross which was bulleted into the net by Dalglish. Millions of Scots across the globe, yelled 'We've Done It.'

Soon afterwards Ally dashed on to the pitch, embraced his players, smothered me in a giant bear hug, and the partying began in earnest. In the space of four months, we had bested England, drawn with Argentina, routed the European champions and had now delivered the *coup de grâce*. Perhaps in the hours which followed we were all entitled to believe that miracles were possible.

PLEASE CRY FOR US, ARGENTINA!

The 1978 World Cup has been likened in many quarters to a national disaster for Scotland. According to the revisionists, the whole campaign was marked by ineptitude, complacency and incompetence. Most of the blame attaches to Ally MacLeod, a decent, well-meaning individual who was derided for daring to voice his opinion: 'I think a medal of some sort will come', when asked to provide an honest answer of how his team would fare in Argentina. Privately, and I know this from speaking to his widow Faye, Ally was harbouring his own reservations and once remarked to her, as the hysteria neared fever pitch: 'God help me if things go wrong. I will either return as a hero or a villain.' In the intervening years, every mishap which befell the Scots in South America has been heaped on his shoulders, yet that analysis is deeply unfair and simplistic.

There is another aspect of that summer which has quietly been forgotten by the sniffier critics, and that is the recollection of just how much *fun* surrounded the prelude to the tournament. Scots in their millions had a spring in their step; they honestly believed that their players were poised to take the football world by storm, and the game's popularity soared to new heights. With hindsight, once the juggernaut crashed off the rails, much of the sunny optimism disappeared like a snowball in Hades. But I have often wondered whether it was better to have advanced to the edge of the promised land, under MacLeod's influence, or lingered in a comfort zone of lowly aspirations. I have no doubt that, however briefly, his positivity illuminated the nation he loved.

Certainly, whether walking through Glasgow, and being heartened by the super-sized smiles on the faces of count-less wannabe Dalglishes and Jordans, or receiving a special Blue Peter badge in the guise of a Loch Ness Monster with a tartan hat, I relished the manner in which football was bringing communities and families together. Every night, on television, there were adverts featuring the World Cup squad, and MacLeod was everywhere, advertising Maryhill Carpets or supplying pearls of wisdom for Tennent's lager. Faye even cropped up in a commercial for the Co-op, which was offering a trip to the World Cup as the main prize in a competition. ('I had better enter this . . .' said Mrs MacLeod, ' . . . just to keep my eye on Ally.')

I also became, ahem, something of a fashion icon, by the way, when I was approached by Taylor Ferguson, a good friend of mine, who ran a hairdressing salon on Bath Street in Glasgow. Danny McGrain, Derek Johnstone and I trav-elled down to London to take part in trials for a new hair-style, which, Taylor said, was going to be huge. He knew he wouldn't get the punters, the wee guys who were into punk rock, to sit in a salon, with curlers in their hair for an hour and a half, but if footballers did it, they might think 'Hey, I want my hair like that as well.' So Taylor drafted us, and we were happy to oblige; it was the start of a global phenom-enon. With us three Greek gods as models, no one should have been surprised. Soon after, Taylor was inundated with offers: Kevin Keegan, Graeme Souness, Willie Miller, the works. It has even gone down in the language – 'a football perm' – and although opponents used to take the piss and I was initially called a 'poof' by rival fans, they were soon walking around with perms themselves. It has become one of my hallmarks. I haven't had one for years, but I am always refered to as 'the man with the perm'.

The comedian, Andy Cameron, famously capitalised on the patriotic phenomenon with an appearance on *Top of the Pops*, regaling a mystified bunch of mostly English teenagers with his Top Ten hit, *Ally's Tartan Army*, and although one can glance back now and cringe at the lyrics – 'England cannae do it, 'cos they didnae qualify' – this was a rare chance for Scots to rid themselves of their dour, Calvinist image (even if some of them were under the delusion that *schadenfreude* was some kind of German sausage).

So we lapped up the attention, were sent good-luck messages by everybody from Lulu and Billy Connolly to the Prime Minister, Jim Callaghan, and Leader of the Opposition, Margaret Thatcher – after all, we were the sole British representatives. All the while the lyrics of Cameron's infernal song filtered through our heads; 'We're on the march with Ally's Army, we're going to the Argentine, and we'll really shake them up, when we win the World Cup, 'Cos Scotland are the greatest football team.' Ah yes, the potency of cheap music!

For a few months, we were celebrities, feted wherever we went. Advertisers wanted us and we were treated like royalty. Chrysler flew the squad down to London for a TV commercial – and if you looked closely at the film, you might have noticed that most of us were red-eyed, following another night on the tiles. We devised a players' pool, and if an individual did an advert, he got 60 per cent of the cash and the money that was left went into the kitty. I helped sell fridges for ScotMid, and because I was married at that time to Michelle, one of the girls on the Tennents lager cans, I couldn't go anywhere without being offered a drink in exchange for an autograph. It was brilliant – while it lasted – but the wee guys in their bunnets who poured lager down our throats genuinely thought that all we needed to do was turn up in Argentina and FIFA would hand us the World Cup.

I suppose if we had been pragmatic about it, we might have recognised a few worrying signs in the lead-up. The news, for instance, that we had been drawn in the same group as Peru, Iran and Holland, was merely regarded as confirmation that we could begin planning our strategy for the later stages of the competition. As some wag (and I don't mean a wife or girlfriend) was later to point out we should have taken heed of that very first portent of doom. Peru, Iran, Scotland, Holland – PISH! MacLeod peremptorily dismissed the South Americans as 'a bunch of old men' and didn't bother to check them out, while our draw with the Iranians seemed fortuitously designed to allow journalists and pundits to make 'hilarious' links between Irn-Bru and 'Iran-Peru'. Even the evidence of an unconvincing Home Nations Championship, during which we drew 1-1 with Ireland and were beaten 1-0 by England, with Steve Coppell clinching victory for the visitors at Hampden, did nothing to dampen expectation levels. Injuries to Danny McGrain and then Gordon McQueen – both of whom had been talismanic figures in the qualification stages – were shrugged off by the manager with the response: 'Ach, I feel sorry for both the lads concerned, but we have plenty of strength in depth.'

Ally also persevered with Don Masson and Bruce Rioch, apparently unconcerned that the midfield duo had recently suffered such miserable form that Derby County had placed them both on the transfer list. As for the absence of Andy Gray, that was difficult to fathom, but MacLeod was loyalty personified and he stuck to his instincts.

Behind the scenes, though, resentment was starting to fester over – what else – money, and issues such as bonus payments to players if we progressed from our section. To be honest, I couldn't have cared less about these matters, I was jetting off to the World Cup, and that was all that concerned me. But some of the other players, predominantly those based in England, wanted to nail down details prior to us leaving Scotland, only for the subject to be put on hold until we had arrived in Argentina. That was one area where the SFA and not MacLeod should be criticised for their lack of professionalism, as it merely served to store up trouble for the future.

Yet, as we prepared to venture on the Cup trail, none of these things felt particularly significant. The spirit among the squad was fine and while finalising our preparations at the Dunblane Hydro, we basked in the celebrity spotlight, constantly surrounded by film crews and interviewed by gushing luvvies. Rod Stewart turned up one afternoon in his helicopter, participated in a hastily convened session and shared a meal with us. Predictably, the pictures were splashed all over the next day's tabloids.

The media attention was overpowering, and we were grateful to Ally for allowing us an evening off before our departure, when he informed us: 'I want you all to go and enjoy yourselves, and if you fancy a good bucket, fine, because this will be your one chance at R'n'R before the hard graft commences.' He decided to split up the players into groups of three or four, and told us not to head in the same direction, for obvious reasons. I joined forces with the gregarious Joe Harper and Derek Johnstone and we chose to travel into Falkirk, where we ended up in a night club called Maniqui. As soon as we had strolled through the door the owner spotted us and invited us upstairs into a plush VIP chamber, which was already occupied by several other people, and we just sat there, enjoying a few beers and some banter.

Regrettably, Joey supped to excess, and once he had a drink inside him, he didn't walk away from confrontation if it occurred. There was this one guy in the club who kept noising him up and swearing at him and, although Derek and I did our best to keep the peace, Harper grew increasingly angry and told us: 'I'll f***ing sort him out.' We reckoned it was time to leave, so we dragged Joe downstairs and I booked a taxi, but just as the cab was drawing up, this same idiot appeared out of nowhere and shouted: 'Hey you, I want a f***ing word with you, you sheep-shagger.' He just wouldn't shut up; he was hurling abuse at the Aberdeen player, and then suddenly sprinted towards Joe and aimed a swipe at him.

It was a bad, bad move. In the next few seconds, after Harper had ducked out of the way, he pummelled his assailant in the face, and there was blood all over the place. The boy's mouth had been completely splattered. I stood there, aghast, then bellowed at Derek: 'Christ, we have to get away from this now or the story will be all over the papers.' So we leapt into the taxi and dashed off. The three of us sneaked in the back door at the Dunblane Hydro, held a quick pow-wow, told one another that we had to keep this a secret between us, and went to our beds. However, at 2am, there was a knock on the door, and the unmistakable voice of Ally MacLeod rang out: 'You have to come down to the lobby, the polis have arrived.' As I got dressed, I had this image of my picture splashed all over the tabloids and of missing the World Cup in disgrace. Yet, once we had joined the rest of the bleary-eyed players, and spotted the cops, we realised that some of our team mates had landed themselves in even bigger trouble. The story was that Kenny Burns and Don Masson had gone to Perth, borrowed this car off a lad, and had apparently wrapped it round a lamp post. But we were told to return to our rooms and I never heard anything more about it, so maybe it never happened, or perhaps Scotland's police were as excited about the World Cup as everybody else.

You might have imagined that, following this fiasco, the

SFA would cut to the chase and decide to get us on the first plane to Argentina, pronto. They might have wanted to, but there was no chance. Some bright spark at the association had thought it would be a brilliant idea to have an open-top bus parade inside Hampden, and charge the fans 50p for a seat and 30p on the terraces for the privilege of seeing us in the flesh . . . and all this before we had kicked a ball. It was just embarrassing, and a rip-off. I couldn't help recalling 1971 and how we had beaten Celtic in the League Cup final, without Thistle laying on a bus. Now, here we were inside the national stadium, being cheered to the rafters by 30,000 supporters, who seemed oblivious to the fact there was, as yet, nothing to celebrate. I winced. Yet that experience summed up the collective mania which had gripped the nation.

Frankly, I couldn't make any sense of it. Suddenly, normally quiet, reserved people were as high as kites and children were running around wearing T-shirts, on which were printed the words: 'We're going to win the World Cup'. The scenes which greeted us en route from Glasgow to Prestwick Airport resembled a scene from *Braveheart*, with the whole region around Fenwick Moor – a place which is usually a barren landscape – transformed into a patchwork of Caledonian paraphernalia. The fans were there in their tens of thousands, adorned in kilts and tammies, in their football strips and with their scarves tied on (in the middle of summer!), joyously singing *Flower of Scotland, Scotland the Brave* and *Ally's Tartan Army*. The noise was overwhelming and heaven knows how many folk we passed on that journey. They were everywhere, on the grass verges, hanging from trees, standing on viaducts above us . . . filling up every available blade of grass in wishing us a fond farewell.

This carried on for about thirty miles and when we reached the airport, it was bedlam; we couldn't even find our own families. And then, in a flash, I found myself stuck behind a wire fence, unable to get out again, and I vaguely recall waving goodbye to my loved ones. There was such breathless pandemonium that it was both exhilarating and a bit scary.

Ally was in his element, a showman who savoured the more theatrical aspects of whipping up a crowd into a frenzy, and he had generated a mass adulation amongst Scottish soccer fans that you couldn't achieve today. For the home-based members of the squad he was fantastic, but several of the Anglos, including Masson, Rioch and Archie Gemmill appeared to consider him, well . . . 'joke' may be too strong a word, but it seemed to me they were accustomed to being the centre of attention, and he was cramping their style. I think they expected their managers to be dour, stolid individuals, in the mould of Don Revie, or Bob Paisley. They had never encountered somebody such as MacLeod, who was, basically, an entertainer. Up until then they had only had to deal with his extrovert nature for two or three days, on international duty, but they were in a new situation at the World Cup and I detected a dearth of respect and a lack of understanding for the balancing act Ally was striving to pull off.

That said, we faced problems from the moment we touched down in Buenos Aires. Without having any knowledge of us, the Argentinians immediately branded us a bunch of bevvy merchants. No sooner had we arrived than complete strangers were approaching us in our hotel and inquiring if we fancied a whisky – I have never drunk the stuff in my life – and I guess we should have foreseen the difficulties which lay ahead. Even before then, while we waited to receive our World Cup accreditation documents – a process that lasted a couple of hours – a string of beautiful women approached us, put garlands round our necks, and gave us all a kiss, as the prelude to our pictures being taken, photographs which would return to haunt us.

After that, we climbed into the team bus and drove to our hotel at Alta Gracia, and, perhaps predictably, it was a dump. I don't know what possessed the SFA to check us into such down-at-heel accommodation, or whether any of their staff had bothered checking out the facilities in advance, but they hadn't done their job properly in this and so many other regards. Worse still, the blazerati were staying in the same location, so while we were there to train and play, they were intent on schmoozing and social-ising with the other delegates. That is how the locals gained the impression that we were running up drinks tabs faster than the hotel employees could count the till receipts. In fact, the only time we consumed alcohol was when we were granted a day off. We were stuck in that hovel for three weeks, cracked up as world-beaters outwith the camp, but simmering with resentment inside the squad.

Nor did relations improve when we finally arranged a meeting with the SFA to discuss what bonuses and other ex gratia payments they were willing to lay on the table for us. Ideally this should never have muddied the waters in Argentina, but our players' association, comprised of Don Masson, Lou Macari, Archie Gemmill and Kenny Dalglish, were determined to pin down the governing body on specifics and rapidly discovered themselves trapped in an impasse with the organisation's president, Willie Harkness, the secretary, Ernie Walker, and a bevy of other stuffed shirts from Park Gardens.

At the initial talks, Harkness mentioned a ballpark bonus figure, which was derisory, and Macari retorted: 'That's f***ing shite. Unless you raise the stakes, we're not playing.' I was a little-league character, who had been thrust into the spotlight, so it was immaterial to me whether we picked up some extra cash, but most of the others were at major clubs and refused to be treated like second-class citizens, so the mood grew seriously nasty. Indeed, our representatives dug in their heels, and for a while there was a definite possibility that the squad would refuse to play unless their grievances were addressed. In retrospect, I guess many of our supporters will be wondering how the Scotland party could have contemplated such an extreme action, but it has to be appreciated that we were not speaking of Beckham-sized fortunes, but £100 payments for every game we won. This was hardly asking Harkness and his cronies to break the bank. All their stinginess did was to foment another unnecessary disagreement and reinforce the impression that they had tried to sweep the issue under the carpet.

Looking back, mishaps and misadventures seemed to occur almost every day. Before we had even launched our campaign, Ally offered us the chance to explore the neighbourhood, so I traipsed off with Harper and Derek Johnstone. We left the hotel grounds and, calm as you please, sauntered through the exit door – security was the last thing on our minds – and unwittingly stumbled into a diplomatic incident. Our tour of Alta Gracia provided minimal thrills, but on our return to our base we lost our bearings and despite spotting where we were supposed to be, couldn't find a way back home. Eventually, we caught sight of this fence, and Joey said: 'That doesn't look too high, why don't we just climb it and jump over on to the other side?' Derek and I nodded, and we had clambered towards the top when I looked down, and nearly shat myself. 'Christ, boys, have a swatch at that.' We were directly above a trio of police officers, carrying machine guns, aimed in our direction. They meant business, we didn't have our accreditation passes with us, so they hauled us down and stuck us up against the wall. For a few seconds my whole life flashed before me. 'Is this how it is going to end? Lying in the dust with my pals, shot as suspected terrorists?' And, lest anybody imagine I am exaggerating, don't forget this was only six years after the atrocities at the Munich Olympics.

All we could be grateful for was that we weren't in Chile. The officer in charge arrested us and led us away and we had to explain our actions to a couple of World Cup administrators, who lectured and hectored us about how we had to be much more careful in the future (no, really!) This little incident sparked my first ever appearance on TV – outside the sports bulletins – on *News at Ten*. When I phoned home, my mother, Jean, sounded distraught and she said: 'Are you okay, son, are you fine, are you no hurt? We saw you surrounded by all those soldiers and we were scared for you.' So was I, but deemed it prudent to laugh off the business as an innocent misunderstanding. Nobody within the SFA was amused.

Yet what did they anticipate? It was symptomatic of their chronic inability to attend to the basics that, although there was a swimming pool at Alta Gracia, it was utterly devoid of a trace of water for the duration of our stay. In that kind of environment, with players growing stir crazy, twiddling their thumbs and counting the cracks on the wallpaper in the ceiling, it is amazing how quickly animosity builds up, and you have to bear in mind that we had no diversions from the tedium of our hotel. We were even restricted in the number of telephone calls we could make, and whenever we ventured outside our rooms, the bureaucrats seemed to be en route to another function.

Eventually it reached the point where I actually relished the prospect of training sessions, but there again, my estimation of Ally's methods wasn't shared by everybody. He didn't adhere to the philosophy that you had to do everything by rote or follow the perceived wisdom of some

European coaches that constant repetition breeds players who can operate in rigid formations. Instead, MacLeod would organise impromptu games of Tig or keepie-uppie, and ask players to hop on one leg, then the other. He was clearly trying to foster camaraderie by persuading us to relax and enjoy ourselves, rather than making us dribble the ball through cones for hours. I was happy with this approach, as were the majority of the squad, but some of the Anglos refused to participate in what were supposedly bonding exercises, and this sparked a fair amount of friction. The dissenters argued that it was kiddies' training, beneath their dignity, and though Ally kept on smiling and exhorting them to accept that it was part of the drill, they flounced off and, within the space of a few days, it was remarkable how quickly morale had plummeted.

In that light, maybe our anti-climactic performance against Peru on 3 June wasn't wholly unexpected. Under Jock Stein I can recall hour-long team talks which contained an incredible amount of detail, but with Ally, it was all brush-strokes and Rob Roy-style rhetoric. One of the travelling press corps had warned me that the Scots should beware of conceding free kicks, given the presence of Teofilo Cubillas in the opposition ranks, and yes, we should certainly have been clued up on the outstanding talent in his country's history (Cubillas was the only Peruvian to be included in Pele's list of the world's greatest living footballers in 2004). But when I broached the subject with the gaffer, he simply laughed and responded, with reference to Cubillas: 'Och, forget him, lad, he's nothing special.' It was astonishing, really. Here we were, in South America, surrounded by journalists and football officials from other countries with an expert memory of the trickery and sleight of foot this gifted individual had demonstrated in lighting up the

1970 World Cup, and we were treating the fellow as if he was a geriatric nonentity. It was hubristic, it was absurd, and it cost us dearly, and all for the want of doing a little homework on our opponents.

Yet there was little sign in the early stages of our tussle with Peru of how spectacularly the wheels would fall off the chariot. Joe Jordan, characteristically gritty and no-holds-barred in his methodology, sent us into the lead in the fourteenth minute. Superficially we looked in control, despite occasional signs that Juan Munante and Juan Carlos Oblitas, allied to the gifted Cubillas – who may have been nicknamed 'Nene' (baby), but impressed me as a fully fledged superstar – all had the pace to run us ragged if we weren't careful. To this day, I am convinced that if we could have secured a second goal – and we had opportunities – or if Don Masson had converted his penalty early in the second half, we would have beaten them.

Our travails began in earnest on the stroke of half-time when Cesar Cueto benefited from Cubillas' unimpeded foray into our box and equalised, and it was a worried dressing room at the interval, if for no other reason than MacLeod had no new instructions for us, despite the menace Peru had posed. The trouble was that neither Ally, nor any of his associates within the governing body, had bothered to assess our adversaries, and whether you regard that as complacency or arrogance or stupidity, it undeniably left the Scots looking like amateurs. But for Masson's gaffe, we might still have escaped with the spoils, but the longer the contest progressed, the more the confidence and swagger visibly drained out of our leading luminaries. Although MacLeod replaced the ineffectual Rioch and Masson with Gemmill and Lou Macari in the seventieth minute, the tide had turned inexorably in favour of our rivals. The ubiquitous Cubillas sent them in front a couple of minutes later, and then, while we were striving to regroup in readiness for a final shove, we conceded a free kick.

It is one of those sickening vignettes, forever stored in a goalie's memory bank. I prepared my wall, and was satisfied I had worked out the angles, but I couldn't have bargained for Stuart Kennedy and Macari moving their heads out of the way of Cubillas' superb shot, and the ball whistled past me as I stared in disbelief.

I wasn't alone. On the terraces the Scottish fans retreated into stunned silence while the frazzled MacLeod looked on in anguish, his face cupped in his hands, a picture of tortured incredulity which was famously captured in celluloid and will doubtless be wheeled out every time a Scotsman involved in that fixture pops his clogs. Within ninety minutes he had been transformed from a merry sprite into a wreck, and when the game concluded, it felt as if it was the end of the world. I will never forget the way the supporters turned on us. As we left the stadium we caught sight of them, flinging their scarves away and swearing at us. These Tartan Army foot-soldiers had shelled out substantial amounts of cash to travel to South America and were entitled to vent their spleen. They had been promised ambrosia and served up offal. Nevertheless, the scale of their fury was incredible, and the media waded in, not least the English broadcasters, who had probably grown sick to the back teeth of the Ally MacLeod/Andy Cameron axis.

Obviously, defeat was depressing enough in itself, but, being Scotland, why stop at misery on the pitch when we could further plumb the depths offstage? It was almost with a weary shrug of resignation that our campaign slumped from bad to worse with the news that Willie

Johnston had failed a drugs test and was on his way home. Much energy, probably too much energy, has been devoted to this business since it erupted, and once again it highlighted the schism between the Scots-based personnel and the Anglos as Johnston's transgression developed into a front-page story throughout the world. Several others in our squad could have shared the same fate – Masson, to his credit, admitted that he had ingested the same drug, and others virtually confessed they, too, were culpable – but I have to admit that I couldn't get steamed up into a lather of moral indignation over the episode.

As professional players I suppose we should have known what substances we were taking. Willie had tested positive for Fencamfamin, which contained similar properties to amphetamine and cocaine, but I gather that he only swallowed them after his own team mates had assured him they were kosher. This followed information they had received from the medics at their clubs in England. I just don't believe that Willie was a cheat, and I regard this as a cock-up rather than a conspiracy. Before every match, the SFA's medical advisor, Dr John Fitzsimmons, would come into the players' rooms and ask us if we were taking any medicines from a list which he carried around with him. We didn't have a clue. As far as we were concerned, once he started spouting out the scientific names for this or that cough syrup or hay-fever remedy, it was time to jump off the train before we reached Gobbledegook Central. I am sorry if that sounds flippant, but if you were looking for evidence of a team on performance-enhancing drugs, you would hardly have wasted your time with Scotland during our first two matches at the World Cup. As for me, if I was suffering from a cold or the shivers, I grabbed an Askit powder or a couple of aspirin and that was as technical as it got.

* * *

On reflection, what *was* rife on these overseas trips was the use of sleeping pills and I would estimate that nearly three quarters of the squad regularly sought out Dr Fitzsimmons when we couldn't nod off. He handed the tablets out like sweeties and they zonked you. But the rationale was straightforward – you were in a foreign country, thousands of miles from home and family, you were in a strange bed, and feeling restless. So, bingo! You popped a little sleeping pill, and were fine.

Ultimately, I still think that Willie was made a scapegoat and the SFA simply panicked, ensuring that Johnston was branded Public Enemy Number One back in Scotland. In my view, the whole affair was handled deplorably, and I am sure the wee man would have gained more comfort by staying within the squad than by having a blanket shoved over his head and being sent packing like a criminal. What made his treatment all the more hypocritical is that Willie earned a life ban from international football, and yet this happened in a period when drug-taking was rife in sport, and where you could guarantee a flurry of doping scandals every time the Olympic Games came around.

Within twenty-four hours, the hysteria and media feeding frenzy were suffocating. We couldn't escape though, because we were forced to attend an SFA function to nibble canapés and vol-au-vents and make small talk with a load of people in blazers. Not unnaturally we felt uncomfortable, standing there with all the composure of a battalion of tanked-up members of the Tartan Army trying to climb up an escalator.

I found myself next to Ally MacLeod, who had taken a few drinks and was seriously depressed, convinced that the world was out to get him. All of a sudden, Trevor McDonald, who was an ITV reporter at that time, appeared, flanked by a camera crew, in search of fresh interview material for *News at Ten*. Ally tapped me on the shoulder and said:

'Hang on, there's that bastard who's been stitching me up – let's go and have a word with him.' Joe Jordan and I immediately looked at each other and echoed the other's words. 'Oh f***, this is all we need.' Anyway, as Trevor marched towards us, he said to Ally: 'Hello Mr MacLeod, can we discuss the Willie Johnston matter and have a chat about your views on drugs in sport?' The manager stroked his chin briefly, then replied, with only the merest hint of a slur: 'Och don't be silly, Trevor. Willie would never have taken drugs – not on top of all the alcohol he had swallowed the night before.' Several jaws collided with the floor. Those of us who knew him recognised that this was Ally's notion of an icebreaker, a joke, but it sounded even worse once ITV's editing desk had done their worst, and all we could do was cringe in the corner.

Amidst this disintegration, the Iran game came and went almost unnoticed. Personally, it was one of the worst matches in my career; we did everything but pound them into submission, and I barely touched the ball, but still lost a bad goal – my fault – at my near post. It was one of those situations where the winger has to choose to shoot or make the cut back to his strikers. I guessed that he was planning the latter option and, in the blink of an eye, Iraj Danaifar, a player who wasn't even a household name in his own living room, had equalised, and we were slip-sliding away to hell in a handcart. Until that gaffe, on the hour mark, it had appeared that we might have regained Dame Fortune's blessing. Iran's Andaranik Eskandarian had gifted us an own goal in the forty-third minute, which should really have eased the strain on us. Despite creating stacks of chances, the 1-1 outcome was manna from heaven to the increasing number of news journalists who were jetting out from Britain with orders to dish more dirt on the Scots.

*　　*　　*

In this noxious atmosphere, with our critics baying for blood and our future in the tournament dependent on us beating Holland by three goals, we switched off the grins, tucked away the kilts and assumed a full-blown siege mentality. There would be no more Mr Nice Guys, or cosy chats with the media, and one hundred per cent focus on the reason we were in Argentina in the first place. Essentially, we had sat down together and decided that the best response to being everybody's whipping boys for the previous week was to let our football do the talking and deliver the message: 'F*** you all!'

It was one of those scenarios where the identity of the opposition didn't matter. We knew that the Dutch were a terrific team, ranked among the favourites to hoist the trophy, and that in normal circumstances the odds were stacked against us to an impossible degree. But this was an exercise in proving to our detractors that we weren't a joke, that we could actually play, and the news from Scotland that Ally's home had been vandalised and his family abused in the street, merely stiffened our resolve.

Graeme Souness had replaced Masson, who had endured a dismal tournament, and from the outset, we were in control. Kenny Dalglish was unlucky to have a goal disallowed for supposedly being offside, and it was typical of our entire Argentine experience that Rob Rensenbrink should open the scoring, against the run of play in the thirty-fourth minute. It came after the Dutch were awarded a dubious penalty when Stuart Kennedy made what I thought was a perfectly fair challenge on Johnny Rep, but we battled on. I later suffered the debatable honour of being presented with an award by FIFA, because, as it materialised, Rensenbrink's goal was the one thousandth in the history of the tournament – aye, it would have to be rattled in against the Scots.

Despite falling behind, we refused to crumble and Kenny Dalglish's nimbly executed equaliser on the stroke of the interval was the least we deserved for our domination. Inside that dressing room in Mendoza the mood was one of near fatalism, a collective attitude that we were climbing Everest with crutches on, but when you have combatants such as Jordan and Souness and Dalglish in your corner, you are never going to be accused of lacking guts or pride. Perhaps if we had entered the World Cup with this to-hell-with-them disregard for the niceties of international football, we would have fared better than smiling politely at receptions and polishing our diplomatic skills.

At one-apiece, the equation was the same as at the start, but when Gemmill converted a penalty in the forty-seventh minute, the first inklings that we might be wandering into Hollywood territory became evident. Suddenly we could hear our supporters again! It was strange to listen to *Flower of Scotland* being cranked into full volume after the silence of a mausoleum throughout the Iran tussle (the 8,000 attendance in Cordoba told its own story). But, like a punch-drunk boxer who looks destined for the canvas and then suddenly gains a second wind, we swarmed around our Dutch adversaries as the encounter raged on and I honestly believe they were growing rattled, particularly after Gemmill conjured up one of the greatest goals in soccer history.

That goal! Poems have been dedicated to its memory, a ballet written in its honour, and I suppose I shared the emotion of the rest of the team when the ball hit the net: a mixture of jubilation and 'Jesus Christ, why couldn't we have done this in our earlier games?' Obviously, I was in my domain at the other end, and if you study the still frames from the scenes leading up to Archie's fireworks you'll find me sitting on the ground, just watching the action. I had little to do during that period, and was as entranced as everybody else when the wee man started his magic, sparking panic in the Holland defence, as the prelude to polishing off his own carnival act with an incredible degree of ice-cold aplomb. When he stuck his arm in the air at the climax, and his team mates rushed towards him, I recollect glancing to my left and noticing a section of the Tartan Army going into raptures and screaming their backing. It reminded me of how narrow the margins are between being viewed as icons and idiots.

At 3-1, with over twenty minutes remaining, our priority should have been to keep in their faces and refuse to allow them time to settle, but this is easier in theory than practice. The Dutch were a class act and the last thing they wanted was to wind up as the victims of the biggest mugging in World Cup chronicles. This would surely have been their fate if we had managed to breach their ramparts again. In short, when Rep, who has since admitted that he cheated to gain his side's earlier penalty, was permitted room to amble into shooting distance and crashed his effort past me, I wasn't particularly surprised. Gutted, yes, sickened, yes, but the truth is we had always been staring at oblivion and we were facing a side who went on to reach the final.

If I had a pound for every time friends, critics and armchair pundits declared it was a bad goal to concede, I would be as rich as Andrew Carnegie. However, let me argue my case. I reckon I had made pretty good contact with the ball and had done enough to push it over the bar, so I couldn't believe it when it finished in the net. But, credit to Gemmill, he later admitted that the shot had deflected off his foot, which had adjusted the trajectory, and from that moment on I was always struggling. It is, of course, irrelevant, because within twenty minutes we were uneasily reacting to the most pyrrhic of victories, a 3-2 success which, in the normal run of things, would have been regarded as a tremendous result, but which simply brought into sharp focus the inadequacy of our previous performances.

I recall normally tough-as-teak people crying their eyes out at the finale. It was characteristic of Scotland that we should take our supporters to a waiting room perched halfway between paradise and purgatory, offer them hope, and then crash to earth against a spectacular montage of the good, the bad and the truly appalling. But I am afraid we weren't in the mood for philosophical discussions that evening – the opposite in fact. Most of the players were enraged with how we had been stitched up by the tabloids, and by Gordon Airs of the *Daily Record* in particular, some of whose trumped-up reports had been littered with fanciful embellishments to say the least. It had reached the point where we were almost frightened to look at the papers.

There were tales, for instance, of how Joe Jordan was supposed to be chasing all these women across the pampas. We knew that it was pure, unadulterated crap, but you can just imagine how Joe's wife, who was in hospital expecting a baby, felt as she surveyed this litany of gratuitous, offensive tittle-tattle. This was invariably accompanied by the infamous photographs of the team at our accreditation process being smothered with kisses and bedecked with garlands by a clutch of beautiful FIFA-recruited hostesses. It was manipulation, deception, call it what you will, but the pictures were cropped and the headlines penned specifically to generate the impression that we were a bunch of sozzled philanderers. The end result was a climate of distrust and suspicion between the 'news'-gatherers – I use the first word in the loosest sense – and the squad, which, pre-1978, had been pretty harmonious.

But, considering we were in South America, we were in no position to refute the flow of drivel which was rolling off the presses in our homeland, and, in my view, the *Daily Record* was amongst the worst offenders. Not their sports desk, incidentally, but their news operation. Eventually, following our elimination, Gordon McQueen, a restless spectator on the sidelines, whose absence through injury had been a critical blow to our prospects, confronted Airs, after spotting him in a bar surrounded by hospitality girls. 'See you mate, you have caused a lot of trouble for us with your garbage. How would you like it if I phoned your wife and told her that you were out on the pull, drinking with a bunch of beauty queens?' But the journalist was unrepentant and replied. 'You can do what you like. I'm not married, so it's not a problem and, in any case, I am only doing my job.' That was a stock answer from these guys, and a difficult one to counter. The bottom line was that they had been sent to Argentina by their papers, they had to justify their expense accounts, and they didn't seem worried as to how they swung it. Yet, matters were never quite the same again between us and the press, the majority of whom had shared our optimism but, as the precursor to twisting the knife, were now perfectly happy to declare they had all the while been apprehensive.

As for Ally MacLeod, he was destroyed: a shell of the man he had been a month earlier. I remember waking up at 6am one morning – this was only forty-eight hours before we returned to Scotland – and the sun was shining, so I decided to grab some fresh air and collect my thoughts. I was toddling around on my own and had turned this corner of our hotel when suddenly I caught sight of Ally. He was curled up in the foetal position on a park bench, completely oblivious to everything else in the universe. I didn't know how to respond, so I just inquired quietly:

'Are you all right, boss?' But he didn't say anything; he simply sat there in a ball, distraught, dishevelled, in despair.

Of course, once the dust had settled on our Cup exit the recriminations began in earnest. Lou Macari went to the management and asked if he could go home a couple of days early, was granted his request, and promptly rushed back to Manchester and his story subsequently appeared in a tabloid, reputedly for a five-figure sum to the player. This, in the 1970s, was a massive amount of cash. Whether Lou spoke to the paper or not, this account, which was a highly selected version of events, went down like a cupful of vomit with his team mates – so much for the loyalty you might have expected from one of the luminaries of our players' association.

By then any concept of esprit des corps had flown out of the window. Some of the squad recognised their international careers were over, so why not inflame an already aggravated situation with an extra injection of breast-beating and public buck-passing? Macari and others blamed the SFA for a string of offences, some of which were valid, and heaped scorn on Ally, which again was partially justified, and seemed happy to hold everybody accountable for a disastrous campaign – except themselves. It made some of these articles ever-so-slightly puke-inducing. After all, as somebody who was in the squad throughout the whole experience, it was plain that we didn't measure up against Peru, and were awful against Iran, so it was laughable for anybody to indulge in hatchet jobs. The truth is we all bore some responsibility for our failure and should have been mature enough to admit it.

It would also have been refreshing to have heard a 'mea culpa' or two from the SFA. Between the Iran and Holland matches we spent a night at the same hotel where the Dutch were staying, and it was the lap of luxury: their wives were with them; their facilities were in a different league from what we had endured at our paltry resort and there was a professionalism about their set-up which exposed the SFA for the second-rate bureaucrats they were.

After our elimination we had to travel to Buenos Aires in a bus which veered off the main highway, and began puttering down this increasingly dodgy-looking dirt-track towards a hotel that wouldn't have featured in any of the tourist brochures. On and on we went, until the bus ground to a halt at this doss-house. It must have had about eighty rooms, and made the Bates Motel seem like the Ritz by comparison. Obviously, the SFA panjandrums weren't billeted there, just the players, and the amenities were so bad that I actually burst out laughing – think of a decrepit version of Fawlty Towers, staffed by a dozen Manuels, and you may be able to envisage the skid-row nature of this place.

But what the hell; I was starting to unpack my bags and preparing for an evening with the cockroaches, when Martin Buchan marched in, asked what I was doing. There was no way that a Scottish international football team were staying in such a dump, he said, and told us to return to the bus immediately. Then he personally instructed the driver to collect all our luggage and take us to the Hilton. Once there he called the SFA officials downstairs and forced them to get the whole business sorted out as quickly as possible. Martin was masterful, and it was a victory of sorts, but it only emphasised the governing body's intransigence and exposed their limitations. Thus it was a sombre, dejected bunch of us who eventually boarded the flight home.

On the plane I was sitting with Joe Harper and Derek Johnstone and we worked ourselves into a lather, worrying what lay in store. 'Is this going to be as bad as some people are making out?' I asked. 'Will there be a lynch mob at the airport?' inquired Joey. 'Do you think the stewardesses might find a pie for me?' wondered Derek. Apart from catching a glimpse of the occasional copy of a Scottish tabloid, on which the words 'Shame' and 'Disgrace' featured in large print, we had heard everything only second-hand. When our jet landed at Heathrow we thought to ourselves: 'Hang on a minute, all the Anglos have buggered off,' and so had most of the Scots boys, sneaking away on hastily arranged holidays to the Continent. By the time we were ready to depart for Prestwick the only people left on board were Ally MacLeod, DJ, Joey, myself and a couple of others, and it didn't require a genius to realise that we were going to cop all the flak.

Then we noticed Ally, pouring himself a few drinks. He was clearly psyching up for the ordeal which lay ahead, although I reckon that armour-plating might have been more useful than alcohol. As we were approaching our destination, and our descent had almost concluded, I looked out of the window and exclaimed: 'Blimey, there are an awful lot of luggage attendants on the tarmac . . . and a helluva load of baggage handlers as well.' Joe whispered to me: 'What the f*** are we going to do here?' And I said, without pausing for a moment: 'We are going to let Ally climb off the plane first and watch what happens.' Even then it was a slightly surreal atmosphere. None of us had a clue what we were meant to be doing. Nowadays you have rafts of PR and media managers to construct a damage limitation strategy, but in 1978, we were the chattels, the SFA were the lords of the manor, and we were simply flung to the wolves.

So we gathered our stuff, thanked the cabin crew, and the plane doors opened. Ally actually went to the top of the stairs and began waving in a celebratory manner to the assembled throng. I don't know whether this was through drink or not, but Ally being Ally, he had clearly persuaded himself that he could calm the booing and win over the baying pack with a few cheery gestures. He discovered pretty swiftly that he couldn't. So the lot of us were bundled by security officers on to a bus. The atmosphere was poisonous: scores of our compatriots were jeering at us, giving us V-signs, and employing the sort of language which is euphemistically described as 'industrial', but is often used by folk who haven't done a day's work in their lives.

As a relatively young man – I was twenty-six – I could scarcely comprehend how dramatically the mood had shifted in the space of just over a fortnight. People were snarling and spitting at us, they were irate and simply couldn't contain their fury. It struck me then that Scotland suffers from a terrible lack of perspective when it comes to football. After all, we had managed one win, one loss and a draw in three matches, which was as good as or better than we have done in any World Cup since 1978. And yet the same Tartan Army troops who had bought into the far-fetched dream that we would carry the trophy home – an idea which none of the players ever promoted or propagated – were now screaming for vengeance. It was unsavoury at the time and, to be frank, time hasn't diminished my unease at the memory of those scenes at Prestwick or those which we endured for the next few weeks. Players, their families and children were routinely sworn at by strangers in broad daylight.

So, what did we learn? The most important lesson was that you can't aim for the stars without getting the rocket motors running sweetly on the launch pad. When you are embarking on a mission with twenty-five people involved there has to be a happy environment, a sense of shared purpose, both on and off the field. In Argentina that never happened, whether due to the irritating trivialities such as the pool without water, the omnipresent tension bubbling under the surface between the SFA and the players, or the lurking threat of strike action.

The association should have learned from their involvement in the 1974 tournament; it wasn't as if they were wandering into uncharted territory. But if anybody checked out our accommodation in advance, they should have got their arses kicked. I was sharing a room with Jim Blyth, the reserve goalkeeper, and it was tiny: it had just two beds, no windows, no television or anything which might have offered a release from the tedium. There was simply nowhere to go, and it was torture.

People always ask me: 'Alan, you have been to the World Cup three times with Scotland, that must have been fantastic,' but I can honestly say that while it was an honour to represent my country, I never really enjoyed any of the competitions. There is this myth that it must be wonderful always to be the centre of attention, and the focus of so many people's expectations. While I was used to criticism, and accepted it when it was merited, the hounding and harassment reached a completely new level in Argentina. When it got to the stage where news reporters were pestering our families and hanging around in our communities, and the seedier elements of the supporters were flinging bricks through players' windows, it marked the start of a deeper malaise which has plunged further in the last three decades. I definitely have sympathy with the modern-day stars, condemned to suffer the blight of journalists scavenging their rubbish bins and photographers permanently parked outside their houses. It is an invasion of privacy and I don't care how much money these players are earning, they are still entitled to go home, shut the door, and relax.

However, the rot set in rapidly in Argentina and the lies which were peddled should have been exposed and denounced by the SFA. According to the allegations, we were searching for sex and drugs and alcohol – forget about rock 'n' roll – and that reputation rapidly snowballed. I remember one day in Alta Gracia and a bunch of us had walked into the town to this small café, where we ordered a few bottles of mineral water and Coca Cola. It was a sweltering afternoon, and we were just trying to relax. All of a sudden, while I was talking to Graeme Souness, I noticed this flash going off. 'Did you see that?' I asked Graeme. 'I think there is somebody in there taking pictures of us.'

Initially he thought I was being paranoid, but a couple of minutes later, there was another explosion of light, and when we investigated we discovered a photographer was hiding under the table inside the café. He had worked out an angle from which it appeared that we were surrounded by glasses of beer and spirits, which actually belonged to other customers. We grabbed the film off this guy, but the damage had been done – I don't know whether he had been accompanied by another snapper, but there were pictures of us in the Argentinian dailies, supposedly bevvying at midday in our Scotland tracksuits. Your faith in human nature takes a little knock when you realise that people are earning a living by crawling around in the gutter, doing their utmost to land their compatriots in trouble.

Certainly, I don't think that Ally MacLeod ever quite recovered his previous ebullience and joie de vivre, once he confronted the wrath of his nation on his return. From a human aspect, I have always been supportive of the manager, not least because everybody else, or nearly everybody, has put their side of the story of the 1978 World Cup, either by selling their reminiscences to newspapers or publishing books. Ally never did that, although he had a massive take on the whole episode: the players he liked and disliked, the way in which he was hung out to dry by the SFA, and the behaviour of the committee men who rode on his coat-tails, but were posted missing when he required their support.

But then, I got on famously with Ally; he was a surrogate father to me, and he couldn't have done more to dispel the opinion, which was regularly voiced in some quarters, that I was the weak link in the squad, because I wasn't at Manchester United, Liverpool or the Old Firm, but rather on the mean streets of Maryhill. He was pressed on this subject repeatedly and constantly stuck up for me. Shortly before we ventured to Argentina, he halted one reporter in his tracks with the forecast: 'As far as I'm concerned, Alan Rough will be *the* best goalkeeper at the World Cup.' Unwittingly, he was heaping pressure on me, but he didn't mean it to be off-putting; he was simply demonstrating his unwavering faith in me and I was appreciative of his loyalty.

There's no doubt he cracked up amidst the wreckage of Scotland's campaign, and you would see him wandering around the Alta Gracia complex, a solitary figure, with this vacant expression on his face. But, regardless of the mistakes he made, in underestimating Peru and not checking on their strengths, I willingly put my hand up and confess that the majority of the team would never wish to be involved again in anything as shambolic as our display against the Iranians. When Ally needed us to dig him out of a hole, several of the really big names – they know who they are – went AWOL on that dire night in Cordoba, and they should have been looking at themselves, instead of foraging around for scapegoats. I count myself in that condemnation – although not as a 'big name' obviously, not then anyway.

Ultimately, the World Cup was a watershed. It dashed the aspirations of thousands of supporters, who subsequently sought refuge in the self-deprecating ranks of the new-fangled Tartan Army, a non-fighting force which stockpiled a substantial stash of gallows humour, and which has subsequently lent much-needed humour to humiliating results against such giants of the international game as Costa Rica, Belarus, Moldova, the Faroe Islands and Morocco.

The relationship between the media and the national team was also transformed, to the point that nowadays any trust has broken down irretrievably between the protagonists and the young, sharp-suited little guys you see at press conferences. They don't want to waste time forging a bond with a player or a manager; they are only interested in writing columns from the comfort of their ivory tower, and sticking a stiletto in people's backs. When I was rising up the ladder, I had no problem in sharing a beer with the likes of Brian Scott, Ian Archer, Ray Hepburn and Rodger Baillie, and while the 'fans-with-typewriters' phenomenon wasn't ideal – some of the stuff which appeared, pre-Argentina, was more PR spin than honest journalism – it was preferable to the present situation.

I should know, having switched sides, so to speak. Whenever I am on international trips with Scotland for Real Radio there is an extremely clear-cut 'Us and Them' mentality between the players and the hacks. At the airport, you will hear one player remarking: 'There's that bastard, from the *Record*, who slagged me off last week.' Then his colleague will reply: 'Yes, and there's that wee tube from the *Sun*, who thinks he knows more about tactics than the rest of us put together.' It has created a dank vibe, where there is no mutual respect, and part of that process was fostered in the made-up claptrap which poured forth in 1978.

Typically, though, the SFA orchestrated what I have always regarded as a cover-up of which Richard Nixon would have been proud. Having conducted their own inquiry – which was hardly likely to conclude that they had acted like a group of eejits, was it? – they banned Willie Johnston (for obvious reasons), Don Masson (for his admittance of having taken the same substance) and Lou Macari (for the newspaper article) from playing for Scotland ever again and their annual report concluded that: 'Scots everywhere should be ashamed.' It would have been pleasing if they had conceded that their own deficiencies were a contributory factor in that shame, but I don't remember any of their administrators ever admitting they might have erred in their choice of facilities, in dealing with player payments, and in orchestrating a climate of suspicion and hostility by routinely, complacently ignoring the players' wishes.

In the final analysis, it was nobody's finest hour, and I was relieved to escape and resume my existence in the shadows at Partick Thistle. And you don't say that everyday. I was even pleased at the prospect of renewing hostilities with Bertie Auld, and although there were indications in the weeks following Argentina that many Scots were wandering around in a state of trauma, it did not linger long in my mind. Let's not forget that it was only a football tournament. We tried, we failed, we were disappointed, now it was time to get on with our lives. After all, as that profound philosopher, Anon, once said: 'Shit happens.'

7 PICKING UP THE PIECES

The hangover from Argentina wasn't cured quickly. It felt like the aftermath of a dozen Hogmanays rolled into one. On the international beat, Scotland suffered a miserable sequence of results for the next couple of years as a new generation of players struggled to adapt to life at the highest level. My own sunny conviction that we should forget about a past we couldn't change and concentrate on the future wasn't shared by many of my colleagues. Perhaps with hindsight they were entitled to be sceptical, now that the adulation had been replaced by a morbid curiosity as to what lay ahead.

Away from football this was a turbulent period in British history. The Scottish devolution vote was lost by a narrow margin in the spring of 1979, an outcome which some observers have argued was partially due to the crisis of confidence suffered by many Scots, following the traumas of the World Cup campaign. Personally, I think anybody who clings to this argument should look at the facts; but there was no denying the wind of change sweeping over the country, after a winter of discontent, which subsequently brought Margaret Thatcher to power, and transformed Scotland into a guinea pig for her more controversial policies.

Everything seemed to be changing, except my own circumstances. The Russians invaded Afghanistan, Ronald

Reagan came to power in the United States and unemploy-
ment soared across the heartland of the Central Belt as
traditional industries were ravaged. But every morning,
oblivious to the dismal tidings in the press, I wandered
into Firhill, changed into my kit, and fulfilled my obliga-
tions, striving to remain as professional as possible, even
though I was starting to regret signing that six-year contract.
By this time, all of my old team mates from the League
Cup triumph had long since departed Maryhill, so the only
signs of constancy were Bertie Auld and his bunnets and
cigars and me.

He was still as volatile as ever and flung pelters at me
when I took a free kick outside the box against Cow-
denbeath in the Scottish Cup in 1978, claiming that my
behaviour was complacent and would negatively affect the
rest of the side. We were like Walter Matthau and Jack
Lemmon in *The Odd Couple* by that stage and the torrent
of abuse he aimed at me was usually more from habit than
any genuine displeasure.

In any case, Thistle eventually won that tie against the
Fifers, which marked the start of a creditable Cup streak,
with further victories secured against Hibernian in a replay,
and Dumbarton. That steered us into a semi-final meeting
with Aberdeen, who were in the process of developing an
excellent squad, which was to become the precursor to the
Pittodrie club becoming one of the behemoths of the
domestic game, who would enjoy European success within
the next five years.

Even at that point, I was impressed by the fashion in
which they played – their brio and panache only matched
by a tough-as-teak approach to defensive chores. They built
on all these facets of their play with Ferguson's arrival and
it was no surprise to learn that the Govan man was to
slacking what W. C. Fields was to temperance. If Partick's

124

fans were hoping that the Dons might be fazed by the prospect of a trip to Hampden, they were proved sadly misguided, and unfortunately I helped to make the Pittodrie men's job a lot easier than it might have been by gifting them a brace of goals and generally enduring one of my shabbier evenings in the Thistle cause.

Auld was incandescent at the interval, his vitriol reserved for me in particular, but prior to his expected tirade, I stuck my hands up and apologised to him and the rest of the team for my howlers, which halted him in his tracks. Sadly, it didn't stop our opponents and although we battled admirably in the second half, the metronomic Joe Harper added another goal and the visitors to Glasgow eventually triumphed 4-2. It was the third time they had defeated us in the space of nine days, with the redoubtable Joey getting on to the score sheet in every instance. He was turning into a genuine nuisance for me, in a professional sense – we were close friends off the pitch – and I recall thinking at the climax of that match that he would have been better saving his goals for the final, which was eventually won by Rangers. None of this provided any consolation for our fans, whose aspirations of conjuring up another famous Cup triumph had been dashed by my mistakes and the clinical finishing of our rivals.

All the same, Thistle continued to combine the sublime with the absurd and I suspect that inconsistency was one of the reasons we attracted such a disparate assortment of fans: you never knew what was coming next. They developed a fine line in repartee, and had a crack for every occasion. Their sharp, quick-witted banter was a far cry from the sectarian bilge which emanated from the Old Firm. Thus we lived in our private playground, oblivious to changing trends elsewhere, and achieved more than we had any reasonable right to anticipate.

The following season, for instance, we propelled ourselves into another decent Scottish Cup sequence and conceded just one goal in the competition while beating Stirling Albion, Airdrie and Dumbarton, en route to a semi-final showdown with Rangers. We fancied our prospects in this game – the Ibrox side were in transition – and I pulled off a terrific save from Tommy McLean. Everybody in the Partick colours quite rightly believed we had clinched victory when, with only a few minutes remaining, Bobby Houston beat Peter McCloy with a header, only to be adjudged offside by a linesman, who was presumably a distant relative of Mr Magoo.

It was a desperate decision, and we were understandably frustrated at the death, with some choice words being reserved for the myopic official. But that was as nothing to our consternation when we dominated the ensuing replay and thoroughly outclassed Rangers, only for Derek Johnstone to scramble the match's solitary goal after we had carved out a string of opportunities of our own. 'How the f*** did we lose that?' was a common refrain in the dressing room, and even Bertie, who was normally as difficult to please as the Rev I. M. Jolly, wore a pained expression and conceded that the better side had lost.

These were strange times for me. When you are eighteen or nineteen you never imagine that you will do anything else except play football, but by the end of the 1970s, several of my friends were politely inquiring whether I had any other irons in the fire. In the event I had plenty of soccer left in me but once I became tied into a protracted contract at Partick, I was aware that I might have committed myself to them for the remainder of my professional career, considering how fickle sport can be.

At the finish of a particularly gruelling training session, one of the Thistle directors came up to me and asked: 'Alan, how do you fancy running a pub?' And there was me, the fellow who didn't know how to pour a pint or change an optic, or tell the difference between Bruichladdich or Buckfast, suddenly being invited to take charge of a Glasgow hostelry. It was a crazy suggestion, but at the time it seemed the most natural thing in the world, and although many players are often temperamentally unsuited to running a tavern, it kept happening. You had Jim Baxter, Billy McNeill, Walter Smith and a whole host of other internationalists with their own bars, so what was the problem with following their example? You could have written my knowledge of business on the back of a postage stamp, yet soon enough I was in charge of this pub in Maryhill – close to the stadium – which I called 'The Goal Post', eagerly awaiting a flood of customers with connections to Thistle.

That didn't happen, but one of my few regulars was Arthur Thompson, the Glasgow godfather, confidant of the Krays and a man whose contacts book extended to every section of the underworld. While struggling to combine the dual responsibilities of football and running a bar I gathered that whisky prices were poised for a steep increase, and ordered a dozen crates of the stuff, before heading off to Belgium for a testimonial match. On my return, I learned that somebody had stolen part of my delivery, which had been sitting unguarded in the yard. I shrugged my shoulders, but, within a couple of days, as I was sitting alone in the pub (an all too common occurence if I'm honest), this chap walked through the door, said 'Hello' and asked if I was Alan Rough. I nodded and he stuck out his hand and introduced himself. 'Pleased to meet you, I am Arthur Thompson. I hope you are settling in all right, and I want you to feel comfortable here, because this is my patch.'

We chatted for a few minutes – I had heard his name being bandied around, but had no notion of the power which he exerted in the city – and then he added: 'By the way, I like football and it's in my interests to see Partick doing well, so I will do what I can to help you. Incidentally, I gather you had a wee problem the other day with some drink going missing. Let me see if I can assist you, because it's nice to be nice.'

Within an hour of Thompson leaving the premises, this wee Glasgow worthy lurched in with a crate of Scotch, placed it on the counter, and spluttered: 'Hi there, big man, I'm really sorry, I didn't know that you were a friend of Arthur's. Apologies for causing you any trouble.' That must have been Thompson's idea of laying out the welcome mat for me and, initially at least, I was grateful, oblivious to the gruesome details of his numerous criminal links, the regular assassination attempts which he survived, and of his associates' stranglehold over their community. At one time I even hoped that by having him as one of my best customers it would attract publicity and persuade all the locals to flock to my gaff.

Of course, that was wishful thinking, and the venture was a disaster. The council had knocked down the neighbouring houses, so I was on my lonesome. There was no demand for another licensed premises, and nobody came in during the day. Also, there was no entertainment (apart from drinking and looking at my perm and garish selection of jumpers, that is) and, frankly, I didn't harbour a burning desire to be stuck behind a counter for hours on end, so I hired a manager and he brought in his cronies. With hindsight Tennent's may as well have put me in charge of a finishing school for debutantes in Chelsea. I didn't have a financial advisor, who might have extricated me from the mire, and after three years, when I added everything up, I found that I had lost a fortune, and was £30,000 in debt, at the beginning of my testimonial season!

This proceeded excellently, and my organising committee arranged a golf day, a gala dinner, and a match against Celtic, which attracted a massive crowd. Regrettably, somebody had fixed the ticket prices at £2 across the board, which wasn't too clever, but I still reckoned I would pocket the jackpot when the cash was totted up. When David Campbell, one of my best mates, announced to me: 'Right Alan, we have worked out how much we have raised for you and it comes to the grand total of £31,000.' I replied: 'That's great, that's bloody marvellous.' But then David flung a spanner in the works revealing that I would not be getting a penny of it. After asking why the hell not, he said, as sensitively as he could in the circumstances: 'Because you owe the brewery £32,000!' I was snookered, in the clouds one minute, down the tubes the next, and that single incident encapsulates the topsy-turvy nature of my life at Firhill.

My career on the field was also undergoing changes, not all of which were favourable. I've mentioned previously that in the aftermath of Argentina, Scotland suffered a depressing sequence of defeats, losing 3-2 to Austria in our opening European Championship qualifying match, with Archie Gemmill cruelly encountering Rudyard Kipling's twin impostors, by contriving an own goal which cost us a point in his first match since his magnificent effort against Holland. We were subsequently beaten 1-0 by Portugal in the Euro Championship in Lisbon, and, most disappointingly from my standpoint, were trounced 3-0 by Wales in the 1979 Home International Championship. John Toshack, as snappy and aggressive as usual, seized a hat-trick which prompted my demotion to the bench for the rest of the competition.

Naturally, I was frustrated at missing out on the opportunity to tackle the English again in their own back yard, but the balance between the teams had shifted, and despite John Wark opening the scoring, we were comfortably brushed aside 3-1, with my replacement, George Wood, struggling to contain the hosts in saturated conditions, not that I derived any pleasure from observing his difficulties.

In common with most sportsmen, I wasn't a good spectator, and it was especially difficult to keep a lid on my emotions in the charged atmosphere of Wembley. Jock Stein, who had unsurprisingly succeeded MacLeod as manager, convinced me that he merely wished to check out all his options and, within a week, I had been restored to the first team for a friendly meeting with the world champions, Argentina, in Glasgow. From a distance, all this sounds fairly chaotic, but I had been at Partick for so long that I was accustomed to flux and transition and a revolving-door policy of arrivals and departures. I was also now twenty-seven, confident in my abilities, and not remotely worried about having to scrap for my place. Our international slump however continued unabated when the South Americans rolled into town. We were all captivated by the mesmerising display of one of their newcomers, a young lad called Diego Maradona, who feinted and jinked and shimmied and looked capable of doing anything with a football. Obviously, he was still a raw talent, but he already possessed the aura of a superstar in the making.

Maradona was blessed with pace and boasted the quality which distinguishes the truly great from the very good – an apparently endless amount of time on the ball. It made him altogether too hot a proposition for a side as shorn of confidence as the Scots, scoring once and proving instrumental in his team's 3-1 win, with our only goal coming from Arthur Graham. One of the men assigned to mark him was Iain Munro, the St Mirren defender, and although he, like the rest of us, suffered a torrid evening, Iain was as pleased as Punch when he managed to get his hands on a tape of the match later on in his career. He was less happy with yours truly, mind you, after I borrowed the video from him, and watched the game, before leaving it in the machine. A week later, Iain asked me if I could give it back to him, and I did so, thinking nothing of it. But within a couple of hours, he phoned me and said 'What the f*** has happened here? I've put the tape on and all I can hear is "Hi ho hi ho, it's off to work we go".' Suddenly it dawned on me that the kids had taped over his precious possession. Replacing Maradona & Co with *Snow White and the Seven Dwarves.* I was a bit embarrassed, but then I suppose I had only replaced Scotland with the creator of Micky Mouse! Some might say the kids knew what they were doing.

Understandably, Stein was pragmatic in defeat. He recognised that there was no quick fix, urged the supporters to judge his stewardship on how Scotland performed in the 1982 World Cup in Spain (providing we qualified, of course). He knuckled down to an arduous task with the same relentless application which had epitomised his stewardship of Celtic throughout their halcyon period of European Cup glory and nine domestic titles in a row. I can picture him now, his beady eyes scrutinising us on the training ground. If MacLeod had been an improviser, Stein was the master planner; Mr Meticulous, a gnarled character who had seen everything on Planet Football and who didn't tolerate laziness or indiscipline.

His appointment was a coup for poor, bedraggled Scotland, and the Tartan Army began to scent renewed optimism following their temporary disenchantment, which had been deepened further by Scotland's dismal sequence of results in an abortive bid to reach the European Championships in 1980. It further helped that the World Cup qualifying draw was kind to us, with two countries from Scotland, Sweden, Portugal, Israel and Northern Ireland assured of entry to the main event. Although it would have been folly to disregard the last two of these sides, Stein rapidly decided where the major battles would be won or lost and, methodical to a fault, spelt out the message that we required a tangible reward from our opening tussle in Stockholm if we were not to be dragged into the mother of all dogfights for the next thirteen months.

I revered Stein, but was a little scared of him as well. Early in my tour of international duty I had been invited down to Seamill for an under-23 match and Jock was in charge of the team, with George Wood in line for the keeper's slot. Anyway, on the Sunday, the pair of us were bored in our hotel room, so we nipped off to the Marine Grill, had a couple of gin and tonics and, feeling in the mood for a night off, slipped out of the hotel in search of extra refreshment. We were mindful of the midnight curfew which Stein had imposed, but didn't manage to get back to Seamill until well after twelve.

Initially, we imagined that we had escaped without punishment. Our next move was to call room service and order a large plateful of sandwiches, along with a couple of pints of milk – as you do when you are feeling no pain – whereupon George's phone rang. It was his wife, and he began whispering sweet nothings down the line. In the midst of his conversation there was a knock on the door and there was Stein, bellowing: 'Where the f*** have you two been?' I kept trying to apologise, but he was in full throttle, calling me everything under the sun. George, who was still on the phone, missed all the flak, while Jock raged on. Within a few minutes, steam was virtually coming out of his ears, and the more I strove to placate him, the angrier he grew, until eventually he picked up this big tray of sandwiches and flung them all over me. I was standing there with a glaikit expression on my face, with bits of prawn and gammon and lettuce and tomato dripping from my hair and oozing down my shirt – it was farcical. Then he asked: 'Who the f*** bought the milk?' And I was sufficiently terrified that I replied: 'It's mine as well, Mr Stein.' So he lifted the glasses, poured them over my head and stormed off, leaving me looking like a stooge from a Laurel and Hardy film.

All that night George and I sat fretting. We concluded that we would be despatched home in disgrace, signalling the end of our international careers. We had worked ourselves into such a state that we didn't really believe things could get any worse. Thus we turned up for training the next morning at the ground of Troon Juniors, and, pretty quickly, Stein announced that everybody else could go back to Seamill, but insisted that George and I stay where we were. We slouched towards him, thinking to ourselves: 'Oh no, this is it.' He called us to attention and said briskly: 'What you did was out of order, it was completely unacceptable and this is what I do with players who break the rules.' Then he murdered us on that pitch for the next hour and a half, inflicting on us one of the most gruelling sessions I have ever experienced in my life. Within an hour, we were both knackered, dead on our feet, nauseous, but Jock displayed no mercy. 'You two seem to have trouble with deadlines. So I want you to know that there is no time limit on this shift. You will carry on until the two of you have been physically sick, and if you ever break a curfew again, then it will be twice as bad the next time round. These are my rules, I am not interested in coaching drunken footballers, so if you are unhappy with the situation, you can f*** off and I will find people who don't flout my authority.'

From that moment on I realised that Stein hadn't earned his fearful reputation lightly. If he believed you were guilty of slacking, he wasn't going to tolerate it. He had mastered the art of rumbling miscreants at Celtic and it was ingrained in his mind to the extent that he had a pathological hatred of footballers over-indulging in alcohol. All of which ensured that when the Scots began their quest for a berth at the 1982 World Cup finals, we knew there would be no hiding place for those who transgressed.

It was a message worth heeding, given the scandals which had plagued the Scottish game in the previous decade. These ranged from Jimmy Johnstone's troubles in a rowing boat at Largs through to the brawl in the Copenhagen nightclub which had abruptly terminated the careers of several talented players. And, although there were still several members of Stein's team, myself included, who relished the opportunity to unleash the shackles and socialise, there were an increasing number of individuals in the mould of Alex McLeish, Willie Miller, Alan Hansen and Gordon Strachan, who were model professionals, concerned with new-fangled aspects such as diet and nutrition. Their attitude reflected a belief that soccer players could no longer prosper on talent alone.

It was no coincidence that the majority of these lads were under Alex Ferguson's tutelage at Aberdeen. He was another boss who had no patience with wasters and womanisers, especially if it clashed with his preparations or threatened to undermine morale. So, essentially, Stein and Ferguson were eggs from the same nest.

I was relaxed about this transformation. Anything which helped foster success and nurture professionalism had to be encouraged, and Jock was nothing if not thorough in his tactical analyses of opponents. Our qualifying campaign was marked by his recruitment of various players to carry out a specific role. But he also insisted that we had to be adaptable and capable of changing our game plan when it was required. Against the Swedes, for instance, in September 1980, Stein was unperturbed by the late call-offs of Graeme Souness, David Narey and Kenny Burns, and deployed Miller in midfield, positioning him in front of the back four to thwart the counter-attacks of the Scandinavians. And the ploy worked, albeit not without anxiety. We had benefited from an early goal by Strachan, but the hosts were dangerous opponents and I was frequently pressed into service, which was the scenario that I most savoured. Better in my book to be active and wholly involved in the action, than try to stay focused with everything happening sixty or seventy metres away.

Despite Sweden's increasingly frantic attempts to attain an equaliser, I had more difficulty with the Austrian referee, Franz Wohrer, than I did from any of their strikers. The cause of this lay in the fact there were no ball-boys behind my goal and on one occasion I was forced to run round to retrieve the ball, which had gone behind some billboards. Unfortunately I caught my foot in one, plunged clean through, and was unable to extract myself, which was rather embarrassing. Herr Wohrer failed to see the funny side and accused me of time-wasting, and I was in peril of seriously incurring his wrath before my colleagues showed him I was genuinely stuck. Jock was understandably delighted with the victory, but the quizzical expression on his face as he congratulated me at the death carried the subtext: 'Ach, Alan, we cannae take you anywhere.'

None the less, it was a significant triumph and Souness returned for our next fixture against the Portuguese at

Hampden a month later. The majority of our supporters and the media thought it would be a stroll – how speedily the lessons of Argentina had been forgotten! – but, to be fair, we had encountered the same adversaries earlier that year and trounced them 4-1, with goals from Dalglish, Andy Gray, Steve Archibald and Gemmill, so the fans had good reason to be optimistic. What none of us could have anticipated was the sumptuous quality of the performance from Portugal's keeper, Manuel Bento, a world-class exponent of the art. He was sensational that night, resisting everything we could fling at him, and appeared to grow in stature. We carved out chance after chance, only for the Benfica stalwart to hold us, almost single-handedly, at bay.

Sometimes a goalie will find himself in a situation where he feels unbeatable, and it is a glorious sensation, which should be relished at all costs, because it doesn't occur very frequently. For my part, I had experienced something similar during our World Cup qualifying match against the Welsh strikers in 1977, and I also recall a sustained joust with Ally McCoist, when I was at Hibernian and he was with Rangers, where he would probably have amassed half-a-dozen goals on any other day, but couldn't defeat me for love or money.

Bento's heroics were in contrast to my own dearth of activity and I was trusting that it wouldn't develop into one of those tussles where the opposing goalkeeper produces twenty excellent saves as the prelude to his team's lone attack which results in a deflected goal. But mercifully, that didn't happen, and despite some mutterings from the terraces, Stein declared at the end that a win and draw – allied to two shut-outs – constituted an acceptable launch to our bid, and there was no need for us to fret over the outcome.

Our next foray abroad was to Tel Aviv the following

February, and although the result was satisfactory – we emerged with a hard-fought 1-0 success when the endlessly probing, sniping Dalglish capitalised on an accurate right-wing corner from John Robertson (the Nottingham Forest and not Hearts version) – it was an uncomfortable ninety minutes for me. The potency of the Israeli forwards in the first half forced me into making several saves, but I also had to overcome the consequences of my superstitious nature. In common with many keepers I have my good-luck charms and a pre-match routine which mustn't be altered in any regard. One of these involved wearing white socks whenever I was playing for Scotland. However, on the morning of the game, it was decided we were switching to our red change strip and the diktat was passed down by the SFA secretary, Ernie Walker, that we would be wearing red stockings. I was not a happy boy because it was messing up my ritual, and yet a hasty check of my kit revealed that I only had one pair of white socks – and they were filthy, from my having worn them at training the day before. Nervously, I approached Jock and explained the situation to him, half expecting him to send me packing in a flurry of invective, but he understood that 'goalies were different' (his expression) and eventually told me: 'Never mind about the red ones, wear whatever you like, and I will take the rap if there is any comeback.'

This was a weight off my mind and our physio, Jimmy Steele, promised to have them cleaned and ironed prior to the kick-off. Unfortunately, however, he stuffed them in a sports bag and forgot to dry them. I wrung them out in the dressing room before we trotted out onto the pitch, but as soon I was in the open air the water began to seep through my boots, which was hardly ideal. On the other hand, I wasn't inclined to raise the issue with Jock again – if I had done so, he might have fingered me as some flake, obsessed with mumbo-jumbo. So, oblivious to this puddle inside my boots, I stayed focused and recorded another precious shut-out. I knew I was right about the colour of my socks being critical . . .

We had already gathered significant momentum from these displays, and the crucial period in the qualifying series arrived in the spring of 1981 when we amassed three points from Northern Ireland and Israel (this was in the days when a win earned only two points). The Portuguese in the meantime had surprisingly gone down in Belfast. By this time the Tartan Army, a tad less gung-ho perhaps than the regiment of the mid-1970s, but still passionately committed to the campaign, were beginning to scent that another World Cup trip was just round the corner. Stein, however, was too canny to raise expectations in public, and his pronouncements were opaque and brilliantly constructed to prevent the media from dashing into print with jingoistic nonsense. He was leaving nothing to chance and demonstrated the savvy and deviousness which is the hallmark of most great managers. Meanwhile his incessant scouting missions and discussions with his coaching assistants highlighted Jock's unerring belief in being methodical.

As expected when two home nations lock together, that Scotland-Northern Ireland affair at Hampden was not for the faint-hearted, and it gradually developed into an engrossing, bruising encounter between two sides who refused to yield an inch to the other. I was soon in the wars when Willie Hamilton, the rambunctious visiting centre forward, charged into me and walloped the top of my shoulder. But although it proved a struggle to continue, I didn't want to be regarded as a soft touch by either my opponents or Stein. Inwardly, however, I was cursing and

Hamilton subsequently shattered my hitherto one hundred per cent clean-sheet with a header which I came desperately close to parrying away. Fortunately John Wark, a lively, industrious, and underrated performer, secured an equaliser, but despite my efforts to stay on the pitch, I was in agony by the eightieth minute and had to be replaced by Billy Thomson.

It was a sickener, and our 1-1 draw meant we were in the unusual situation of having a better record away from Glasgow than at home. I missed the end of the match when the doctors who attended to my injury decided to call an ambulance to ferry me to the nearby Victoria Infirmary for examination. On a normal day this wouldn't have caused any problems, but the vehicle didn't arrive until twenty minutes after the game had finished. Predictably, it took an eternity for us to crawl through the traffic jams and streams of supporters walking blithely along the road. There was a crowd of nearly 80,000, which suggests that those smart-arses who said that Scottish football had died post-1978 were talking through their posteriors. Luckily, the initial gloomy diagnosis of my shoulder injury was awry. Yes, it throbbed and ached like blazes, but I was given an injection, there was nothing broken, and I was back in fine fettle for our return meeting with Israel on 28 April, when we furthered our World Cup objective.

It was an 'interesting' contest, with sufficient talking points to fill a couple of my radio programmes. Most importantly, a couple of sweetly struck penalties from John Robertson and a Joe Jordan goal ensured there were no further Hampden hiccups, but I was forced to leap acrobatically to block a terrific shot from Beni Tabak in the early stages and the visitors tackled and scrapped with a ferocity which belied their lowly international standing.

Indeed, the result was still in the balance when Andy Gray came on for Dalglish twenty minutes from the climax, and almost immediately fell, as if pole-axed, in the box to earn Robertson one of his spot-kicks. Gray made the mistake then of telling everybody in the dressing room how he had kidded the Swiss referee and Stein went ballistic.

It demonstrates why Jock was so respected wherever he travelled: namely, that he was hard, but fair; he admired effort and endeavour, and loathed slacking, but, above all, he abhorred cheating in whatever guise. In plain terms, Andy had gained us a penalty, which had virtually booked our place at the World Cup, but that was immaterial to Stein. He warned the player never to repeat his gamesmanship or he would be consigned to the wilderness for as long as Jock was in charge. I have to admit that there were a few incredulous glances when he began haranguing Gray, but the manager told us he hated to think that we might relinquish a goal in similar circumstances and demanded that we adhere not merely to the rules but the spirit of the rules. It was a reminder of the code by which he plied his trade and I can think of several modern bosses who would do well to heed Stein's message. Those managerial figures who develop a blind spot whenever one of their star names perpetrates an outrageous foul or tumbles in the box are unfit to lace Jock's boots.

Once he had cooled down, we could bask in the knowledge that we had almost sealed our Spanish passage and as April turned into May, I was involved in my third success against England, at Wembley, where another Robertson penalty was ample. In this instance, so unlike 1977, there were no grandiose post-match declarations of intent – we still had some work to do and Stein was too streetwise to gift the media anything which might return to haunt us. But there was definitely a rising swell of expectation around a squad, blessed as it was with a mix of seasoned warhorses and burgeoning young colts.

Sweden, whose bolt was shot, certainly offered us scant threat when they ventured to Hampden in September, and were brushed aside 2-0, with Joe Jordan and John Robertson scoring the goals, the latter with his fourth spot-kick in four matches. This was one of those tussles where we enjoyed so much possession and territory that our opponents were always destined to concede fouls in and around their area, and they paid the price. The stadium erupted at the finish, and any scepticism amongst the support had clearly been replaced by renewed pride and joy, but Stein was still the soul of cold realism. Inwardly, I suspect that, although we had strung together a fine sequence when the pressure was on us, he appreciated that we were not World Cup-winning material.

Yet his first priority, qualification, had been assured and despite being burdened with an extensive injury list (Jordan, Danny McGrain, Alex McLeish, and the two Davies, Provan and Cooper) for the return tie with Northern Ireland at Windsor Park, Stein was aware that containment would be adequate. And so it transpired, with our opponents also guaranteeing their passage to the World Cup. Meanwhile there were greater concerns about matters off the pitch.

This, of course, had nothing to do with football and everything with the religious divide which had sparked incessant violence between various terrorist organisations in Northern Ireland. Sporting organisations simply tip-toed round the fringes of the crisis. Security was paramount in Ulster, and it was a case of getting safely in and out for the match and to hell with sightseeing visits! There were guard dogs outside the grounds of our hotel at Dunadry, and armed plainclothes officers wandering around the building – a wake-up call for those of us who lived in Glasgow to the scale of the tension and sectarianism which were endemic just a few miles across the Irish Sea.

Thankfully, the fixture itself passed without incident – I was praised for one save which I knocked on to the top of the bar – yet otherwise it was an insipid contest, which fulfilled the traditional definition of the more tedious Old Firm occasions – 'Nil-nil, nae football.' But, for once, I was merely relieved to be on the journey home as soon as possible, and able to bask in the knowledge that we had played seven of our eight qualifying ties and remained unbeaten. I wasn't to know at that stage that I would miss out on the concluding game when I suffered a freak accident at the Palacio Hotel in Estoril, ahead of our climactic tussle with Portugal: I tripped on the marble stairs and fell on my ankle on the day of the match. Despite Billy Thomson being forced to fill my boots at the eleventh hour, and the Scots succumbing to a 2-1 defeat, we were en route to Spain. For some of us, it was the chance to seek redemption and to exorcise the spectre of 1978.

It was also time to bid adieu to Partick Thistle, but that can wait awhile.

MORE PAIN IN SPAIN

Lessons had been absorbed from the gaffe-strewn 1978 World Cup. That much was evident in the lack of hype which surrounded the build-up to our next involvement in the competition. It wasn't just that Jock Stein was far too worldly-wise to indulge in over-blown forecasts, or that some of us in the squad were older and wiser from the bruises which had been sustained in Argentina, but there was less emphasis on Scotland, given that England and Northern Ireland had also qualified for the tournament. Our downplaying of expectations even extended to our official song, *I Have a Dream*, as written by B.A. Robertson and performed by John Gordon Sinclair, to which we provided backing vocals. Whereas *Ally's Tartan Army*, the anthem of choice four years earlier (although not the official song – that accolade went to the classic smash by Rod the Mod *Ole Ola*), bragged that we were on our road to South America to bring back the Jules Rimet Trophy, the 1982 offering was a self-deprecating exercise in poking gentle fun at ourselves. Perhaps that is why you could listen to it without blushing.

Before we left for Spain, the squad had to go to London for an appearance on *Top of the Pops* and that is as close as we came to being accorded A-list status. For some reason the BBC decided that we had to fly down the night before the live broadcast, so we enjoyed an evening's plush hospitality, prior to arriving at the studios at midday for a rehearsal. What the producers didn't tell us was that they wanted to put us through our paces three times prior to appearing live at 7.30pm. Perhaps inevitably, this was asking for trouble, given that we all knew the lyrics. These rehearsals passed quickly, leaving us plenty of time to sit around and while away the hours in the BBC bar. By the stage we were close to going on air, several of the players were out of their faces (not me, of course . . . Irn-Bru only; honest Guv). Added to which you had these farcical scenes of us all being kitted out in tartan jackets, an act of cruelty which should have been reported to Amnesty International.

Looking at the clip today you can see us all swaying to the music, with several of the more sober characters stopping the others from falling down. John Robertson had been asked to hold a football, but he was completely plastered and so glassy-eyed that he had forgotten the words of the song and was reduced to a state where he was lurching in front of the cameras, slobbering nonsense. He can't remember a thing, which highlights the dangers of sitting around in the green room too long. Fortunately, John Gordon Sinclair and B.A. were true professionals, and served up an excellent live version, which helped the song towards the summit of the charts.

Jock, as you might imagine, wasn't into pop music, but he was meticulous in every other regard. As soon as we learned in January that we had been drawn in the same group as New Zealand, Brazil and Russia, with our matches scheduled for Malaga and Seville, in the warmest part of Spain at the height of summer, Stein checked out all our opponents. Not exactly the same as Ally . . . He also spoke to a variety of doctors about how best we could combat the heat, and cast his gaze over the itinerary and accommodation to guarantee that we avoided being stuck in the kind of decrepit, down-at-heel joints, which happened in Argentina. He had obviously researched the reasons behind the 1978 fiasco, and vowed that there would be no repetition: if Scotland lost out, it would have nothing to do with factors outwith football.

Thus it was that Jock took us to Portugal for a week of acclimatisation and we stayed at the splendid Penina Golf Club, designed by Henry Cotton. We were nearby the popular Algarve resort of Praia da Rocha and, despite the temperatures approaching 100 degrees, managed to fit in a couple of fixtures against a local Torralta team as well as enjoying a few rounds of golf, amidst amenities which could hardly have been better. Certainly, there was nary a murmur of dissent, and the 'Wow' factor increased when we advanced from there into Spain and clapped our eyes on our World Cup base, deep in Tony Jacklin country at Sotogrande, where a training pitch had been pegged out for our benefit. Our hotel rooms also had windows and TVs and, praise be, there was plenty of water in our swimming pool. It couldn't have been more different from 1978 and, as we stretched our legs, and Jock checked out the location, prior to calling us together for a meeting, we had no complaints. It was an ideal holiday resort and we reflected on the prospect of sunbathing in luxury.

But of course Stein had other plans; we were there on a mission, and he was one of the most single-minded, formidable people I have ever encountered. Woe betide anybody who dreamt they could pull the wool over his eyes, and, from the outset, he was master and commander of our party. On arrival, at our initial team get-together in Sotogrande, he told us: 'Look, we're just off a flight, so I want you all to get up to your rooms, unpack, and grab a couple of hours' sleep.' His instructions could hardly have been clearer. Jock rammed home the message that he didn't want us lying out in the sun, and risk being burned – as had happened to me and the Thistle boys on our trip to Malaysia a decade earlier; I didn't think I'd mention that to Jock just at that moment. Not that I'd learnt anything, of course. Footballers being footballers, we all splashed on the suntan oil and dashed out to our verandas as rapidly as we could. Naturally, Jock fathomed that we would do this, and within ten minutes he walked along the outside of the hotel apartments, nailed absolutely everybody, asked us what the hell we were doing, and, much as a parent might react to a naughty five-year-old, sent us to our beds.

From then on we obeyed his orders explicitly. Why not – everything was better on that trip: the facilities, the quality of training, the fact we were occasionally permitted to cool off in the pool, the standard of service and the food . . . we could find no complaints on any score. We were also heartened by a visit from Sean Connery who lived in Marbella, and whose name carried sufficient clout for him to be able to squeeze through the tight security cordon to pay us a call, wish us good luck, and entertain us with that oft-imitated voice. We also had a rare laugh at the gaffer's expense when he nipped off in a World Cup vehicle with the rest of his backroom staff, but without warning the guards in Sotogrande what he was doing . . . and a police car swooped on them under the impression the motor had been stolen. Jock then had a hard time convincing a throng of officers he had made an honest error. It proved that he was human, which was pleasant, because there were many other occasions when we thought we were in the company of the Almighty himself.

As the start of the tournament beckoned, Stein added to our knowledge of our rivals and spent hours in the video room, analysing their strengths and weaknesses. Gradually, methodically, he went through the three games on the schedule, and his homework was first-rate. New Zealand, our opening adversaries, had been forced to travel tens of thousands of miles to qualify and had played a remarkable fifteen matches in the Oceania section, so you couldn't fault their commitment. Jock's conclusion boiled down to a fairly straightforward assessment: 'We should beat the Kiwis, and patently the more goals we can score the better, but I am not going to heap any pressure on you to defeat Brazil,' he told us, succinctly. 'We know their reputation, and it would be daft for any of us to rush into print with declarations that we will roll them over, but I want you to enjoy the experience, and soak up the atmosphere, because you should consider yourselves privileged: not too many Scots have ever gained the opportunity to meet the Brazilians at a World Cup, so I hope that you can seize it with both hands. As for Russia, that is the contest which will determine whether we progress any further in the competition and we have to be completely focused on that. I have watched them, and they are an extremely capable side, but we should not be frightened of them. They are beatable, but to achieve that, we have to be totally professional in our outlook and finish off our chances.'

It was typical of the man. There were no histrionics, no grand gestures, but rather a measured approach to the task which confronted us. As for New Zealand, he recognised that while this was classic banana-skin territory, if we approached the tussle professionally, they were to soccer what we were to cricket, we should be too good for them.

This was exactly how it panned out, though not without several scares along the way. Mind you, we would have been spared these frissons if everybody else had performed with the same sharpness, penetration and intensity of Gordon Strachan. He proved the catalyst for sustained mayhem on the right wing, individual brilliance which pushed us into a situation where we led 3-0 at the interval, with a brace of goals from John Wark and another from Kenny Dalglish. It was a glorious illustration of Strachan's talents, and a fresh reminder of how he and his Aberdeen team mates had blossomed under Alex Ferguson. Unsurprisingly, Stein was purring with pleasure throughout his half-time talk. On the surface, the hard work had been achieved, and now all that remained, in his estimation, was for us to capitalise on our superiority by completing a 5-0 or 6-0 victory, which would ensure that goal difference didn't become a factor . . .

If only it was that simple with Scotland! But instead of reasserting our authority upon the resumption, slackness crept in. A pass back from Danny McGrain was intercepted by Steve Sumner in the fifty-fourth minute, to reduce our advantage to 3-1. Then, as the underdogs discovered a second wind, they pegged matters back to 3-2 in the sixty-fourth minute with a fine effort from Steve Wooddin, which, briefly at least, shattered our composure, silenced the Tartan Army, and left Stein clutching the air in exasperation on the touchline. We couldn't afford to offer such charity and my instantaneous response was to say to myself: 'This lot won't score twice against the Russians.' (And they didn't.)

Eventually, we regained our poise and goals from John Robertson and Steve Archibald, a substitute for the ineffectual Ally Brazil, yielded a 5-2 victory, but there was little celebration at the whistle and the glowering displeasure from Stein was indicative of our general disappointment. It might have been different if we had struggled to break the deadlock, or wilted in the heat. Instead, bolstered by Strachan, who ran himself into the ground for eighty-four minutes before David Narey entered the action, we had established a magnificent platform for success and then done our best to undermine it with sloppy mistakes. That was what rankled with Stein, and he let us know it. It was irrelevant that never before (or since) have we accumulated five goals in a World Cup game. What mattered was the figure on the debit sheet.

So there was no rest in the build-up to the meeting with the Brazilians and at Jock's insistence, on the morning of the match, I suffered one of the worst hours of my life on a training pitch. The manager had identified the fabled South Americans' strength at corners, which they could swerve in every direction, and decided to put me through the wringer by testing me at set-pieces. 'They are going to be targeting you, so we had better get ready for that and build your confidence,' maintained Stein. Yet if that was the purpose of the exercise, it was lost on me. He picked Joe Jordan, Andy Gray and Gordon McQueen as his hitmen, and, for sixty minutes John Robertson did nothing but despatch corners for these three to attack, and they weren't too particular about snaffling a bit of me as well.

In fact, I was battered to pieces in the process as they hurled themselves at me with the same ferocity as if I had been Peter Shilton. As a psychological preparation, it was scarcely ideal. To be frank, when you are trying to concentrate on looking at the ball, but you can hear Andy, Joe and Gordon charging towards you, it is pretty scary, and I was covered in bruises and bumps even before I had embarked on the hellish coach journey from Sotogrande to Seville.

It was probably my only criticism of that World Cup itinerary. I have no idea whether there was an alternative route we could have taken, but it was as if we were traversing the Rocky Mountains. One minute this rickety old bus was puttering uphill, the next creaking downhill, and the trip seemed to last forever, without respite or even any illusion of comfort. Most of us were frazzled by the time we climbed off the vehicle. When we eventually reached the ground, however, the atmosphere was wonderful, with so-called 'rival' fans mingling together, dancing sambas and shaking maracas, and you have to bear in mind this was in a period when football violence was a depressingly regular occurrence throughout England and across Europe.

Mercifully, there was not the slightest hint of trouble between the supporters in Seville – on the contrary, they forged this immediate bond and the camaraderie was tremendous. Unfortunately, that wasn't the only thing which was obvious when we reached our destination. There was also the weather. It wasn't sunny, as it had previously been during the campaign, but humid, utterly stifling, with the temperature over 100 degrees, which made the short stroll into the stadium resemble walking into a wall of heat.

Jock looked concerned at the conditions and said: 'Let's get out early on to the pitch and sample this.' Which was fine for me – I was simply standing in my goalmouth and dealing with an assortment of shots, and it was a pretty gentle session. But within a couple of minutes the likes of Alan Hansen and Kenny Dalglish and Asa Hartford were dripping with sweat, their warm-up (hah!) strips absolutely soaked in perspiration and I was already asking myself: 'How on earth are we going to last nine minutes in this, let alone ninety?' It was unbelievable; a pressure cooker which sapped your strength and made you feel faint, and when Jock returned to the dressing room his team talk revolved around the necessity of retaining possession and striving to set the tempo, which would be nothing more than walking pace if we could help it. Although he was renowned for his wisdom and his attention to detail, he knew he had no control over the elements and the sight of wee Strachan, bearing an uncanny resemblance to a beetroot – and this prior to kick-off – did

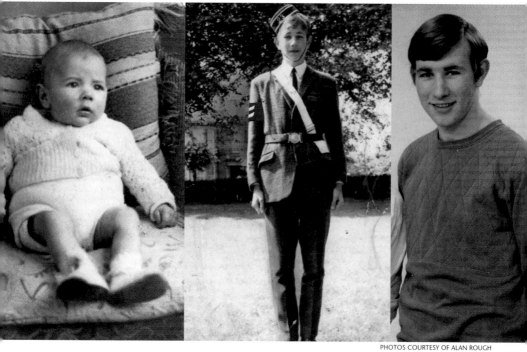

Before...

...and after. The start of a global phenomenon.

There was no surprise at a 4–0 half-time scoreline.
Except that it was in Thistle's favour!

SUNDAY MAIL, October 24

JAGS... THE GIANT-KILLER

They have Celtic on the rack

BY ALLAN HERRON

THE UNBELIEVABLE was happening out there on the saturated turf of Hampden Park — the Thistle fans were standing there chanting: "We want four . . . we want four" after only 30 minutes of this incredible final.

We were watching it, but we were hardly capable of digesting it. Celtic, one of the giant successful sides of all-time in British football, were being outclassed and humiliated by Partick Thistle in a major cup final.

I thought I had seen everything in football, but this was the most astonishing match I have ever seen in my life—because the whole pattern of the play seemed somehow totally unreal.

Thistle, just eight months out of Second Division football, were absolutely magnificent as they ignored the impressive record of Celtic and weaved their devastating patterns of attack, deception and uncovering toward the

• All eyes on the ball as Evan Williams is beaten for a second time by a tremendous Bobby Lawrie shot in 15 minutes, with the Celtic defenders looking slightly shocked

• The scorer is the man with his hands in the air—DENIS McQUADE. It's Thistle's third goal in 38 minutes and Celtic left...

SUNDAY MAIL

SUNDAY MAIL

No way through for
Dixie and Kenny as
I take the brunt and
Alan Hansen looks
hard as nails.

The Jags in Europe.
Not something you
can say every day.

It wasn't always
sunshine, smiles and
cigars with Bertie.

ACTION IMAGES

SCOTTISH NEWS SERVICE

1976. Scotland 2 England 1. Sweet.

1977. England 1 Scotland 2. Sweeter still. I wonder if those goalposts will see the day out.

EMPICS

MacLeod and Stein both brought a huge amount to the Scottish national team. We should cherish their achievements.

SCOTTISH NEWS SERVICE

World Cup 1982. My 50th Cap. With such silky skills on display the Brazilians must have been terrified of us.

UNDAY MAIL

SUNDAY MAIL

Aye, it's a tough life being a footballer. The pressures of photo calls, hanging out with Wham! (sorry, Charlie Nicholas I mean) and discussing literature with team mates…

Signing for Hibs. Things were tough at the club but under Pat Stanton we had good times.

Earning a draw at Pittodrie in 1984.

Four months with the Orlando Lions was just what I needed after my departure form Hibs. And meeting up with Bestie was the icing on the cake.

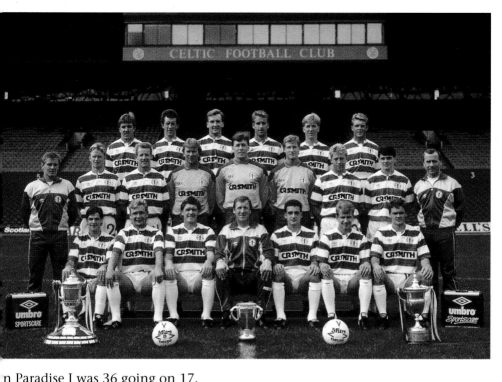

In Paradise I was 36 going on 17.

Reunited with Ally. Number 1 again.
No wait – that's the number of
first team games I played.

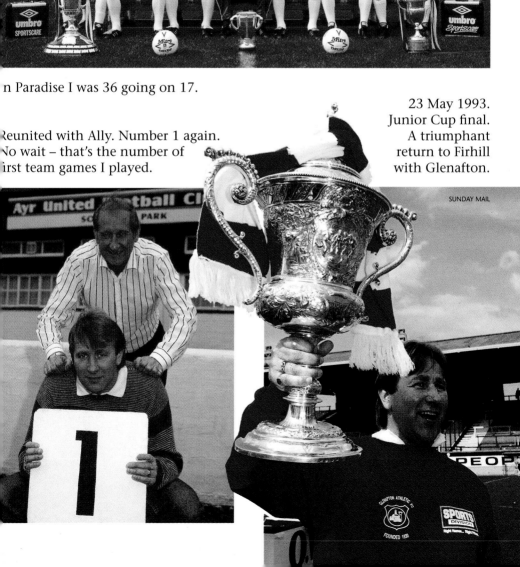

23 May 1993.
Junior Cup final.
A triumphant
return to Firhill
with Glenafton.

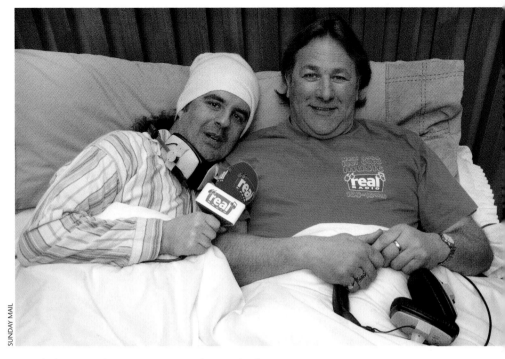

Eric 'n' Ernie. Or is it Ewen and Roughy?

At home with Sarah, Lucy, Maggie and Alan.

nothing to dispel the feeling that what always promised to be an arduous job was turning into an impossible one.

It was doubly dispiriting to survey our opponents who were wearing the smallest shorts I can remember on international duty. They were standing there unruffled, devoid of any signs of sweat or discomfort, but ready to dazzle another admiring audience with their pyrotechnics and prestidigitation. They appeared so relaxed: they had all these different gears which they could crank up to whenever the mood or the situation demanded. They started at a stately canter, and were clearly reining themselves in (perhaps they were wary of our explosive power from the outset . . . or, on the other hand, perhaps that is just their style), before David Narey scored a magnificent goal – a goal which was absurdly described as a 'toe-poke' by that impresario of smugness, Jimmy Hill. From a distance, I recall leaping up and down in the air with jubilation, before the suffocating heat halted me in my tracks. I should have known that at that precise moment it wasn't the Brazilians who should have been worried – it was us. We'd wounded the lion – now we were in for it. Despite Scotland's lead, our adversaries didn't panic or relinquish their control and you had to marvel at the fashion in which they swept like waves from one place to another.

I know that Brazil went on to experience a disappointing World Cup by their own lofty standards, but it was still an education to watch them stringing sixteen or more passes together, contriving intricate forays and perpetrating labyrinthine passages of play. They were constantly toying with us, even when we were winning, and yet they weren't interested in humiliating the opposition; it was all about searching for beauty and elegance on a football pitch. Although I couldn't have known that my fiftieth cap would be against these superstars, I was thrilled by their exploits and I was one of the men striving to hold them at bay. Eventually, of course, the mercurial Zico provided the equaliser with a free kick, and while I was frustrated that all our homework had come to naught, you can't really hope to joust with giants without sustaining injuries.

Subsequently I received a great deal of condemnation for conceding the goal. Both Jock and I had attempted to study their methods to the nth degree, but there is only so much planning you can undertake. We knew they had myriad options. Zico, Eder and Socrates were all dead-ball specialists, and we scrutinised miles of video evidence on how they lined themselves up. But you have to comprehend that they were in a different league. In Scotland, when you conceded a free kick, almost centre of your goal, you assembled your wall at one side and stood as cover at the other side. So far, so straightforward, and no decent Scottish keeper would have been frightened of defending these positions, on the domestic circuit.

However, this was Brazil and they were on an altogether higher plane. Jock had told me that Eder took most of their free kicks, but that the other two would be hovering nearby, and my mistake lay in focusing excessively on him. Whatever he did I had decided I was going to react to it, so, when the trio stood round the ball, and Eder feigned a move to take the kick into my right-hand corner, I anticipated that line of attack and made a slight movement in that direction. Once you do that, the striker recognises what is passing through your mind, and, in a twinkling, Brazil changed their plans and intimated that Zico would be their kicker. As this was happening, I had edged a little bit behind my own wall, and when he struck his attempt, I never truly saw him hit it. Had I done so, and if it had been in my line of sight, I could probably have stopped it, because the ball was only a couple of feet away from me. But I had been suckered and it may as well have been a couple of miles. Sure, I was annoyed, because we had contained them for thirty-three minutes and if we could have gone to the dressing room 1-0 ahead, it would have certainly allowed us to regroup and maybe have forced them to alter their style.

Jock wasn't going berserk or flinging teacups at us. He merely exhorted us to be patient and show perseverance and keep possession as often as we could, but I don't genuinely believe that he imagined we could win in these circumstances. He wasn't being defeatist, just practical, and I reckon that Stein's principal concern was that we didn't lose anybody to injury or serious dehydration ahead of the pivotal clash with the Russians.

It might have developed into an intriguing battle if we could have stemmed the Brazilian tide for the first quarter of an hour in the second half, but sadly, we allowed their defender, Oscar, a free header in the forty-eighth minute and he wasn't so profligate as to squander the chance. From that point, it was exhibition stuff, albeit with a clinical edge, and our boys were slack-jawed with a mixture of incredulity and exhaustion the longer the clock ticked on. Their third goal was a piece of magic from Eder, who gratefully accepted Serginho's exquisite service, and chipped me with the delicacy of Tiger Woods on the fringes of the green. The majestic Falcao applied the *coup de grâce* in the eighty-sixth minute, via the post. Basically, it was a tough old night for us, and I actually believe we did fairly well to restrict them to 4-1, given that our midfield players were knackered for two-thirds of the encounter. It wouldn't have been overly surprising if we had ended up conceding seven or eight.

The thing about Brazil was that they were fluent, they performed with the natural rhythm of a bossa nova, and although the term 'beautiful game' might be a cliché, they provided ample testimony to the fact that football *can* be a wondrous thing when it is played with that level of panache and pizzazz and precision. Granted, it is never enjoyable to taste defeat, but there were many instances where our lads were chasing shadows. To their credit men such as Graeme Souness, Alan Hansen, Willie Miller and Gordon Strachan, despite being dead on their feet by the climax, couldn't have given more to the cause, and our fans appreciated that. There was no booing at the final whistle here, nor was it any disgrace to yield to a side of that quality. But the consequence, as in 1978, was that we had to win our last match to advance further in the competition.

Jock was very phlegmatic; he had witnessed everything in the soccer canon, and nothing fazed him. For our part, we were told that, if we qualified, we had nine days to wait before the next round, and the SFA had decided we would be granted a £500 bonus and allowed to go away on holiday, wherever we desired, for the weekend. Suddenly, our thoughts turned to exotic locations, such as Cannes or Monte Carlo – I fancied Morocco – but Jock, characteristically, reminded us all that we would be heading nowhere except Glasgow unless we knuckled down to the serious business.

I can't rationalise, but despite the bonuses and rewards dangled in front of us, the tangle with Russia was a bit of a non-event. Ultimately, things just didn't click for us; there was a tension in the air, which hadn't surfaced earlier, and which did not dissipate even when Joe Jordan, restored to the fold, opened the scoring after fifteen minutes. From then on we should have been masters of our own destiny, but our captain, Souness, had already been booked, which restricted the level of aggression which he could display, and where we should have been fired up by taking the lead, it was as if we slunk back in our shells. This is one instance where I certainly don't take the blame for our problems, but although we quickly discovered that our opponents were no world-beaters, we lacked cohesion and toiled to crank up the momentum which might have brought us a decisive second goal. We were tense, bloody tense, and the butterflies wouldn't budge.

At the interval Jock advised us to get the basics right, and forget elaboration, but his message went unheeded, the malaise continued and it was symptomatic of the match that Aleksandr Chivadze should level matters on the hour when he unwittingly swerved his shot past me after failing to strike it properly. One or two of our lads looked disconsolate when they should have fathomed there was ample time to retrieve the situation. It was almost as if we were preparing for the roof to cave in, and there was an inevitability about the manner in which Hansen and Miller, normally two of the most dependable, classy defenders in Europe, conspired in a disastrous mix-up in the eighty-fourth minute which gave Ramaz Shengelia a clear sprint towards me on my lonesome.

It was the sort of one-in-a-million years collision which appeared to be *de rigueur* for the Scots in World Cup combat. I stood there, watching the debacle unfold and it was simply a lack of communication between the pair. I had plenty of time to weigh up the situation and ponder my choices, but these essentially entailed either running out of the box and hauling the striker down, which would have brought a red card, or wait until he neared me, after which it was in the lap of the gods. Unfortunately, nobody else put any pressure on Shengelia, he was clean through in acres of empty space, and the question was whether he might lose his cool and blast wide or give me an opportunity to dive at his feet.

To his credit though he remained calm, converted the chance, and our aspirations had vanished in a pratfall straight from a Carry On film. Even then, there was sufficient time for Souness to level the score at 2-2 as the prelude to the usual 'Charge of the Light Brigade' from the Scots during an action-packed finale. But it was a lot of sound and fury which signified nothing but our elimination. Elsewhere, England topped their group, and Northern Ireland defeated the hosts to win their section, which merely reinforced the impression that we were our own worst enemies, the kings of wishful thinking. With hindsight, Stein couldn't be held accountable – there was no better manager at the tournament – but when you analyse our World Cup record from 1974 to 1982 and discover we had played nine, won three, drawn four and lost just twice, yet failed to progress from the preliminaries, it hints at a dearth of mental toughness. After all, we took the lead in all our three matches in Spain without beating anybody but New Zealand, so it wasn't that we were playing catch-up, quite the opposite.

That was demoralising enough. Nor was it any consolation that we had been involved in what would later unfold into one of the great football tournaments in the chronicles, with Italy, Brazil and Argentina drawn together in the same group. Every game oozed quality, particularly the Azzurri's 3-2 triumph over Zico & Co. We simply had to settle into the role of bit-part players and gaze at the fantastic, controversy-packed semi-final between Germany and France, which the former won 5-4 on penalties (3-3 after extra time), but only after their goalkeeper, Harald Schumacher, escaped any censure whatsoever for a life-threatening challenge on the French defender, Patrick Battiston. That briefly made me wonder if I should have pole-axed Shengelia, and damn the consequences. But I could never have committed a premeditated assault on any opponent and my conscience is clear on that issue. None of which diminished the deflation which engulfed our party as we bowed out of another World Cup.

On the way back to Sotogrande some of us deliberated on whether we really wanted to return to the complex and mope for three days, prior to our flight. Wouldn't it be better to stop off at Puerto Banus, the playground for the affluent yacht-owners and Ferrari drivers, next to Marbella? There was no point indulging in redundant post-mortems or musing on the whys and wherefores of how Scots, en masse, appeared addicted to the principle of so near and yet so far. We would surely be happier escaping the goldfish bowl and enjoying a short vacation. Made sense to us – it won't surprise you. The only concern lay in how Jock would respond to this request. Eventually Kenny Dalglish, as effective a shop steward as he was a striker, explained the situation to Stein who replied without a pause: 'Well, if that is how you feel, fine. I have no problems with your idea and many thanks for all your efforts.' He did add the rider: 'The official bus will be leaving Sotogrande on Tuesday at 6am sharp and if you aren't there, you will have to make your own way home.' But that was fair enough and George Wood, Joe Jordan, Graeme Souness, Kenny and myself hopped off the bus at Puerto Banus for a diversion which proved truly therapeutic. It helped, of course, that Dalglish had a friend in the Holiday Inn management business, who lent us a boat for the remainder of our stay in the Costa del Sol.

We didn't overstay our welcome in paradise – even a diet of lotuses can pall – but there was plenty of Spanish champagne for our party and that sparked a minor embarrassment for me. I had gone ashore for lunch with George and we christened three or four ships, followed by a stroll along the beach. I wasn't in the mood for a dip, but our boat was moored just 100 metres out and my goalkeeping colleague insisted that we swim back, even though I was so light-headed I could barely keep my eyes open.

Predictably, my breast-stroke technique was not of Olympic standard and I was soon floundering around in a splurge of splashing, bubbles and expletives, making barely five metres a minute. Finally George lost patience and barked at me to stand up and take a rest. When I did so, the water only reached as far as my waist . . .

Sun, booze, good food, a boat – God it was tough recovering from our World Cup exit. But we struggled through. Seriously though, it was the perfect antidote to Seville and the single lingering source of anxiety was making sure that I didn't miss the Scotland bus. The other players made their own plans, whereupon I fell in with a group of my compatriots and stayed in their apartment on the last day. 'Look, I can't afford to sleep in, Jock will go nuts, so can you wake me up early tomorrow?' I told them, so we set the alarm clock for 4.30am, and I ordered a taxi, but it was a close-run thing; I arrived at the hotel at 5.55am. And who was sitting there but Stein himself, waiting on everybody and ticking off the numbers. We all made it back, we owed the Big Man that, and, in any case, we knew what he could be like when he was cheesed off.

But, in some respects, Stein's disciplined approach summed up our Spanish adventure. It was low-key, resolutely downbeat, almost as if the SFA had decreed that there should be nothing remotely reminiscent of the scandal-laden campaign in Argentina. It never occurred to me at the time as I trudged off the field, a disconsolate figure after the draw with Russia, that I was in effect kissing international football goodbye. But I was on the wrong side of thirty, I had posted over fifty caps for my country, and several of us were destined to be allowed to fade quietly out of the spotlight.

Should I have been thinking along those lines? Perhaps but, unlike today, where youngsters are actively encouraged to pursue academic qualifications and get ready for life after football, playing the game was all I knew and I had spent the previous decade engaged in a love affair with the sport. This blinded me to the reality that, sooner or later, there would be a time when I would be too old to continue pulling on the goalie's jersey. Whether with Partick or Scotland, I was protected from the daily grind of worrying over the source of my next pay cheque. As we returned home, I had several pressing concerns to address; they wouldn't wait forever. And yet I was convinced that if one door closed, another would open. And it did.

I was lucky that way. All it took was the phone to ring and I was on the carnival trail once again. In retrospect, it was hardly a wonder that some of my friends imagined I had a four-leaved sprig of clover permanently stuck to my back pocket.

SUNSHINE AND SHADOWS

By late summer in 1982, it was clear that I needed an amicable separation from Partick Thistle. The club had been terrific to me, with Eddie McCulloch nurturing me as a teenager, Dave McParland easing my path into first-team football, and Bertie Auld, regardless of his temper tantrums, coaxing and cajoling me into training regimes beyond the call of duty. But, while I was appreciative of all their efforts, my record of 624 appearances for the Firhill organisation, including 418 league outings, was ample evidence that I could hardly be accused of being a fly-by-night. Despite the several prospective transfer deals which might have sparked my departure to England – whether to Hull City with Terry Neill, or to Middlesbrough with John Neal (who approached me a few days before the Scotland-England match in 1978, only to pull out, an hour before the kick-off) – I was starting to think that I might be destined to spend my whole career at the one organisation. In the aftermath of the World Cup in Spain I was beginning to reckon that my international stint was finished, and although I was never the sort of individual to trudge around with a petulant lip, or the confrontational type who would demand so-called 'crunch' meetings with managers, there was no question that after thirteen seasons at Thistle, I needed a fresh challenge.

*   *   *

Peter Cormack was now in charge at Partick, and I recall popping into the reception area of the stadium one Thursday afternoon and being informed by the secretary, Molly Stallon, that the gaffer wanted a chat with me about my contract situation. He wasn't at his desk, so I pressed Molly for more information and she declared casually, as if discussing the weather: 'Oh, I gather that the club has decided to sell you to Hibernian for £60,000.' I was dumbstruck at this, but bit my tongue, and awaited Peter's arrival. When he finally appeared, he noticed me standing with this inquisitive expression on my face, invited me into his office, and asked: 'What is it?' I replied that I was under the impression that I was on my way to Hibs and he looked genuinely surprised, before remarking: 'Well, that is the first that anybody has told me about it.'

The Partick directors, a brethren forever on the verge of financial penury, had apparently implemented the decision and neglected to let their manager in on the secret. Suddenly it dawned on me that I had never been involved in transfer negotiations, and hadn't an earthly as to the procedure I should follow. 'Aha,' I reasoned, 'Peter is a man of the world, he has been on the merry-go-round, so I will pick his brains.' Eventually, once I had enlightened him on my ignorance of these matters – for me, the concept of contract discussions extended about as far as picking up a pen and signing a piece of paper – he flitted away for a rapid chat with a couple of the directors, who were still in the building, then confirmed: 'Well, from what I gather, you have to travel through to Edinburgh tonight to see their chairman, Kenny Waugh, who is promoting a boxing event, and thrash out the personal details of the move with him.'

This was all happening so quickly that a hundred different things were flashing through my mind and I was in a whirl. 'Erm, Peter, you have played with Liverpool, you are used to dealing with guys in suits, how much money do you think I should be looking for?' He drummed his fingers on his desk, scribbled a few figures down in a notebook, then announced to me, with all the solemnity of the Chancellor of the Exchequer: 'Let's see, if it is a three-year contract, I think that if you received between £10,000 and £12,000, that would be fantastic.' All of which sounded pretty impressive to me in my naivety. And so I left Firhill in the twinkling of an eye and without any of the teary scenes which might have been anticipated.

As excited as any teenager, I leapt in my car and ventured to Edinburgh, where I briefly met the Hibs manager, Pat Stanton, at the Royal Scot Hotel. It was on then to Kenny's function at the Oratava Hotel, where the place contained so many people dressed like penguins, I might as well have been an Arctic explorer. With hindsight, it was no mystery as to why we had to settle this business with such haste. Kenny was clearly pre-occupied with boxing matters during our meeting, and when he shook hands, and exclaimed: 'How are you, Alan?' and I responded, 'Fine, Mr Waugh, we have a lot of things to discuss,' I should have guessed we would not be indulging in small talk. In fact, as sponsor of the next bout, he had next to no time at his disposal.

It was a curious, nigh-surreal occasion: I was battling with a variety of emotions, and concluding that this was probably the biggest moment of my life, whereas Kenny's thoughts were elsewhere, and he just halted me in my tracks with the words: 'Right, the most important thing, son (he always called me that – and he still does), is to thrash out the size of your signing-on fee, so what sum do you have in mind?' He possessed this brisk, no-nonsense, my-time-is-money manner, which could initially be quite intimidating. I was also in unfamiliar territory, so I wavered for an instant, recalling Peter's guidance, and wondering whether I wasn't pushing my luck, when he interjected: 'Okay, let's agree on terms, we want you on a three-year deal, so is £25,000 okay with you?' There was a pause and I thought to myself: 'What! And that eejit, Cormack, was about to sell me up the creek!'

I was so completely stunned that I nodded my approval on the spot and it was only once Kenny had marched away that I realised that I hadn't asked him about wages, or expenses, or bonuses – or, in fact, any of the issues which should have been central to our conversation. I hadn't signed anything either, so I returned to Glasgow with a large smile on my face, and absolutely nothing finalised from a legal perspective.

It had been a momentous few hours, but the very next morning brought another twist in the tale when I was sitting at home, scanning Friday's newspapers and the telephone rang. It was John Greig, the then manager of Rangers. 'Alan, I have been reading speculation in the tabloids that you might be poised to join Hibs and I need to find out if these stories are true.' I answered: 'Well, I met Kenny Waugh last night, and we have agreed a signing-on fee, but I haven't put pen to paper on a deal as yet.' John continued: 'Look, I want you to come to Ibrox, so can you sit on this until Monday? I will get together with my board, and I am confident that I can persuade the directors to go for it. But please don't mention this to anybody until the start of next week. Fine?'

Fine? Only twenty-four hours earlier I had been treading water at Firhill; now, I was being courted by a couple of the biggest organisations in Scotland. What I didn't appreciate at the time was that John was experiencing a crisis at Rangers – this was at a time when they were being surpassed by Alex

Ferguson's Aberdeen and the crowds were drying up drastically – but it would still have constituted a decent move for me. I felt akin to a struggling actor who finds himself transformed from one of the extras, sitting behind Ken Barlow in the Rover's Return, into a situation where he is being offered leading roles from Steven Spielberg and George Lucas at the same time, and I was as content as I had been for years.

But, when I woke on the Sabbath the saga took a new turn when I picked up the *Sunday Mail* and the headline 'Rough for Rangers' was splashed all over the back page, in the kind of typeface which is normally reserved for assassinations and Royal weddings, and I guessed that I would be heading to Easter Road after all because the Old Firm weren't in the habit of signing players via the media, and John had obviously been shafted by somebody in his circle. To his credit, he rang me on the Monday, he sounded terrible, and said to me: 'Alan, I am very sorry at the way this has unfolded. Circumstances have conspired against me. I didn't mention this to the board, but I look pretty stupid and the deal just isn't going to happen.' I had no doubt as to his sincerity, and his tone was that of a fellow at the end of his tether. I wasn't a Rangers fan – I had always been a supporter of their Old Firm rivals – but I would have been totally professional for them if I had walked through the gates at Ibrox, and would have been very happy to work for John. Remember he was one of the most courageous, committed characters ever to represent his club and country. However, it wasn't to be, and in some respects, that was a relief, considering I had already given a verbal pledge to Kenny Waugh.

Luckily, as I came under the influence of Pat Stanton and his assistants, George Stewart and Jimmy O'Rourke, and met players such as Jackie McNamara, Ralph Callaghan and Bobby Smith, I found myself in my element. There was an instant rapport between us which compensated for the often harum-scarum nature of footballing affairs at Easter Road in the early 1980s. For instance, within a few days of my arrival, Pat turned to Jimmy one morning and asked: 'Where are we training today? Are we heading off to Leith Links?' But the latter replied: 'Naw, we cannae, the police chased us aff that park yesterday.' So Pat followed up with: 'What about Liberton?' At which Jimmy told him: 'Nope, we've messed that place up, the council are doing it up at the moment.' Eventually, Pat said wearily: 'So, what you are effectively telling me is that Hibs FC, one of the proudest soccer institutions in Scotland, has nowhere to go and train?'

Then, finally, O'Rourke, a quicksilver individual, with an eye for mischief and a heart the size of a lion, provided a tonic for the troops, by concluding: 'No problem boss, we can always chance it at Holyrood.' Thus it was that we trotted off with our kit, oblivious to the fact that no formal arrangements had been made, and, en route, Jimmy let slip to the manager: 'By the way, Pat, we have only got two balls available for training purposes today.' Stanton was on the point of despair when his colleague added: 'But then, who's counting? I've only got two balls to my name, but I am still swinging with the best of them.' Quietly, in the background, I was privately reflecting: 'What the f*** have I walked into here?' Once we reached Holyrood, Pat split the players up into the Firsts against the Reserves and we were just starting to enjoy ourselves, when suddenly we heard this whistle in the distance. It was the park police. McNamara screamed at me: 'Alan, hurry up, get down and hide until he has gone away.' And the twenty-five of us had to dive on to the ground and lie low, until the bobby had passed us by.

It seems farcical now that Hibs should have been involved in such a scenario – whatever happened to all the cash which they must have raked in during the glory days of the Famous Five, not to mention the star-studded line-up of the Seventies? – but the management team were my kind of people, there was no standing on ceremony, they mucked in and were glad to get their hands dirty in a common cause. Pat was a gentleman, an avuncular fellow, who treated everybody as if they were his favourite nephew. And he talked to people rather than shouting at them, while George and Jimmy revelled in their roles, relished a laugh, and boasted a terrific sense of community spirit. This was crucial to Hibs at the time because they were, quite simply, hanging on by the skin of their teeth, surviving on the most meagre of budgets, and eking out modest results without a sugar daddy in sight.

We were all earning peanuts – I was on £170 a week – and half-a-dozen of us travelled through from Glasgow every day. It even reached the stage where the club wouldn't grant us expenses, so some of us used to fiddle our three-month rail passes and alter the dates on them, which would probably provoke outraged headlines in the tabloids today, but which merely seemed a big joke at the time. Pat was always in a parlous position with the board – there was never significant money to strengthen the squad – and he was regularly forced to sell his leading youngsters. I sympathised with his plight, as this was not an entirely different environment from Partick, where expectations were permanently low.

Nor did it help that, after helping the team climb up the table during my first season in Edinburgh – when I made my debut in a 3-2 defeat against Celtic – we then amassed a paltry seven points from thirteen fixtures and were once again staring at the spectre of relegation when I broke my ankle. It happened on a frozen pitch at Bayview, in a Scottish Cup replay against East Fife, which we lost 2-0 – an outcome which heaped further pressure on Stanton. That incident was doubly galling as, although I was in agony, the home club's doctor convinced me there was no fracture. So I journeyed back to Glasgow, only to be forced to hobble off to hospital in the middle of the night to find nobody on duty in the X-ray unit. On the Sunday morning I learned what I had dreaded – that the bone was indeed broken – and that left me consigned to a plaster cast, and months on the sidelines, twiddling my thumbs and bemoaning the fact the referee had permitted the Fife game to proceed. As things turned out, we warded off the ominous presence of relegation, finishing safe but in the lower half of the division.

That spell on the periphery allowed me a breather to cast a glance over the rest of the leading Scottish clubs. It simply reinforced my conviction that the Hibernian board had left Stanton becalmed. All right, we couldn't expect to compete with the Old Firm in terms of revenue or supporter numbers, but we were also lagging badly behind Aberdeen and Dundee United, both of whom were regularly challenging for major honours, and one of the keys to their success was continuity. The Dons, in particular, inspired by Alex Ferguson, with chairman Dick Donald acting as the paterfamilias, illustrated exactly what was possible outside the Glasgow goldfish bowl. Their triumphant advance to the European Cup-Winners' Cup final in 1983, where they famously defeated Real Madrid 2-1 on a sodden evening in Gothenburg, was one of the few instances where I felt envious of several of my former international colleagues, including Gordon Strachan, Willie Miller and Alex McLeish. Fair enough, I had accumulated fifty-plus caps for Scotland, so I was hardly in a position to complain about missing out on the major occasions, but it was perplexing to me that a club with the history and pedigree of Hibs could be content to settle for mid-table mediocrity (at best). Meanwhile their transfer policy ensured that whenever they unearthed a talented youngster, he had barely made his mark on the Easter Road faithful before the directors were rubbing their hands in glee and touting him for sale.

If I sound angry, part of my exasperation lies in the admiration which I harboured for Stanton, an eminently decent, hard-working individual and one who deserved better at the hands of his employers than to be inched out of the revolving door in September 1984, without being granted the investment and the loyalty to do his job properly. A home loss to Dumbarton settled his fate, but the guillotine had beckoned for months before that. I felt sorry for Pat; although we were also-rans in the championship stakes, I simply don't believe anybody would have fared much better in the circumstances. If he had a fault it was that he was possibly too nice to cope with the more brutal aspects of football – telling kids they weren't good enough to turn professional, for instance, or pulling an old-timer aside and informing him his contract wasn't being renewed. But integrity should never be regarded as a vice, nor bullying as a virtue, and, frankly, some of the values which seeped into Easter Road as the 1980s rolled on suggested we had gone through the looking glass or entered a parallel universe.

With Stanton's departure, along with Jimmy O'Rourke and George Stewart, the managerial role was handed to his second-in-command John Blackley, a former Scotland colleague of mine. He proved to be significantly more intense and competitive than his predecessor – if John thought that anybody wasn't pulling their weight, he bawled him out – while Tommy Craig was also recruited to Easter Road and soon started exhibiting the methodical qualities which have earned him widespread respect across the football circuit in Scotland and England. Blackley didn't hang around, making a shrewd signing in Gordon Durie, and he also snapped up the likes of Steve Cowan and Gordon Chisholm. Tommy in the meantime endeared himself to the squad with the intensity of his academic approach to training: he was akin to an absent-minded professor, beavering about in his own domain, and organising everything to the nth degree. The rest of us were often amazed by his work ethic.

I recall that the first day we hooked up with John and Tommy the latter had booked the grounds at Fettes College, and had completed preparations for the session so thoroughly that when the rest of us turned up in the team bus, there were so many cones lying on the ground that I half expected a couple of aeroplanes to land on the grass. That vignette summed him up: he was incredibly organised, his office at the club was plastered with wall charts and to-do piles and blackboards covered in chalk. He was one of those rare people, blessed with the ability to work on twenty different tasks and chores at the same time, without losing focus or forgetting his priorities. He and John were a good combination, a frost-and-fire partnership, and despite our continuing fiscal woes, there was a less dishevelled look to Hibs and we recorded some notable displays in the Cup competitions, even if our league form was at best erratic, and at worst, chronically bad.

Perhaps if Blackley and Craig had secured a trophy, they might have been given more time to settle into their roles, but 1985 was a frustrating year at Hibs, considering the opportunities which the team orchestrated without earning any tangible reward in terms of silverware. By that point the club's youth system was unearthing some splendid prospects, none more impressive than John Collins, who was my boot boy and who engaged in the thankless task of scraping the mud off my footwear with the same purposeful intensity which characterised his attitude to training and playing. Right from the outset there was no larking around, no descent into bad habits: instead, Collins was smartness and professionalism personified and I recognised that he was going to be a star, right from his first fledgling steps in the Hibs cause.

Earlier in my career, Alan Hansen had shown a similar single-mindedness and there is an inevitability about the progression of certain players which means it isn't a surprise when they shine on the biggest stages. It is not so much that they are selfish, as absorbed with being the best they can possibly be, striving to push themselves to more exalted levels. For the majority of footballers, simply being involved and paid to play the game is sufficient.

Our 1985 League Cup campaign was a frustrating experience, not least because when you beat both halves of the Old Firm in any tournament, you expect to win it. It was so typical of Hibs that we weren't afraid of Rangers or Celtic, but seemed to find new means of losing to Aberdeen whenever we tackled them. On our road to the final I managed penalty saves against both the Glasgow giants, and the disgruntled expression of Ally McCoist's face from a few yards away when I blocked his shot is still ingrained in my mind.

One or two of our players responded to these victories by remarking that this might be our season, but I wasn't convinced. Let's not forget that Aberdeen in the mid-1980s was an incredibly talented club, and the team they despatched on to the Hampden turf for our encounter epitomised their strength – the side was replete with oft-capped internationalists, from Jim Leighton, and the stalwart defensive pairing of Miller and McLeish, through to Eric Black and Billy Stark. Although we brought a massive travelling support along with us from Edinburgh, I can't claim I was particularly optimistic in advance. I was keenly aware that we had had less joy against the Dons during my period at Easter Road, than any other opponents in the league – including Hearts.

In the build-up, I walked around the stadium and reflected that this might be my last appearance in an occasion of this magnitude. As far as I was concerned, there was no prospect of my regaining my Scotland place. Leighton and an emerging Andy Goram were now dominating the goalkeeping berths, and while I was still enthusiastic about soccer, and relishing my residence at Hibs, I was beginning to ponder, at last, I know, life after football and it wasn't a pleasant concept. I hadn't amassed any savings (big surprise), I was no intellectual genius (although obviously I hide it well), and my past experience of owning a pub had demonstrated that I was to that profession what David Brent was to running an efficient office.

None of this should have been important on the day of a Cup final, but I was thirty-three which in sporting terms meant I was edging towards the veteran tag. As I waited in the dressing room, I could only hark back to the heady scenes on my first visit to the national stadium, in the same competition, with Partick in 1971. Now, as then, we were rightly bracketed as underdogs, in light of Aberdeen's list of achievements in the previous three or four years. But, in this instance, there was to be no romance, or tales of the unexpected, and despite the vocal exhortations of our supporters, and the fact the match was being screened live on television, it was as flat as a pancake, and we were, quite frankly, never in the hunt.

Before the kick-off, I tried to convey the message to the

younger members of the team that they had to savour the atmosphere, soak in the memories, and revel in the spotlight. These kind of afternoons don't happen too often in anybody's career. I also recalled the way in which Partick Thistle had entered the arena against Celtic with absolutely no trepidation – we had nothing to lose. I might as well have been speaking to the stones on the wall. Quite simply, we froze; we were like rabbits in the headlights, and Aberdeen surged forwards in waves, and had scored twice inside twelve minutes through Black and Stark, with John Hewitt sparking panic amongst our defence every time he embarked on one of his marauding forays on the left wing.

By nature, I am not one of life's shouters; I don't believe any player deliberately sets out to make mistakes and especially in a final. But I was furious at the manner in which we allowed Aberdeen to dominate and bully us into submission, and there was no way back once the second goal had been stuck into my net. We were missing our regular centre-half Gordon Rae, who had been banned for three matches, commencing with the final, but that was no excuse and Aberdeen's early supremacy sucked all the passion out of the contest. We were reduced to foraging for respectability. I hesitate to say we attained even that modest aim – Black subsequently added a third goal, which merely reinforced his team's superiority – and I was a pretty shell-shocked character by the death, even though I picked up one of the few medals in my career.

I suppose it was one of the first occasions when actual retirement entered my thinking. Scary. But once again, I found myself in the right place at the right time. Just as I was wondering about a possible source of future employment, my topsy-turvy world was turned on its head once more when out of the blue, I received a phone call from Jock Stein. It was to invite me to join the rest of the Scotland squad at Turnberry, prior to the 1985 Home International Championship and the subsequent international meeting with Iceland in Reykjavik at the end of May. I had assumed that my international career was long finished, and Stein was typically frank with me as soon as I climbed down off cloud nine. The pair of us were having a meal at the Ayrshire hotel, with Jock's assistant, Alex Ferguson, and the Big Man said gruffly: 'You know something, Alan, you are very lucky that you are back in the fold.' I briefly imagined he was going to qualify that remark, by imparting some piece of wisdom or shaft of wit in my direction, but he was deadly serious and said in a matter-of-fact fashion: 'The truth is that I never picked you.' I was mystified as to what he was talking about, but he continued: 'Three weeks ago, I was at home with my wife Jean, and I was telling her that I needed to find a third goalie for the World Cup qualifying campaign. Well, we discussed a couple of names, and then she inter-jected: "Why not bring back Alan Rough? I really like him and he has never let you down." I wasn't sure myself, but she can be a pretty convincing character witness and she is the only reason that you have returned to the fold.'

Clearly, I felt grateful to Jean, if ever-so-slightly deflated, but it was simply terrific to be involved at that level again. All of us were in high spirits following Richard Gough's goal, which had earned Scotland a 1-0 victory over England at Hampden. We travelled straight from the stadium to the airport for the important qualification match with Iceland, one in which I nearly participated, following a curious injury sustained by Jim Leighton. On the Monday evening before the fixture, Jim and I went to the cinema with Graeme Sharp and Andy Gray (the latter pair had arrived late because Everton had played Coventry on the Sunday). I can't remember exactly what we saw. It was a re-run I'm pretty sure. Perhaps the *Magnificent Seven* but something tells me it was *Eskimo Nell*! If you've seen it perhaps it will go some way to helping explain how Jim managed to strain his neck watching it. He couldn't turn his head by the end. Of course it might have been the *Magnificent Seven*, I just can't remember . . . Anyway, as you can imagine, this was considered hilarious by the rest of us, but the Aberdeen keeper, who was my room-mate, wasn't remotely amused – especially when he returned from the physio, Jimmy Steele, with a hot water bottle tied to his neck and orders to go to bed. It wasn't exactly cutting-edge medical science, and neither of us slept much through a combination of his discomfort, the constant daylight, and my best efforts to relieve the tension with a series of protracted anecdotes.

Worse still, Steele's old-fashioned treatment didn't work on Jim's neck, and I was told to prepare myself to fill his boots against Iceland. We trained the next morning on a plastic pitch, adjacent to the match stadium, and it was both exhilarating and peculiar, because so many new personnel had joined the team since my previous appearance that I was now considered one of the old geezers in the ranks. I was put through my paces by Jock and Alex and it was one of the toughest sessions since that gruelling set-piece work-out with Joe Jordan, Gordon McQueen and John Robertson in Spain three years earlier. But I was in my element, I dived all over the place, and could detect that both the gaffers were satisfied that I could handle the pressure, if required. Elsewhere, Jim was having liniment rubbed into his neck, and initially, the prognosis wasn't promising, but he was granted a late afternoon deadline to declare himself fit or otherwise for that evening.

It was touch and go, and I have to admit to a faint twinge of disappointment when Jim's pain eased and he informed Stein he could play. But I wasn't so selfish as to want to benefit from another person's misfortune – he was the man in possession of the number one spot. In any case, Jim and I have been friends from the moment we met. I was just delighted to be in the thick of things again, even if the bench has never been my preferred position.

As it worked out, I was surplus to requirements, because Jim was in magnificent form, producing a string of marvellous, acrobatic saves. I don't know what was in that liniment, but my God, it worked! His form was pivotal to our 1-0 success, with Jim Bett breaking the deadlock in the last five minutes, after the ubiquitous Leighton had blocked Teitur Thordarsson's penalty. It was a grim, gruelling struggle and a generally unconvincing performance on our part, but we had secured the spoils due to Jim's heroics and that result heightened our hopes of reaching a fourth successive World Cup.

There still remained considerable work to do to achieve that aim, and we knew we would face a serious test of our mettle in the crucial encounter with the Welsh in Cardiff on 10 September: what we couldn't reasonably have imagined was that the occasion would bring us both victory and shroud us – and the rest of Scotland – in sadness.

Looking back on it now, as we prepared for the match, Jock didn't appear well; he slouched around the team hotel in Bristol, which wasn't his normal demeanour, and there was none of the effervescence and spontaneous wit with which he used to relieve the tension in the camp. More tellingly, whereas he usually loved his food, everybody noticed that, in the days leading up to the tussle, he would nibble at his plate. He was surviving on morsels, and his brow seemed constantly furrowed.

At the time, we just dismissed these symptoms as evidence that even Stein, one of the legendary managers, could fall prey to anxiety and tension. Certainly, none of us suspected anything more sinister, and yet I knew him better than the majority of the squad members and noticed that he seemed vague and blunt, where he had previously been magisterial and sharp as a tack.

For example, I had staved three fingers while playing for Hibs against Celtic on the previous Saturday. In bygone years, this might have led to him blowing a gasket or sending me home, but he simply glanced at me with a weary, care-worn expression and remarked: 'It's OK, you won't be needed.' Suddenly, from being a masterful presence, this industrious son of the Lanarkshire coalfields, who could command loyalty and inspire fear amongst the most battle-hardened veterans, looked old and grey.

Oblivious to these concerns, the kilted regiments of the Tartan Army had travelled to Cardiff en masse, and when I strolled out during the warm-up – I was immensely relaxed, because I was in agreement with Jock that I was superfluous – I couldn't help thinking how masterfully Stein had kept the supporters in the palm of his hands. Whatever happened on the pitch, we were a seasoned bunch who would contrive, one way or the other, to gain the required result and satisfy our followers.

In the early exchanges that seemed a rather optimistic assessment, with Mark Hughes sparking fury by lunging into several tackles. But Mike England had definitely stoked up the Welsh dragon and we were under the cosh, particularly when Hughes pushed his country into the lead in the thirteenth minute. Thereafter, they launched a string of assaults on our goal, and it was a fraught encounter for Leighton, who was lacking his normal composure and committed a few blunders. It was tense for everybody, or everybody that is but me who, as much out of curiosity as anything else, went out on to the pitch with the other substitutes at the interval. There was nary a hint of the pressure cooker which was set to explode.

As anybody who knows me will appreciate, I enjoy a crack and a practical joke, and while the Welsh Dragoon Guards were regaling the audience with their triumphal tunes, wee David Speedie and I decided to have a carry-on, kicking a ball over the soldiers' heads and trying to skelp them on their bearskins. In the midst of this nonsense, Brian Scott, the Celtic physio, suddenly came sprinting on to the park and shouted at me: 'Alan, you have to get off the field.' I asked why and he almost spat out the words: 'Because you will be playing in goal in the second half.' It sounded so ridiculous that I actually burst out laughing and told Brian: 'F*** off, you are just winding me up, do you take me for an idiot?' And he replied: 'No, no, this is serious.' I still didn't believe him and Speedie was also convinced that I was the victim of a prank, so I was about to flounce away from Brian when he marched up to me and said, in as emphatic a tone as I have ever heard: 'Look, it is not a f***ing wind-up, get into that dressing room now, or there will be hell to pay.' It was an offer I couldn't refuse.

When I entered, it was pandemonium. There were teacups splattering off the walls and Jock Stein and Alex Ferguson were cursing and screaming at each other in the toilet area. 'You never told me that Jim wore f***ing contact lenses,' bellowed Stein. 'That's because I never f***ing knew it myself,' replied Alex and the veins on the temples of both men were absolutely bulging. This was football at its most visceral, and primitive – I think if any of us had gone near either of them, we would have been thrown in the lavatory. The place was like a boxing ring. You could smell the sweat and sense the adrenaline and I remember asking myself: 'What the f*** am I letting myself in for here?' But it was patently clear we were in the midst of a crisis, an unforeseen situation which had totally destroyed the composure of the management duo.

Eventually, as the histrionics abated – a little – Jock walked towards me and although it would be pleasant to report that his final words to me were some dazzling bon mot or piece of wisdom, which I could have stored in my memory for posterity, he just said: 'You're f***ing on!' That was it, nothing else, no advice or salutations, merely an abrupt confirmation that Jim Leighton had lost a contact lens, and that I would have to step into the breach.

So I changed into my gear with no time to mull over the ramifications of World Cup qualification – or not – before striding out with my colleagues for the second half. Scotland were trailing, and the players were now flustered and befuddled. We were also up against highly charged opponents, who roared into every tackle as if it was their last, and we had to claw back the momentum, gradually. Moreover our fans, for once, were being out-sung by their Welsh counterparts. The hosts had dominated the opening forty-five minutes, and might have been two or three goals in front, which would have left us staring at mission impossible. The balance, however, shifted in our favour the longer the action raged on and, despite having to make one decent save to thwart Mickey Thomas, my job became more and more straightforward as my defence stemmed the threat of Hughes and Ian Rush. Indeed, within fifteen minutes or so, much of their earlier sting evaporated and they had run themselves into the ground, at which point Stein elected to send Davie Cooper into the fray, as we searched for an equaliser.

That next half-an hour is etched in my mind: the surge of joy which engulfed me when a shot from Speedie struck

Dave Phillips on the arm and the Dutch referee, Jan Keizer, awarded a penalty which was coolly converted by Cooper; the ensuing confusion which enveloped us when we noticed some kind of commotion in the Scotland dug-out; the frantic gestures from people in the surrounding area and the slow realisation that what I had initially suspected might be an outbreak of crowd trouble was something worse for any of us who loved the inimitable Stein.

At the climax of the 1-1 draw, we were all jumping up and down, with sheer relief as much as elation in the dressing room, when Ferguson entered with a ghastly pallor on his face, and terminated the celebrations. 'Look lads, there is no easy way to tell you this,' he whispered, 'but Jock has had a heart attack, and we don't know if he is dead or alive, we are still trying to find out the exact details.' We just shut up; we were all devastated, and the shock was accompanied by a numbing unreality. Big Jock, the lion of Lisbon, the hero of nine titles in a row for Celtic, and the man who had poured himself into the task of resuscitating his nation after the debacle of 1978 – he couldn't be dead, could he? We all sat there; nobody said a word for minutes on end, impervious to the sight of officials milling back and forward and we shed tears. Somebody said that he was still alive, then eventually, following what felt like an eternity, the news filtered through that he had died. It was the most sombre, depression-laden group of young men you could ever have encountered who journeyed to Cardiff Airport, engulfed in a fog of grief and incomprehension.

In essence, football had been put in its place. For that night, and for many days afterwards, we were blubbing like children. If there were any celebrations amongst the Tartan Army, it could only have been because they didn't know what had happened. There can't have been another occasion in the history of Scottish football when a triumph, of sorts, was so completely overshadowed. Mike England, to his credit, spoke emotionally and passionately about his overwhelming sadness, not at the result, which had been reduced to an irrelevance in the circumstances, but at the loss of a giant among men, a genuine hero.

With hindsight, the burden placed on Stein for so long must have taken its toll; it would have been more surprising if it hadn't. He had recovered from a car crash, he had walked away from Celtic with a dignity which would have proved beyond the majority of us, considering what I believe to be the shabby treatment he received from the Parkhead board, and he had forged an alliance with his prodigy, Ferguson, in whom he recognised many of the qualities which he had displayed as a younger man. But, whether on European assignments or World Cup missions, he remained the same down-to-earth, hard-driving character, whose persona was forged from his roots.

For instance, on that final crusade in Bristol he had scanned our hotel's expensive restaurant menu, and discovered that one of the players (I'll give you a clue: his initials were AR) had ordered lobster and smoked salmon. When the food appeared he clocked me and sidled over, before inquiring: 'Would you be having that today if you were at home?' It was his way of reminding us that we weren't on holiday, we were representing our country, and that we should regard it as a privilege, and not take anything for granted. On a previous trip abroad, he had spotted a group of Scotland fans and he turned to me and observed: 'You know, Alan, these are the folk who really matter, the hard-working lads who shell out hundreds of pounds to support this team, and ask nothing more of us than that we offer them courage and commitment. It might be that we are never going to win the World Cup, but these guys believe in us and think we can. And there are thousands of them who would die happy if you gave them one solitary chance to pull on a Scotland shirt.'

I have never forgotten that message, nor its inherent core values which epitomised Jock Stein. He would probably have been embarrassed at the tributes which were penned in his honour after that fateful evening in September. But he deserved them all.

10

A WORLD CUP FAREWELL

The tearful scenes which followed Jock Stein's death guaranteed that Scotland's bid to qualify for the 1986 World Cup in Mexico became even more highly charged in the build-up to a play-off, scheduled over two legs, against the Australians. The SFA installed Alex Ferguson as a stand-in for Stein, and it was hardly surprising that the Aberdeen manager encountered problems in straddling the club-country divide. At Pittodrie he had developed a side in his mould; he was fully aware of his men's strengths and knew them, not simply as players but as human beings, with all their accompanying frailties, quirks and idiosyncrasies. There wasn't, however, similar scope to forge that relationship in the Scotland job, given that he only met up with his squad around once a month.

Ferguson, a famously volatile and fiercely competitive personality in the club environment, was uncharacteristically calm and even restrained after picking up the torch from his mentor, Stein. Perhaps it was the knowledge that soccer shouldn't be a matter of life and death and that Jock had borne a tremendous strain for too long. Certainly, Alex treated us like adults, while he and his coaching staff, including Walter Smith, Archie Knox, Andy Roxburgh and Craig Brown, prepared methodically for the clash with the Socceroos. He was determined not to squander Jock's legacy, but there was also an undercurrent of sadness around the squad.

I didn't feature in the match at Hampden on 20 November, which was preceded by a stirring send-off provided by our supporters for their late manager which guaranteed that anything that followed was likely to be anti-climactic. The Australian encounter had always promised to be an arduous experience, not least because our rivals were well-organised, and every bit as tenacious as you would expect opponents to be from Down Under. The Scots had to forage for even glimmers of opportunities and show patience in unlocking a well-organised defence. The match was goalless at the interval, but Ferguson urged us to maintain our discipline and not grow frustrated, pointing out that we could ill afford to lose our shape and risk going to Melbourne in arrears.

Moreover he was far from the raging bull that some of us had anticipated. Mind you, this wasn't a normal international and it would be crazy to pretend it was business as usual. On the contrary, in the days leading up to the game, whenever we spoke to our supporters at the team hotel the conversations kept returning to anecdotes about 'big Jock', and memories of how he had kept Jimmy Johnstone on the leash by establishing a network of contacts amongst publicans across the west of Scotland. Stein's shadow dominated the occasion.

Eventually, when the action resumed, the lads succeeded in upping the stakes and creating several good opportunities, but it was still a relief when Davie Cooper delivered a marvellous, unstoppable free kick in the fifty-eighth minute and, as a tidal wave of emotion swept around the stadium, Frank McAvennie added a second on the hour. To their credit, the Aussies refused to buckle and although we pressed for the third goal which would have made the second leg academic, we were thwarted by a mixture of striking deficiencies and last-ditch heroics. Our adversaries must have wondered what they had walked into as the salutes to Stein reverberated from every corner of the ground for the last half an hour of the contest.

Afterwards, Ferguson was concise and precise. We had taken just one stride on the Mexican trail, and he recognised that without leaping up and down. It was plain that he was fully aware of his priorities and he has subsequently spoken of how he reacted to Stein's demise. Clearly he blamed himself for not appreciating that Jock had been unwell throughout the second half in Cardiff. But Alex had no need for such self-recriminations. The Big Man departed us on the field of play where he had thrived and he had stamped his impression on the world, and that is not a bad epitaph for anybody.

Bolstered by a two-goal cushion, we reckoned we were in pole position to advance to the World Cup, but the Australian coach, Frank Arok cautioned us to 'pack our sunscreen' for the return leg, intending to stage the fixture in extreme temperatures. That simply served as a warning, and we flew to Melbourne a week ahead of the tie on 4 December. Once more, I was under no illusions as to my prospects of playing: scant to non-existent. But I was friendly with Graeme Sharp and David Speedie and when we touched down in Australia, I looked forward to spending some time off with them, and the luxury of being able to do what I liked. Alex Ferguson decided to visit one of his relatives in Oz, and in his absence, Walter Smith granted us all a day off to work on our golf handicap, or head along to the local racetrack. The only proviso was that we had to be back in the hotel by teatime, because we had been invited to attend a large function by a group of Scottish expatriates, and the management had lent their blessing to the proposal.

Hence it was that Graeme, David and I popped off to a nearby golf course and the thought that we might suffer in the heat didn't cross our minds. Our round started at 11am, with 100 degrees already showing on the thermometer, and it climbed by ten degrees or more, but we carried on with that stiff upper lip for which the British are renowned. The golf finished with the scores level, so we organised an impromptu skins event, and we were just knuckling down to that challenge when wee David said 'Oh boy' out of the blue and promptly passed out from sunstroke. He just collapsed in a heap, and was obviously struggling, so we took him back to the hotel, and suggested he grab a few hours' sleep. He looked decidedly peaky, and had turned lobster-pink. As the senior member of the party, I concluded I would let him stay in bed and relax for the evening. However, by 6pm he maintained that he had recovered, there were no ill effects, and he said to me: 'I am absolutely fine, there is no problem, so let's go out and party!' I had my reservations, but he was adamant and, in that mood, there was no halting him.

He was soon staggering around, drunk as a lord, and barely capable of standing on his own. Not unusual for some in the party but definitely for Davie. I glanced at the lad and thought to myself: 'God, I wish I had persuaded him not to come.' And, suddenly, in walked Walter Smith, who approached me and asked: 'Where's Speedie?' I was a bit flustered and mumbled: 'Erm, he's just about to pass out on the couch over there, so there's no point trying to talk to him. He's plastered.' Smith was furious. He pointed at Graeme and I and said, with all the affection of a speak-your-weight machine: 'Right, this is a balls-up, you two were put in charge of him and you had better get a grip of him, because he has been booked to appear live on *Grandstand* later this evening. Take him back to the hotel and sober him up smartish.'

We were both flummoxed; there was about as much chance of us achieving that as of stopping Rolf Harris playing his blasted didgeridoo. But the BBC had requested an interview with David as part of their build-up to the qualifying match, and we had to do our best to oblige. So I took one of David's arms and Graeme the other, and the pair of us dragged him to the studio link between Melbourne and London. By then he was babbling interminable nonsense, shouting 'How's it hangin', big man?' to strangers in the elevator. 'If we pull this off, it will be a f***ing miracle,' I said to Sharp.

We didn't and it wasn't. Bob Wilson, the former Scotland goalkeeper-turned-sports anchorman, was on the line, and the plan was that he would lob a few easy questions over to Speedie. You have to remember that while it was around midday in Britain, it was late on Saturday night in Melbourne. We tried to prop David up, between passing him orange juice and mineral water. But it was futile. He was sozzled. As we stood in the studio, like the Three Stooges, Bob began by asking: 'Hi there, David, how are you enjoying yourself over there and how is the Scottish squad acclimatising?' Whereupon, our team mate replied, rather stylishly I thought, 'Ach, f***ing nae problem, big man, how's yourself?' At that moment, we heard this producer screaming into the microphone: 'Get him off the f***ing air this instant!' and there was a breathless announcement that the satellite between Blighty and Australia had malfunctioned. End of transmission.

Mercifully, there were no hitches when we switched our thoughts to the match itself and despite a gutsy, battling performance from the hosts, Jim Leighton was at his imperious best and repelled everything which they flung in his direction. The joust eventually finished in stalemate, at 0-0. Alex Ferguson seemed satisfied enough, but you sensed that he would be as pleased as punch to get back to Pittodrie, amongst his true soulmates, rather than being forced to deal with the different dynamics of the national structure. I can't blame him for that. He had tried to lay the foundations of hard work and commitment, but the process cannot be organised in weeks, let alone months. Even when Alex moved on to Manchester United, it was three or four years before his men embarked on the honour-strewn run which would steer the club to Champions League glory in 1999.

Basically, he has always been at his happiest when working with youngsters, assembling teams on the basis of trust and mutual respect. In common with Jock Stein he never approved of players hitting the bottle, or believed in the adage that the team which drinks together wins together. Thus, despite his attempts to forge a club-style relationship with the Scotland players, he found it difficult: he had to work with individuals in the mould of Frank McAvennie and Mo Johnston, devil-may-care characters, who insisted on doing their own thing, regularly waved two fingers at the blazerati, and who made up their own rules. All of which was anathema to Ferguson.

This may suggest that I wasn't enamoured of Alex, but that isn't the case at all. I guess I was just surprised that he permitted us so much leeway, both on that excursion to Australia and throughout our 1986 World Cup campaign. I suspect that because he had inherited another person's squad – and from a comrade he had admired immensely – he felt he had to maintain the status quo. But I detected strains beneath the surface, not least in his relationship with Graeme Souness, which broke down completely in Mexico.

In the prelude to us flying over to the tournament, via Santa Fe, which had been chosen as the ideal location for high-altitude training, Graeme had been appointed player-manager of Rangers. The buzz within the Scotland camp was that Ferguson had fancied the job himself. It may have been nothing but hyped-up tabloid speculation, yet there were reports that the former Ibrox player had even been interviewed for the post and, whatever the veracity or otherwise of these stories, I can confirm that there was unquestionably tension between the two men during the tournament. At nearly every meeting the players held with Alex – and Graeme was the head of the players' committee, so there were plenty – they seemed to end up at each other's throats, or become embroiled in shouting matches, frequently over the most trivial of matters. It was hardly conducive to fostering a climate of unity. Being on the periphery I was baffled by these spats, but they kept occurring and one of the most serious disagreements was sparked by what should have been a side issue: the number of overseas phone calls that the players were allowed to make.

In retrospect, it appears absurd that this should ever have been a contentious issue, but the SFA had decided that squad members should only be permitted one three-minute call twice a week. This was pretty pathetic for those with wives and young children, particularly when you consider the wads of cash swilling around in the governing body's coffers. As soon as he heard the details, Graeme went ballistic, and told us: 'This is f***ing ridiculous,' and elected to fight our corner. It developed into a really big argument between him and Alex, with the pair bawling at each other. Certainly, they were a contrasting couple: Ferguson, the Govan shop steward, whose routine response to footballers demanding excessive pampering was similar to Jim Taggart being informed about another murder in Partick; and Souness, the Edinburgh-born property-owning capitalist, with a penchant for personal grooming and a belief that players were part of the entertainment industry and worth as much money as any Hollywood film star.

The consequence of all of this, was that the campaign was bogged down from the outset. We should have been in with a fair prospect of qualifying from a group comprising Denmark, Germany and Uruguay – particularly given the expanded nature of the tournament and the fact that three of us were destined for the later stages. But we never gained any momentum. Our first match, against the Danes in Nezahualcoyotl (a pronunciation to induce nightmares amongst commentators), with Souness as captain, was an unmemorable contest. Although Ferguson had targeted that as one of the fixtures we were capable of winning, neither Richard Gough nor Charlie Nicholas could profit on opportunities during the first half. The Scandinavians secured the only goal in the fifty-eighth minute when Preben Elkjaer-Larsen gained the break of the ball in a tussle with Willie Miller and it was an uphill struggle thereafter. They were a good side, and already boasted some of the players who would feature in their European Championship triumph in 1992. While we might have seized a draw or snatched victory with the rub of the green, they had the likes of Michael Laudrup, Jesper Olsen, Soren Lerby, Frank Arnesen and Jan Molby. They were no slouches whether demonstrating silky passing or indulging in hefty challenges, and the hapless Nicholas was on the receiving end of a vicious tackle by Klaus Berggreen near the climax, which earned him a yellow card (it would have been red these days) and sparked a grand old stramash.

I hadn't really fancied our chances from the moment I heard the draw. It was also a frustrating competition for me, because although I was in the squad, I wasn't seriously involved with the rest of the personnel. For the first time in nearly twenty years I was out of the equation, third in line behind Jim Leighton and Andy Goram, and I wasn't so naïve as to imagine that I would be recalled to the fold, short of the other goalkeepers being abducted by aliens. I guess I should have viewed the trip as a holiday, but that wasn't how I had envisaged my international career ending, and it was hard to stay focused and motivated. Graeme Sharp was pretty much in the same boat, and we soon grew fed up loitering around the hotel, so we devised a series of private games in a variety of sports, from tennis to tiddlywinks, to occupy our minds.

If anything, I enjoyed myself more en route to the competition than I actually did in Mexico. Between a couple of warm-up matches in Los Angeles, for example, we had a taste of the Hollywood lifestyle when Rod Stewart turned up at our hotel and requested permission from Alex Ferguson for a group of us to have a meal with him. A string of hits ensured that wherever he went it was invariably to the strains of *Do You Think I'm Sexy?* There was nothing confidential about this LA assignation because Rod laid on a massive, chauffeur-driven limousine for half-a-dozen of us – Graeme Souness, Frank McAvennie, Mo Johnston, Steve Archibald, Graeme Sharp and myself – and if there was something slightly absurd about the OTT fashion in which we were cosseted that evening, it was a reminder that, Stateside, everything is available at a price.

For a few hours at least, we were the playboys of the Western world, dining on oysters and champagne at a swanky restaurant on Sunset Boulevard, with Rod, as usual, more interested in talking about football than the rest of us. We just couldn't believe the luxury of our surroundings. It was a fabulous place – there was even a string quartet in the toilets playing Handel's *Water Music* – but predictably, by midnight our consumption of bubbly had transformed us into Rod Stewart and the Out of our Faces. We didn't care, we were in seventh heaven, and as we negotiated the heavy traffic on the road back to our hotel,

Mo used the car phone to have a merry chat with his mother – in Possil! The rest of us were keen to continue the festivities, and when I was fed the information by that prankster McAvennie that there was a party in a room on the fifteenth floor, I bounded up the stairs and hammered on the door enthusiastically. It was eventually opened – by an irate Alex Ferguson, who asked me what the hell I thought I was doing. That brought the curtain down on a night to remember, but by heavens, we had enjoyed ourselves.

All in all there was a geniality and informality about our stay in America which showed how far the normally strict Ferguson was prepared to let us off the leash. He also allowed us to spend a day at The Downs, the local racetrack (as he had done in Australia – you sort of get the impression he's a racing fan don't you), and our evenings were occupied with a variety of organised functions, such as video race nights, where we were encouraged to indulge in a beer and a bet. As somebody who has always enjoyed the sport of kings, this seemed a pleasant diversion, away from the pressures of preparing myself for a tournament in which I was never going to play. Mind you, I was involved in a bounce game against Northern Ireland in Albuquerque, prior to us venturing to Mexico, and I guess that was my last hurrah in my country's cause. It was a fairly bizarre farewell, because Alex Ferguson and Billy Bingham had contrived an elaborate three-part match which allowed all the squad members to take the field. It was obvious, however, from the outset that the managers had arranged a draw in advance, because I was in goal for the final stages and we were leading 6-4, when the Irish were handed a brace of late penalties. This wouldn't have been so bad, but on each occasion the kicker approached me and told me to dive in the opposite direction to the ball, which was alien to me, but ensured that the proceedings finished with honours even at 6-6. I can just imagine Ferguson entering into any sort of reciprocal agreement with Jose Mourinho or Arsene Wenger – aye, right! – but it summed up the slightly strange nature of the warm-up and when Willie Miller mentioned to me the next day that he had never seen Alex so nonchalant, it suggested to me the Glaswegian wasn't really comfortable in the role.

My World Cup in the shadows degenerated thereafter into a crashing bore. I wasn't required for most of the training sessions, so I watched copious amounts of low-quality American television (not hard – although I did become hooked and could recite the dialogue from *Charlie's Angels*, *Quincy*, *Starsky and Hutch* and *Falcon Crest* better than the actors), jogged to keep myself fit, perused a few sports magazines, and constantly strove to remind myself that I was a lucky boy, even as the days elapsed without me ever feeling that I was in any way central to Scotland's plans.

If that sounds monotonous, what were the options? One afternoon I bumped into Souness, and spent a couple of hours with him, discussing his plans for Rangers, which proved one of the most fascinating experiences of the Mexican campaign. We shared a couple of quiet beers outside his hotel room, and he spoke of how David Holmes, the club's chairman, was prepared to bankroll a revolution at Ibrox by recruiting some genuinely international-class performers. I was sceptical at first, and inquired: 'Who are we talking about here?' Calm as you please, Souness replied: 'Well, I have studied all the good sides in recent years and their success has been based around a spine of a top-notch keeper, an inspirational centre-half, a midfield supremo, and a prolific striker, and that is why I am planning to bring people of the calibre of Chris Woods, Terry Butcher and Trevor Steven to Glasgow.'

I almost spilled my beer in amazement and eventually came back with: 'But what do you need them for, Graeme, when you have the likes of Cammy Fraser, Craig Paterson and Tom McAdam?' He just gazed at me and there was this messianic glint in his face. 'Listen,' he said, 'what we need is a total transformation in the culture of Scottish football. If Rangers are ever to become a truly leading European club, we have to broaden our horizons and change our approach to everything from diet and nutrition, to creating soccer academies, and introducing the kids to good habits.' It was strong stuff, and I have to admit that while I believe the subsequent influx of foreign players has been detrimental to Scottish football, Souness was a genuine visionary and his arguments made a lot of sense.

Another consequence of his radicalism, by the way, was that Celtic's leading lights ironically found themselves in a much healthier bargaining position. As Old Firm combatants they might have battled on the pitch, but they weren't tardy in discussing finance off it, and when the Parkhead lads discovered the likes of Woods and Butcher were on a grand or two grand a week, they soon twigged: 'Why should we have to settle for £300?' That chat with Graeme was one of the most revealing meetings I shared with a team mate, anytime, anywhere. It made me realise he was going to open the floodgates and change the face of Scottish club football.

As for the World Cup, Scotland were coming under severe pressure in advance of the next match against the Germans. By comparison, as I climbed on the team bus, the only thing on my mind was how on earth the Mexicans had been awarded the tournament again after staging it in 1970. I mean, it wasn't as if the locales and the stadiums were on a scale to rival the Maracana or the San Siro or that we were surrounded by breath-taking tropical vistas. Far from it; the venue for the Germany clash was a virtual shanty town and I recall, as our bus weaved slowly along this dirt-track, catching sight of two dead horses lying in the streets of Queretaro. It might have served as a metaphor for our campaign that summer. Finally, on climbing out and entering the arena, we found ourselves in yet another underwhelming venue – the attendance was barely 30,000. It was admittedly an improvement on the 18,000 attendance for the Danish fixture, but still nothing to boast about. My spirits soared when Gordon Strachan latched on to Roy Aitken's service to open the scoring in the eighteenth minute, but our rivals levelled almost immediately through Rudi Voller. From then on they dominated most of the proceedings before Klaus Allofs secured victory after fifty minutes as the precursor to the usual frantic finale.

But it was in vain and, to be frank, I felt literally as well as physically isolated from the action. We had been warned the conditions would probably be sweltering and were advised to avoid dehydration by drinking lots of water. The organisers had also erected a sheltered awning which covered the substitutes' heads, but which was too small to accommodate myself and Graeme Sharp. As a consequence we were forced to sit outside, lathered in sun cream, and we thought to ourselves: 'Ach, f*** this, let's relax!' So we rolled up our sleeves and started talking to a group of the Scotland fans, one of whom asked if we would fancy a quick glance at the *Daily Record*. We were grateful and separated the paper into two parts. After the Germans tied matters at 1-1, we started to read, laughing at what was going on back home.

It might sound disloyal, but the reality of the situation was that we both knew we weren't going to be playing, so there was no point in biting our fingernails and fretting.

Instead, it was feet-up time! When our players walked off at the interval they were soaked in perspiration – they had been caught up in a dogfight, contested at a frantic pace, and seemed shattered. But Sharp and I had nothing else to do except scan the cartoons and grab a glass of juice. As we sat there in comfort I remember, as Souness led his men out for the resumption, he noticed us, and walking over in our direction said: 'Aye, it's good to see that you fellows are really coping with the pressure,' as witheringly and sarcastically as you can imagine. We both felt guilty for, oh, a few seconds. But then we concluded that it wasn't our fault that we weren't on the pitch, so we got back to our lemonade, our sports section and our sunbathing.

In any case, there was enough rancour spreading through the squad without Graeme Sharp and I adding to the management's problems. The team had been stuck in Mexico for nearly three weeks, we hadn't especially risen to expectations, or under-achieved, but the niggles continued unabated between Souness and Ferguson. Frankly, it was a fiasco. As to the phoning home issue, some of us could afford now to ignore the SFA's instructions because Steve Nicol had discovered that we could use the BBC's facilities by climbing through a window into one of their offices. As soon as that became public knowledge, we were on the blower for forty-five minutes to our loved ones and it was all done on the fly.

If anything, this simply accentuated the continued dearth of professionalism which was endemic amongst the SFA's panjandrums. We just had to accept that they were amateurs in comparison to many of the other countries' officials, and yet they had no excuses by 1986. Indeed, matters had definitely improved under Stein; he fought for the players, whether in arranging decent places to stay or giving us priority over the suits. I recall one instance when we were checking into a hotel in Spain, and he spied the SFA brigade doing their best to snaffle the best rooms. Marching up to them he said: 'Wait your turn and get to the back of the line. The players are the important people in this queue, not you guys.'

Sadly, though, we had returned to square one in Mexico, and the mood scarcely improved when we discovered who had been selected for our crucial encounter with Uruguay. Souness, skipper in the previous two matches, was dropped and didn't even feature among the substitutes. Instead the captaincy was passed to Willie Miller, while Paul McStay was introduced for the first time in the finals, along with Arthur Albiston, Paul Sturrock and, to his immense surprise, Graeme Sharp. Some of these selections were, quite simply, baffling, and despite some talk of dehydration having affected several of those who had participated in the tussle with Germany, nobody had been forced to resort to the oxygen canisters which were stored in the dressing room. Moreover Souness was one of the fittest members in the camp; he prided himself on his stamina and taking care of himself, and it was hard to avoid the suspicion that his omission was due to a personality clash.

The press skated around the issue – clearly, they were as mystified as the rest of us, and none of them were keen on crossing Ferguson – but there was no genuine sense of confidence as we approached what had always promised to be an acrimonious meeting with the Uruguayans who merely required a draw, and weren't in the slightest fussy as to how they went about it. Before the kick-off sections of their fans were horrendous, spitting at us from behind the wire fences, and the players weren't much better, nipping the Scots behind the referee's back, aiming sly kicks at our lads' genitals, and generally behaving atrociously. But – and it is a familiar refrain – we should have been capable of rising above their cynical tactics, especially after Jose Batista was sent off in the first minute for a desperate tackle on Gordon Strachan. That ensured we enjoyed a numerical advantage for long enough to have cracked open their defence.

But chances proved thin on the ground, and the South Americans were obviously accustomed to performing with a man short, because they put up the shutters and killed the game. If ever a scenario cried out for a rampaging maestro such as Souness to start orchestrating the tempo, this was surely it. In his absence the Scots simply wilted and, as I sat on the bench, I seriously wondered whether there was any merit in us progressing further in the tournament if it was the prelude to another three weeks of being miserable.

I know that sounds like a terrible admission, but I wasn't alone in being fed up with wall-to-wall re-runs of *Dallas*. After Nicol had squandered our best chance one of the other subs turned to me and remarked: 'God, that was a lucky break for us.' I glanced quizzically at him, and he added: 'Well, Jeez, would it really be such a disaster if we didn't win this?' I could understood his rationale. In the cold light of day we were never in with a shout of hoisting the World Cup in Mexico, and the winners of our tie with Uruguay were scheduled to meet the formidable Argentinians, Diego Maradona et al, in the next round. All we were doing, to some extent, was delaying the inevitable, and that acceptance summed up what developed into a pretty lousy event for us.

In fact, I have never fathomed why there was so little fuss over our elimination in 1986. We collected one paltry 0-0 draw against Uruguay's ten men and were largely unimpressive, whereas 1978 was viewed as a national disaster, we were portrayed as laughing stocks, and our failure has subsequently proved the subject of endless post-mortems and breast-beating. Under Ally MacLeod we had confidence in ourselves and there was a tangible joie de vivre in the ranks. We also stuffed Holland, who just happened to be one of the leading sides on the planet. Just eight years later an ignominious campaign was simply shrugged off with murmurs of 'So what!'

I suppose that expectations had diminished with every passing disappointment, but as I travelled home from Mexico, I harboured all kinds of conflicting emotions. Mind you, the flight was a riot because we were on the same plane as the Northern Irish squad, who seemed determined to drink the flight dry – before we had reached the Atlantic Ocean – and I needed a smart piece of initiative to save us from being swamped. Gordon Strachan tried to get a few drinks for the boys, but the wee man never stood a chance of fighting his way past the Irish to the bar on the plane, and it seemed we would have to sit on our backsides and stay sober. But then inspiration struck. I had a quiet word with one of the air hostesses, and she was happy to let me make an impromptu announcement over the intercom. 'Ladies and gentlemen,' I said, 'Would anybody who hasn't been to three World Cups please return to their seats.' It was crazy, but because it sounded official, the Irish lads responded to the request and Strachan reached the bar after all. As we touched down in Glasgow, I found myself contemplating my own World Cup journey. On a positive note, I appreciated that I was fortunate to have featured in three World Cups, and when I contemplate the names of those who have never graced Jules Rimet's sphere – even in the British ranks, the list includes a collection of gifted individuals, ranging from George Best to Jimmy Johnstone, and Jim Baxter to Mark Hughes and Ryan Giggs – I have to be proud of my achievement. Irrespective of what my detractors might allege, it can't all have been down to luck. But, in the aftermath of Mexico there were also thoughts of what might have been – if Don Masson had converted the penalty against Peru, if Alan Hansen and Willie Miller hadn't collided with each other in Spain, if we had enjoyed a little more good fortune against Iran. Nowadays, when our national football team is at a low ebb and in a state which will require something close to a miracle for the class of 2010 or 2020 to reach four successive World Cups, maybe we should cherish the likes of Ally MacLeod and Jock Stein a little more, and stop lamenting the past. Because, in my opinion, we didn't disgrace ourselves.

The bottom line was that my international career was over, I had amassed fifty-three caps, kept sixteen clean sheets, and been in the spotlight for a decade. This would have been beyond my wildest dreams as a youngster growing up in Maryhill. Yet, upon resuming club activities at Hibs, I couldn't rest on my laurels. Souness had just taken charge of Rangers, Aberdeen remained a formidable force, Hearts had only narrowly missed out on a league and Cup double, Celtic remained a potent organisation, and Dundee United were about to embark on a European run which would guide them to the UEFA Cup final. And as for life on the Leith beat . . . let's merely conclude it was conducted on a smaller stage.

None of which should diminish from the explosive atmosphere and fresh spate of headlines which greeted Souness' controversial Premier League debut in Scotland, and at Easter Road of all places. The newspapers had destroyed small rain forests in preparing their analyses of the likely effects of the Liverpool and Sampdoria star's policy of recruiting a band of high-profile English stalwarts to Ibrox, but as John Blackley and Tommy Craig observed, prior to the kick-off on a sun-drenched Edinburgh afternoon: 'We are not here to make up the numbers. Go out and do Hibs proud.'

During the summer the duo had bolstered the team by signing the likes of Billy Kirkwood and Stuart Beedie from Tannadice and George McCluskey, the former Celtic player, on a free transfer from Leeds United. Beedie sent us in front, as the match swiftly developed into a take-no-prisoners slugfest. Suddenly, following a rash of intemperate challenges, there was a flare up in the centre circle between Souness and McCluskey, which left the latter lying prostrate on the turf. The majority of the players became involved, while I stayed on my line, and watched the fist fight develop. The referee Mike Delaney faced a near-impossible task in restoring order, but was perfectly justified in red-carding Souness for his challenge. He could have sent off two or three others, without them having any grounds for complaints.

In the end we won 2-1, but the result was overshadowed by Delaney booking everybody for their part in the mêlée, except for yours truly. Many people have since asked me why I didn't involve myself in the argument. Couldn't I be bothered to assist my colleagues? Worried I might damage my precious hands if I threw I punch? But there was a simpler explanation, namely that Rangers had earlier been awarded a penalty, a decision with which I had disagreed so vehemently that I had been cautioned. Therefore, if I *had* dashed into the affray, I would surely have finished up sharing the long walk with Souness, which would have done nothing for our chances of securing victory. And besides, what could I have done? It wasn't as if I was Ken Buchanan, and I have never been interested in handbags at ten paces.

But my God, Graeme had got George and it was a sickener. I have witnessed a clutch of ugly sights throughout my footballing life, but George had five stud marks in the back of his leg, like bullet holes, and he was distraught and in agony. I am convinced it was just a rush of blood from Souness, and that he had, subconsciously, been caught up in the hysteria surrounding his arrival at Rangers. But it was a horrible, horrible tackle and when I went up to the players' lounge afterwards, and joined Terry Butcher and Souness, the latter just sat there shaking his head and grimacing. It was clear that he was genuinely contrite. He admitted to feeling embarrassed and I gained the distinct impression that the twin pressures of being player-manager and being flung into such a cauldron had made him lose his control, exactly at the moment he was desperate to stamp his authority – not on poor McCluskey, but on Rangers FC. Not that it offered any consolation to the stricken player, nor diminished the wrath of the SFA, which once again found itself dragged into disrepute as the TV pictures were beamed across Britain.

Unsurprisingly, they resorted to their usual modus operandi by holding an investigation which concluded with Rangers being fined £5,000 and Hibs £1,000, plus an additional suspension for Souness and two penalty points for every player except me. Incredibly, McCluskey was ranked among the culprits, along with Mark Fulton, who had been punched to the ground, and Mickey Weir, who had done his utmost to prevent his colleagues from losing their rags. When this trio submitted appeals to the association and eventually won their case, it was nothing more than natural justice.

Yet, even as the recriminations from that clash were dissipating, fresh storm clouds were brewing over Easter Road, sparked by the realisation that while Hibs possessed the ability to stir themselves and fulfil their potential in some of the bigger fixtures, their form against the so-called lesser lights was utterly dismal. I don't know why this should have been the case, but statistics are invariably revealing and after a meagre tally of three wins in our next seventeen league games under Blackley, it was hardly earth-shattering news when he quit the job, following an abject defeat at Love Street in November.

Briefly, at least, the mercurial, Tommy Craig was placed in charge, and as somebody who admired the little fellow immensely, I reckon that he should have been handed the reins on a permanent basis. But back-to-back losses against Celtic and Dundee United, followed by a home reverse to Hamilton in front of a sprinkling of fans, hardly inspired confidence and the board elected to search for somebody from outside the club. It might have been more honest of them to confess to their own failings and lack of prescience – such as selling Gordon Durie to Chelsea for a knock-down price of £400,000 – but, in my experience, soccer administrators are rarely willing to shoulder responsibility when they can heap the blame on somebody else. The reality, that we had been overtaken by many of our rivals as a direct result of their 'Sell, Sell, Sell' philosophy – which encapsulated Hibs' approach to balancing the books – was ignored in their deliberations.

The local papers were filled with possible candidates, both from within and outwith Scotland, but the directors plumped for Alex Miller. That spelled trouble and heralded one of the few instances in my life where I met somebody I actively detested.

NO TIME FOR MILLER

Most of my friends and acquaintances, I am happy to think, would describe me as a pretty straightforward bloke, disinclined to waste time with political intrigue or engage in confrontation for the sake of it. Down the years, I can perhaps be criticised for my ignorance of money matters or my failure to study the fine print of contracts and other legal documents, but I have never engaged in artifice, whether on or off the pitch.

If I have committed blunders which have cost my teams victory, or slagged somebody off unfairly on my radio programme I will willingly put up my hands and apologise. It isn't in my nature to make enemies – life is too short, and I have lost enough colleagues, from Jock Stein and Ally MacLeod to Davie Cooper and George Best. I have learnt that there are fewer more futile exercises in this world than to ponder on what might have been. Basically, if you are pleasant to me, I will respond in kind, and if that occasionally means searching for the line of least resistance, what is wrong with a little tranquillity?

All of which is a preamble to analysing my relationship with Alex Miller, who walked through the gates at Easter Road at the start of 1987, and immediately made my existence, and that of several of my colleagues, a bloody misery. That's how I saw it. That's how I felt. As a new kid on the block, it seemed to me he was determined to lay down the law, but there is being affirmative and assertive and then there is being a pain in the arse, and, in my view, Miller belonged snugly in the latter category. From the moment he first approached me, and asked me how much longer I expected to remain in football, I felt that he was determined to propel me through the exit door. I accepted that was his right, but I wasn't prepared for the manner in which he sniped away at my resolve.

Obviously I recognised that I was on the final stretch of my career, but when a new manager meets his squad and realises he has experienced performers in the ranks, he can either choose to work with them, pick their brains and absorb whatever lessons they might be able to give, or regard them as deadwood, addicted to complacency, and fling them on the scrap-heap. Perhaps in certain circumstances, this second approach can be justified. But not with me, I didn't think. But, there was no ambiguity about Miller's stance from the outset: he was committed to stamping his imprint on his players, and leaving them in no doubt as to who was boss. For me, Miller was unrealistically exacting in the standards and results he expected from the youngsters, such as Paul Kane, Mickey Weir and John Collins, and treating the likes of myself and Jackie McNamara much as an SAS officer might sneer scornfully at Dad's Army. So he ruled with an iron glove, rode roughshod over the previously accepted practices which are part and parcel of any club, and conflict became inevitable. Soon enough we demanded a meeting with Miller, where some of the senior squad members spelled out the message that we were unhappy with some of the things that were going on. Naturally, that appeared to merely convince him that we were a bunch of malcontents, and several of us found ourselves shunted into the reserves, depriving us of first-team football, presumably with a view to ejecting us from the club.

It was a worrying situation, made worse by my contention I was still in good shape; there was no way I was over the hill at thirty-five. But Miller seemed to have identified me as a trouble-maker, which was patently untrue, and in my book his conduct was entirely out of order. He clearly reckoned he could move me on to some lower-league organisation, and collect Hibs some brass. What he didn't know was that I had a three-year contract in my pocket and was going nowhere.

I had signed the first such deal in 1982, and when I came to re-negotiate it, Kenny Waugh was quite honest and admitted: 'Look, the club is in a financial crisis, we can't offer you the kind of signing-on fee which we previously arranged, but we can provide you with another three year contract with a testimonial at the end of that.' I was satisfied with this, but Miller kept hauling me aside and I strongly felt that our conversations contained numerous loaded remarks on his part about my future at the club which were aimed at encouraging me to flounce off.

For my part I was equally determined that he wasn't going to win, so we both dug in our heels and knuckled down to a war of attrition. The relationship between us worsened every week: I was blamed for every goal we conceded, there was constant friction and relentless negativity towards me, and some of the things he said I felt were outrageous. He didn't want me there, I didn't want to be there either, but although the other senior personnel drifted away gradually, I was determined to hang on for my testimonial year, even though I was working with a guy I hated.

The bottom line was that I knew it was inevitable I would be replaced, but Miller's stance stiffened my commitment to leaving on my terms. And why not? There was one match against Rangers where I produced a string of terrific saves, the majority of them at the expense of Ally McCoist, before Davie McPherson provided a belated equaliser for his side. McCoist actually congratulated me at the final whistle, while the press were glowing in their commendation, and yet there was not a single word of praise from my own manager. He seemed more interested in embarking on scouting trips to England in search of my successor.

Ian Andrews of Leicester City was almost recruited by Hibs, who offered his employers £225,000, and even travelled north to look around the club, but decided to stay at Filbert Street. Miller then turned his attention to Andy Goram, who was then at Oldham Athletic, and didn't bother to inform me that he was in the process of signing one of my international team mates – for £325,000 – so that I knew nothing about the story until I heard it on television. But I had played my last Premier League match.

Even from this distance, I believe his behaviour was appalling. Trying to put into words what I thought of him isn't hard. My opinion was that he lacked charisma and personality and that he was a very average Rangers player who relied on the fact that he had been on the books at Ibrox, yet what had he achieved there? If you study his statistics they seem to me to tell their own tale – a bit-part performer in a crumbling team. Given my experience of him, the fact that he is still involved in the sport at the highest level with Liverpool astonishes me, and every time I spy him sitting in the dug-out, next to Rafael Benitez, I cringe. Perhaps I never saw the best of him at Easter Road, who knows, but to me he always appeared dreich and uninspiring.

I tolerated Miller's behaviour because it takes two to engineer an argument, and when I walked out of the club doors every evening, Miller vanished from my thoughts. However, what really put the ball on the slates was a change in the boardroom at Hibernian, which saw the replacement of Kenny Waugh and ultimately the end to my testimonial plans and my future at the club. I had already organised my testimonial committee, and was looking forward to sorting out all the arrangements – perhaps a golf day, a dinner and even a game against Manchester United or a Scotland select – and getting away from Hibs, when one afternoon at training Peter Cormack, my former team mate at Partick, who was now Miller's number two, approached me and said: 'Alan, you have to go to the boardroom.' We both headed up there and even to this day I can hear exactly what was said. I was told in no uncertain terms that, 'Gordon Rae, who has been at Easter Road much longer than you, will be the beneficiary of a testimonial, and he deserves it.' I didn't disagree with this sentiment: Gordon was an indus- trious, whole-hearted professional, and I certainly didn't want to rain on his parade. He was also a smashing bloke and whether or not you believe in testimonials, loyalty deserves to be rewarded. Then, as I sat there, with a variety of thoughts swirling through my mind, Alex Miller, who was there in the room, added: 'Just to set you straight, by the way, you won't get another game here.' I nearly exploded and demanded to know what he meant. So he continued: 'You can have your golf day, and your dinner, but you won't be picked or play as long as I am in charge.'

And that just hit the nail on the head. It was brutal. One of the more hopeless competitors on *The Apprentice* couldn't have felt more put down. I turned to Peter Cormack, and asked: 'What the f*** is going on?' And he couldn't provide an answer. Perhaps Miller didn't rate me or he believed I was past it – he is entitled to his opinion – but it was the manner in which he went about it which upset me. Common sense seemed to have flown out the window. He didn't appear to have considered what would happen if Andy Goram picked up an injury.

Alex Miller's appointment wasn't exactly good news for me and I sometimes wonder if it was also less than positive for the traditional Hibs values of exciting, expansive play. From where I sat, he seemed to mould a team that believed a point a game would avoid relegation. I dare say he would see things differently, but I can't see us having a beer and a chat about it any time soon.

Ultimately, it was futile to offer resistance, but as I strode out of that room, I pledged that I would leave on my terms. Miller could hector me as much as he desired, but I wouldn't bow to his wishes. Within a few days the situation resolved itself in any case, because I received a phone call from the coach of Orlando Lions, Mark Dillon, who invited me to play soccer in the United States. Suddenly, somebody was chasing my services again; they were keen to fly me over to America, and, frankly, I had already reached the conclusion that anything had to be better than the unpleasantness at Easter Road. So I decided: 'That's it, I'm going,' and asked to be released from my contract. I was told: 'If you leave next week, we are not paying you the rest of your contract.' Things had gone far enough, so I simply replied: 'I don't care, just stick your club up your arse' and I was away from there and as happy as Larry, though I never saw another penny from Hibs.

In the twinkling of an eye, I sold my house and took my wife Michelle and son Alan to the United States with me. When we touched down in Orlando, it was like another world. Mark and his fellow Lions officials said to me: 'Give yourself a week to sort out decent accommodation, and we will allow you to choose from a selection of condominiums, all of which have modern facilities, a swimming pool, tennis courts, a barbecue area, and a double garage, as standard. Take your time – we want you to feel as relaxed and as comfortable as possible.' Thus, we stayed in a five-star hotel for the next seven or eight days, then checked out this luxurious, fully furnished house, and we were all enthralled. Dillon added: 'We will also give you a company car, so let us know what you want.' I wasn't really bothered, but when I awoke the next morning, there was this yellow Ford Mustang convertible sitting outside my door. Everything simply reeked of class and professionalism, especially after life with The Munsters at Hibs.

I realise now that I may not have been a familiar face to people in America, but when they saw my CV and noticed three World Cups, they couldn't fail to be seriously impressed. It was irrelevant that Scotland hadn't achieved anything significant at these tournaments, I had *been* there, and that was enough. They watched the videos, and they saw me in the same frames as the Brazilians, the Germans and the Dutch, and duly treated me and my family like royalty from the minute we landed in Florida.

The first match in which I was involved was against Miami, and with every club being allowed three foreigners, this sparked a notable reunion for me. I was sitting in the dressing room when the coach walked in with the team sheets and I discovered that the Brazilian maestro Zico was in the opposition line-up. My initial response was: 'F***, is this man going to blast free kicks past me all my life?' But he wasn't successful on that occasion, even though we lost 2-0.

In normal circumstances we would have been pretty

deflated at that outcome, but Mark strolled in and insisted that we shouldn't waste breath growing demoralised. It was party time! I said to him: 'Hang on, we have just been hammered and there isn't a lot to celebrate. Besides, who else is going to be at this party?' Then he uttered the immortal words: 'The Miami boys will all be there, along with supporters from both clubs, and we can all mix and mingle and get to know each other better.' So, off we trotted to this massive Sheraton Hotel and the joint was jumping; it was packed to the rafters. As the season progressed, this occurred at all Orlando's matches, and I recall Mark saying: 'Alan, you seem a trifle perplexed with this lifestyle.' And I answered: 'Yes, I am. Back in Scotland, if you get beaten, you generally go home to your bed and try to avoid any flak.'

'No, no,' he interjected, 'you have to move on. You Scottish folk have got it all wrong. Don't you think it would be fantastic if you had your Rangers and Celtic players sharing a pint at Old Firm fixtures and joining a crowd of fans later for a big barbecue?' At which my jaw almost hit the floor. But there again, the Americans had a franchise system, whereby if any side was being too successful, some of their leading players would be drafted by their opponents, and relocated to other cities.

The Orlando Lions also had a baseball team – and they were crap – so the administrators swiftly moved them to Tallahassee. Although they thrived on this system in their indigenous sports, it didn't really work in football. Yet who cared! It was all pizzazz and razzamatazz, about as substantial as a souffle, and you couldn't do anything but enjoy it while it lasted.

One of my abiding memories is of appearing at the John F. Kennedy Stadium against the Washington Diplomats. The game was at 2pm and the temperature was 120 degrees.

We had a couple of South Americans in our ranks and they were used to warm conditions, but even they were toiling and the proceedings unfolded at a snail's pace. Nobody sprinted, nobody moved any faster than they possibly could, it was like chess with a ball, and there were only 3,000 supporters in an arena equipped for 100,000. Then suddenly, in the midst of the (in)action, the MC announced: 'Hello, ladies and gentlemen, boys and girls, the entertainment today will be Pass the Chicken.'

It went like this: they had this massive bird, which they moved around the stands, as music boomed out from the Tannoy, and when the music stopped, the person carrying the chicken won a prize. Down on the pitch, the match was so terminally boring that I remember growing more interested in watching the supporters passing poultry, than passing a football. Another time, when we travelled down to tackle the Tampa Bay Rowdies on Independence Day, we were told it was the equivalent of the Old Firm of US soccer. Yet there was no sectarian chanting, or aggression, on or off the field. Instead, as the tussle progressed, and Roy Wegerle launched an attack down the wing, an organ started blaring out *The William Tell Overture* at the behest of the organisers. None of which exactly helped the concentration of the players.

It was totally surreal and when the fixture ended in a 1-1 draw, suddenly, 40,000 patriotic Americans flooded into the auditorium to celebrate their national holiday, and the atmosphere was transformed from a morgue to the Last Night of the Proms. Maybe that incident shows why I reckon football is never going to be massively popular in the States. Besides, everything there is geared towards adverts, as anybody who has had the misfortune to watch a USPGA tour event will be aware. You watch three or four shots being played before the broadcasters are off for another commercial break, and it soon becomes genuinely exasperating. I know that the Americans eventually staged the World Cup in 1994, but if they had their way, I am convinced they would press for six ad breaks every fifteen minutes. This would unquestionably ruin soccer. In any case, the beautiful game is never going to become an obsession with Uncle Sam or enjoy the same audience share as American Football or baseball, except amongst the ethnic communities.

It's a different situation with their national team, because the authorities have promoted soccer in the colleges and universities. And there is no doubt that the US has a decent batch of players, but I suspect the majority of them will continue to be forced to migrate to Europe to make a living. Yet, during my spell there, you couldn't fault the enthusiasm or commitment of the officials, and when I was told that I had been picked for the All-Stars team, I was delighted. In fact I still have the jersey from that occasion in my house. It turned out that I had been selected because my statistics were superior to any of the other keepers. I hadn't conceded a goal in six hours and had saved more shots than any of my counterparts. I felt like phoning Alex Miller and reversing the charges!

That gained me a place in the showpiece occasion, but Mark Dillon departed shortly afterwards and the owner of the club, Colin Phipps, actually offered me the coaching role at the Lions. It was a tempting proposition, and he delivered the commendation: 'You have really impressed us over here – both as a player and as a human being.' But I was swithering. The main stumbling block was that the Americans had a waiver system; they could get rid of you at any time, call you into the office, tear up your contract and wave goodbye. It meant there was no security if things went pear-shaped. I had to think about my family, and how it might impact on them. This led to a difficult couple of days, but once again, just when I was on the horns of a dilemma, the phone rang and a new adventure beckoned.

I returned home from training one evening, and my then-wife, Michelle – who knew nothing about football and has only attended a couple of matches in her life – told me: 'A Billy McNeill has been ringing you. Who's he?' She added that I had to call him in an hour, and although I began to think it might be a wind-up, I followed her instructions and found myself speaking to the man himself, who was managing Celtic at the time. 'How are you getting on over there? I hope you are in a position to help me out, because we want you to come back to Scotland and play for us. Pat Bonner is going to be out with a serious back injury for five to six months, we have signed this lad, Ian Andrews, but we require experienced back-up, and I have talked to Tommy Craig. He said you got a raw deal at Hibs, but your attitude was spot-on, so what about it?' He finished by asking if I was up for it, and I replied: 'I'll be at Parkhead tomorrow.'

None of this should be implied as criticism of my American colleagues. I was immensely grateful for the faith they had demonstrated in me and, prior to flying home, I enjoyed one final thrill. I was in a hotel in Tampa and discovered that George Best, who was on the books at Fort Lauderdale, was one of the guests. We wound up sharing a chat by the swimming pool, comparing our Stateside experiences. He had always been one of my favourite players, and despite being at the end of his career – his knees had suffered a few kickings too many – he could still excite the crowds with his trickery. It was the first time that I had met him – we subsequently hooked up on several occasions – and he was fantastic, devoid of ego or narcissism. As our conversation flowed he admitted ruefully to having a million friends, and you could fit them all in a telephone box! 'One of the great things about being here is that the fans love you, but they don't want to put you on a pedestal, they simply want to shake your hand and talk about football,' he told me. 'There is none of the negativity you encounter in Britain, where the tabloids seem obsessed with building people up, then knocking them down, and if I want to go for a walk in the streets, I can do it without being shouted at or without some idiot trying to pick a fight or dragging me off to a bar.'

I also asked him about fame and its pluses and minuses and he looked melancholy for an instant before replying to the effect: 'I can't complain. Life has been very good to me, but I wish that I had been as smart twenty years ago as I am nowadays. I would have recognised the hangers-on and the sycophants and I wouldn't have trusted everybody as implicitly as I used to do, when I arrived in the big city and my face was being splashed all over the papers. The thing is that football is wonderful, and when I was at my prime, I felt I could do anything on the field. Beating defenders, dodging tackles, scoring goals . . . none of that was a problem. It was whenever I left the pitch and was back in the real world that my difficulties started and I don't gloss over the reality that I was often my own worst enemy. That is the drawback to fame: it can gain you a seat in the best restaurants, but when you walk off out of these places, there will be a dozen photographers waiting for you to trip into the gutter. I guess I have never been able to understand why they are there. Don't we all have a right to privacy in our lives?'

Best was comfortable in America and when I played my final match for the Lions, against Fort Lauderdale, our outfield players were instructed by Werner Fricker, the president of the US Soccer Federation, not to inflict too many tackles on him. He may have lost his pace, but he could still perform from his magic box if allowed the requisite space. Fricker must have been delighted by the outcome, with Best regaling a sizeable audience with dummies and feints, and a few trademark dribbles, as the fixture concluded in a cosy 3-3 draw. Inwardly, he knew that he couldn't continue much longer, but he was pleased that so many spectators wanted to watch his repertoire.

We might only have exchanged a few words at that initial meeting, but I could detect some of the inner sadness which plagued George, and I was mightily relieved that I have never been forced to battle the same demons. 'Oh, by the way, what was it like, playing in the World Cup?' he inquired, as the prelude to going for a swim. 'That is one of my few regrets in football: that I never had a part to play in the greatest show on earth.' I would gladly have swapped one of my three Cup experiences with him, but sadly, that was impossible. Life may have proved a dreadfully difficult business for George, but few others have done more to enhance the image of the beautiful game.

12 PARADISE AND A REALITY CHECK

As a small boy, Partick Thistle was part of my existence, but Celtic was the club I really supported, even if I never imagined, as the flaccid 50s turned into the swinging 60s, that I would eventually be approached by Billy McNeill to join the ranks at Parkhead. The circumstances were not as I would have envisaged, and I had to pinch myself when, immediately upon my return from the United States, I was met at Glasgow Airport by McNeill, the captain of the Lisbon Lions. He was a character who commanded reverence wherever he went, despite the fact that the majority of the youngsters who thronged the stadium every Saturday in 1988 must have had no recollection of that fabled European Cup victory, beyond what their fathers or uncles had passed on to them.

By the time of my arrival Celtic were in transition, forced to raise the financial stakes to emulate their Old Firm rivals. Graeme Souness had embarked on his personal crusade to revolutionise standards at Ibrox by recruiting the best of British, and David Murray was poised to add momentum to the process in the next couple of years. But while I recognised that Billy had only signed me as cover for the injured Pat Bonner and the inexperienced Ian Andrews, I couldn't have cared less whether I was there for six weeks or six months. No, it was simply a privilege to be affiliated to a club whose core values – providing entertainment, encouraging kids to progress through their youth system, and whose players actually looked as if they were enjoying themselves – were similar to my own philosophy on football.

I also gathered fairly quickly and emphatically why so many talented performers manage to thrive elsewhere yet fail at the Old Firm. It is extraordinarily difficult to explain, but as soon as you march through the gates of either club there is a dramatic shift in mindset from that which exists anywhere else in Scotland and, to some extent, I would argue, in the whole of British soccer. Suddenly it is part-circus, part-goldfish bowl, with an incessant crescendo of pressure being heaped on your shoulders. Woe betide the new Rangers or Celtic signing who doesn't measure up and conform to the rules which lay down that draws are unacceptable; defeats are not to be contemplated, and that if you don't believe that winning every match is part of the pact you have entered into with your supporters, you should seek alternative employment.

Naturally, this entails possessing a thick skin, and the ability to ignore random abuse in the street or with your family in a supermarket or restaurant. You need also to grasp the fact that you are considered public property by the fans in both camps, and it becomes apparent why: for every Henrik Larsson or Brian Laudrup who flourishes in this environment, there will be plenty others – Tore Andre Flo, Peter van Vossen, Vidar Riseth and Harald Brattbakk spring to mind – who will be eaten alive in the feeding frenzy.

Mercifully, as somebody who had grown accustomed to taking stick from disgruntled Scotland supporters and a seasoned campaigner on the Celtic Park turf, I was not about to be fazed by a spot of name-calling or tabloid tittle-tattle. Billy told me, once we had completed the formalities: 'We can't offer you a signing-on fee, but we can provide you with a good wage [it was £600 a week], and every available bonus.' Therefore, whether I was part of the team or not, I collected all the extras when we were winning. This was terrific but I was so thrilled just to be there that I must have resembled a kid being handed a free pass to Disneyland.

In fact I had been handed a year's contract and it was such a joy to be walking in the door at Parkhead every day that Billy used to comment that I was thirty-six, coming on seventeen, which wasn't far off the mark. Mixing with the players, mingling with all the supporters who turned up religiously at training sessions, coping with the interminable photo-sessions and media demands . . . it was a complete transformation from anything I had witnessed on the club circuit before. You have to bear in mind that, at this juncture, the Old Firm's hegemony was under genuine threat from Hearts, Aberdeen and Dundee United, and thus the scrutiny and attention on everything we did was relentless. Fortunately, I relished the spotlight.

Hence the exhilaration which swept over me as I pushed back the years and flung myself around on the training pitch like a youngster. I was determined that if I was called up to the first team I would be ready, and the opportunity soon materialised, though not in the manner I would have wished. At the end of August 1988 Celtic travelled to Ibrox, with Ian Andrews between the sticks, and he suffered a dreadful afternoon as the hosts swept to an emphatic 5-1 triumph. It was their biggest win in an Old Firm fixture for twenty-eight years – which testified to the quality of the side which Souness had assembled. A couple of goals from Ally McCoist, allied to a stunning, venomous volley from Ray Wilkins, and other strikes from Kevin Drinkell and Mark Walters highlighted their potency. Although Frank McAvennie had secured an early equaliser, there was nothing else to cheer.

Even Celtic acolytes had to grudgingly admit the power of the light blue tidal wave which engulfed Andrews that day – their ranks oozed with class and tenacity from Terry Butcher and Richard Gough in defence, through to Wilkins, Ian Durrant and Ian Ferguson as the midfield enforcers. Meanwhile up front McCoist and Walters posed all kinds of problems for Celtic, who fielded players of the calibre of Roy Aitken, Mick McCarthy, Paul McStay, Andy Walker and Tommy Burns, but were never at the races that day. As usual, when the scoreline morphs from a defeat into demolition, the keeper can anticipate a torrent of derision and Andrews soon learned that it is never hard to distinguish between an Old Firm fan with a grievance and a ray of sunshine.

Even as Ian was toiling, I was in trouble of my own in the second-team fixture, staged at Parkhead. With half an hour gone I dived in to collect the ball, and rose to kick it upfield. Oblivious to the normal courtesies in these situations, Scott Nisbet lunged forward and in so doing caught me in the face with his knee. He was sent off immediately, but I was in agony, and the medics despatched me in an ambulance to the Victoria Hospital for X-rays. The diagnosis – that I had broken my jaw in four places – was clearly disturbing, and I was furious that I had sustained such an injury in a reserve tussle, but I was so desperate to be involved at Celtic that I shrugged aside the pain and pestered the doctors to patch me up and allow me to resume my football.

Call it what you will, blind faith, intuition, or stupidity, but I had a feeling that I wasn't far from first-team selection as I turned up at Ross Hall Hospital on the following Tuesday for an operation. The damaged bones were duly pushed back into place, and I needed just three stitches to complete the repair job, and these were removed forty-eight hours later. The specialist informed me that the damage wouldn't have healed properly for six weeks, but it was my decision on how swiftly I wished to return to the pitch. With Celtic flying out to Hungary the following Monday to meet Honved in the European Cup, I discussed the options with Michelle, and neither of us had a Plan B. In blunt terms, I would have travelled with the squad on a stretcher. As it happened, while I was abroad, I didn't need a single painkiller, which delighted me. The care I had from those guys is one reason why I won't hear a bad word uttered against the health service in Scotland. Other nations would love to have that quality of care.

Once I had rallied from the injury, I must confess to harbouring pangs of guilt over Ian Andrews, who needed backing and support, but was being dragged through the wringer. At least 200 Celtic fans would flock to our training facilities every day and I was always accorded a warmer reception than him, which, unsurprisingly, did nothing to boost the lad's confidence. Nor did his mood improve during our foray to Budapest where he conceded a bad goal at his left-hand post. This gave Honved a potentially crucial advantage, without us managing to record an important away goal. The atmosphere reminded me that while my life had moved full circle since my previous visit there, in 1972 with Thistle, our opponents had barely advanced an inch. Their stadium was still decrepit, and there was that same piece of wood where I had written my name all those years ago. But it was strange, the people we met on the streets seemed happier than they had been in 1972. Maybe, beneath the surface they already had an inkling that changes where about to sweep across their country – changes that were sure to make their lives a lot better.

Once again Ian was blamed for the defeat, and you could detect from his body language that he was struggling to hold things together. This was regrettable; he may have been guilty of one mistake in Hungary, but there were plenty of other aspects of the team's performance which weren't perfect.

Indeed, with that reverse, Celtic had lost as many games in the opening month of the new season as they had done in the whole of their previous campaign, and the supporters, irrational as ever, vented their spleen. 'See you, Andrews, you are f***ing useless,' they bellowed at him on the thorough-fares of Glasgow, and his shoulders visibly slumped.

I shared his pain – after all, similar condemnation had been hurled at me, most volubly after the 1978 World Cup when many Scots seemed to think it was all right to march up to the same players they had praised as heroes and patriots a month earlier, and denounce them as effing traitors and wankers and worse besides. But, on the other hand, my sympathy had to be tempered by pragmatism. They say that one man's misfortune is another man's windfall, and the greater Ian's problems intensified, the more prospect I had of being summoned to arms. Yes, sport can be the cruellest of vocations, but in this instance, it worked to my benefit.

Thus it transpired that Tommy Craig, who had moved from Hibs to Celtic, strolled up to me a couple of days later and asked: 'Do you want to play in the first team?' I just looked at him as if it was the daftest question in the world and replied: 'Aye, of course I do, that is why I came here.' He then informed me that, at thirty-six, I would be the oldest goalie since Ronnie Simpson in the 1960s to turn out for Celtic, and I noticed that he was skating around the issue, so I asked him straight out: 'What is it? Come on, I am big enough and ugly enough to hear what you think.' He dithered for a few seconds, and then declared: 'Look, I know you have loads of savvy and experience, and you have turned out in World Cups with Scotland, so you know your trade, nobody disputes that, but, erm . . .' By this point, I was close to picking him up and giving him a right good shake, but he eventually finished the sentence with the words: 'Can you handle it?' It was a strange question to put to somebody with fifty-three caps, and twenty years in the business. I guess that Tommy was entitled to harbour some reservations, because I had spent the previous two seasons frittering around in the reserves at Easter Road or performing in pressure-free Stateside matches, and that is a million miles removed from taking the field in one of the Old Firm's colours. All the same, I was fired up, I was totally motivated and I quickly convinced him that I merited my inclusion.

In truth, Celtic weren't a great side, they were more workmanlike than inspired, and for the next few weeks I was tested to the full. My debut came against Dundee, and as I sat in the dressing room, surrounded by the likes of McAvennie and Aitken, I reflected on the transformation in my fortunes from that desperate spell at Hibs, and inwardly smiled. Sadly, though, there was no fairytale finale: Tommy Coyne seized the only goal of a lacklustre match and the pattern repeated itself when I returned to Easter Road for the first time since I had stormed out in high dudgeon. Alex Miller was still in charge, casting his shadow over Leith and I am afraid that I just couldn't help myself. I remember meeting him in the corridor, prior to the kick-off, and while I should probably have treated him with the silent contempt I felt he deserved, I said loudly in his ear: 'Hi there, Alex, no f***ing bad for a guy who was over the hill, eh? Playing for Celtic!' and he looked at me as if he was ready to explode, so I sauntered off with a swagger, humming the classic jazz tune *On The Sunny Side of the Street*.

But I guess that I should have waited until after the game: Hibs won 3-2 and, just to rub salt in the wound, we were denied an absolute stonewall penalty when Alan Sneddon hauled down McAvennie, only for the referee to wave play on. At that juncture, the contest was goalless, but the episode seemed to demoralise Celtic and they plummeted to a 3-0 deficit by half-time, with Steve Archibald grabbing a brace and Gareth Evans adding a third, after Gordon Rae escaped without a sanction after I felt the full brunt of his boot catching me in the chest as we clashed in the area.

It was another dubious decision – indeed, it was bloody disgraceful, and I nearly chased the official to tell him as much. We were seething during the interval, but although we responded with a stirring recovery in the second period, it wasn't quite enough and I recollect sneaking a peek at the opposition dug-out and I'm pretty sure I saw Miller rubbing his hands in glee. On Saturday evenings such as that you simply wanted to escape, to avoid contact with anybody. So I slipped away, concerned that unless we started winning soon, I might be the victim of the same criticism which had bedevilled Andrews.

He had suffered badly and his self-belief dwindled appreciably. You could sense it in his body language, and following a particularly gaffe-laden session on the training pitch, Billy McNeill and Tommy Craig informed me that they wanted me to play in the second leg against Honved. I was ecstatic: it felt akin to the end of some fantastic dream. If anybody had told me, circa 1965, that all these years later I would be playing in a European Cup match for Celtic in front of a capacity crowd, with the 'Jungle' packed to the rafters, I would have told them not to be so daft.

Prior to the European tie, there was a nervous, tense atmosphere around Celtic – we had made a poor start to our championship campaign and this Honved match was very important. Mercifully, a spirit of fun still lurked under the surface and one or two of the more experienced players relieved the pressure when they sprung a surprise on Tommy Craig. It was his birthday on the day of the Honved tie, and as he was methodically discussing tactics as usual, suddenly a comely female wearing a fur coat strolled into the dressing room. She had nothing else on underneath but a smile and wee Tommy didn't know where to look when she snuggled up to him. But the rest of us were splitting our sides. Laughter is the best medicine in adversity there's no doubt.

It was one of those nights when the hair rises on the back of your neck. The atmosphere was electric, and we rampaged all over the Hungarians, en route to a 4-0 triumph, which could have been even more conclusive. Billy Stark, a talismanic figure for Celtic that season, notched a brace of goals, Andy Walker added another and McAvennie applied the *coup de grâce* with a mesmerising chip, as the auditorium rose to acclaim an artistic demolition job. I remember not so much walking as floating off the pitch, imbued with the sense that I had rarely experienced a more glorious occasion in my life, and that, even on the cusp of thirty-seven, I still had plenty to offer.

The trouble was that hard reality soon interrupted my reveries. I had never been under any illusions that my Celtic career was likely to be anything other than ephemeral. When Pat Bonner returned to action from his injury sooner than anticipated – he was fit for the next stage of the European Cup – the management needed to justify their investment in Andrews, so I found himself consigned to the reserves pretty quickly, and it was tough. I wasn't greedy, given the prizes which had been bestowed on me, and Ian and I settled into sharing the job as second-team keeper, but, to be honest, once you have savoured the buzz of a grand European adventure, languishing in the reserves doesn't really cut it. I was too old to cling to any deluded notion that I might earn new opportunities if I hung around indefinitely. It was an awkward situation, but to his credit, McNeill refused to leave me hanging, and, within weeks, called me into his office.

'Alan, we appreciate what you have done for us, but we paid a lot of cash for Ian, and we have to give the boy a chance, so that probably means you won't be involved in any more games [I turned out seven times for Celtic, five in the league, one in the League Cup and the other against Honved]. I am absolutely happy for you to stay here for the rest of the season, but I think that Ian has got a grip again, so why don't you just enjoy yourself?' I still received my payments and my bonuses, and have no complaints about my treatment, but as the winter advanced I started to wonder what I was doing there. Eventually I approached Billy and confessed: 'I am not enjoying this, I have loved being at Celtic, but I need to keep myself occupied.' And he replied: 'I can understand your position. Leave it with me.'

The very next day, he marched up to me and said: 'Alan, I have spoken to Jim Dempsey at Hamilton. He wants you to go there, on the same wages as we are paying you, and there will also be a big signing-on fee.' I wasn't exactly minted, so this sounded promising, but I asked Billy: 'What will happen at the end of the season? Will I get another year at Celtic?' And, respect to him, he was utterly candid. 'My friend, I can't even guarantee that *I* will get another year, so it is up to you.' Almost immediately, I reached my decision: I would venture to Hamilton and see where that led me.

Financially, it was the right choice, but from a footballing perspective it was the worst move I ever made in my career. I grabbed all my stuff and packed it in a couple of black bags, left Parkhead, this magical theatre, replete with the ghosts of legends, and drove over to Hamilton. I had no sooner arrived at Douglas Park than the thought flashed through my mind: 'What the f*** am I doing here?' It was a hole, a dump. I recall walking through the dressing room and having to bend down to avoid crashing my head off the beams, and I can tell you it was a sobering couple of hours.

Jim Dempsey was a smashing bloke and I have no gripes with him whatsoever. He was obviously a resilient character, undaunted by the scale of the challenge. 'Look, we are giving you all this money, we want you to save us a few championship points in return, so let's give it a blast for the next three months and see how it works out, because I genuinely believe that we have the potential to go places at this club,' he said to me with the enthusiasm which stamps out the true devotee. 'What have we got to lose?' It was a bold statement, but I was facing my own financial problems at the time.

Remember, I had already lost £30,000 on running a hostelry in Glasgow, and my second stab at entering the retail trade had brought a similarly inauspicious outcome when, on the advice of a couple of my Hibs team mates, I opened a sports shop. Nowadays, the television schedules are packed with programmes emphasising the importance of location, location, location, but my emporium was hidden away in a side street in Musselburgh. It was a case of déjà vu. Fairly swiftly this new venture started to suffer, and although I had invested in £10,000 or £12,000 worth of stock, there was nary a sign of the strips, boots and other merchandise being snapped up by any queue of customers. When the call came from the Orlando Lions, I decided to skedaddle off to America and sort out my retail problems later.

While I was abroad, the Sheriff's officers duly closed down the business, and while this was less calamitous than my pub's demise, it was a straightforward case of a footballer lurching into the business world without having any knowledge or experience. At Easter Road, Paul Kane had talked to me about buying flats and letting them out to clients, and several of the other youngsters had mapped out alternative futures in case their soccer careers didn't go according to plan. Yet, as far as myself and the majority of my footballing generation were concerned, we were so delighted that we were earning a wage for kicking a ball around a field that the last thing on our minds was worrying what might happen once we were speeding towards retirement. With hindsight, we stuck our heads in the sand and many of us would come to rue our inaction.

My short stint at Hamilton provided a massive reality check. The simple truth is that they weren't good enough to transcend their circumstances, the club had no training facilities, and we would practise outside on a strip of grass next to the railway station – and I had exited Parkhead for this! Every single day I drove to the ground I could hardly believe I had landed myself in such a farcical scenario. Apprehension was setting in with a vengeance and it was an ignominious time for me. At the end of the season Dempsey, whose confidence in me had rapidly eroded, ushered me into his office and counselled: 'I'm sorry, Alan, I know you have given it your best shot, but it just hasn't worked and we are not going to renew your contract.' And that was the first instance in twenty years that somebody had cut to the chase and told me straight that I was surplus to requirements. I had been effectively cast on the scrap heap.

Of course, I had faced conflict before; Alex Miller had done his best to hand me my P45 at Hibs – but, in an instant, I was a reject, and it was awful. Hitherto, I had been spared the ordeal of sitting at home, waiting for the phone to ring, but as the days passed and the silence became deafening, I recognised that I was existing beyond my means and that it wouldn't be long before this impacted on my family. We were living in a spacious house in Ayr, which had been bought on the back of my signing for Celtic, yet I wasn't completely stupid, and as I gazed out of the window the message kept battering away at my brain: 'You can't afford this, you have to find something else fast.' I had neither wages, nor anything substantial in the bank, and it is amazing how quickly you can vanish out of the picture once one door has been slammed in your face.

Luckily, while out for a constitutional one morning, I bumped into Ally MacLeod, who was now managing Ayr United, and he asked what I had lined up. I was able to answer the question with a shrug and the single word 'Nothing.' He paused for a moment, and then replied: 'Well listen, I have got a young keeper at the club, David Purdie, and I rate the lad highly. How do you fancy coming to Somerset Park as the number two goalie and the coach?' At least somebody wanted me, which was slightly reassuring, but I was to see no action on the field for months on end – I only played one first-team match in a year, against St Johnstone – and it was a tremendous culture shock, never to have the slightest chance of playing regularly.

As for Ally, he still possessed a bit of the old patter, he could still charm the worthies whenever he visited one of the local social clubs, and he was an intrinsically decent human being. But he had no cash to reinforce the United squad. He rescued them from falling off the precipice a couple of times, but this was at the end of his managerial career and the sport had changed out of all recognition from the days in 1977 and 1978 when he held his country in the palm of his hand. I recall asking him once whether he was still bitter, considering how his stock had plummeted in the fractious aftermath of the World Cup in Argentina, but he simply smiled at me and replied: 'Ach son, I've done OK. We would all change things if we could turn back the clock, wouldn't we, but the abuse didn't last long. And, in any case, I never ever stated that we would win the World Cup. I told one journalist that we were capable of gaining a medal, namely a top-three finish, and I still believe that outcome might have been possible, considering the players I had at my disposal. But ach, laddie, life is too short for recriminations and regrets, isn't it?' With which this blithe individual would amble away from training, carrying a couple of bags of ice, towards his pub in Ayr, where he had a thousand anecdotes for the regulars.

For my part, I was fearful of going nowhere. My professional soccer days were dwindling but the prospect of being redundant constantly hammered away at my subconscious and I went through a depressing period. I was close to oblivion. Always a proud individual, the idea of asking people for favours or returning to a humdrum existence outside the playground appeared a huge hurdle to surmount. Without the generous backing of a long-term friend, Donald McCorquodale, a businessman in the west of Scotland, who fixed me up with odd jobs and invitations to participate in some after-dinner speaking, I could have drifted into the gutter or slipped through the cracks.

One of the myths of football is that there will always be employment for the old internationalists, once they have packed away their boots. The reality is far less comfortable. When Jimmy Johnstone died at the start of 2006 the obituarists focused on his role as a Celtic legend. They all agreed that he would never be forgotten by millions of sporting followers, not merely in his homeland, but across the globe. Well, that may be correct, but I can testify that not too many Scots were overly interested in Jinky when the lad was on his uppers in the 1980s, working as a labourer, shrouded in anonymity, digging drains and doing other unglamorous chores to earn a basic wage. One afternoon, as I walked out of Easter Road, I spotted him down a hole, sweating away with a shovel in his hand, and there wasn't an autograph hunter in sight. Nor was there any sign yet of the wealthy benefactors who subsequently came to his assistance, but only after he had been diagnosed with the motor neurone disease which eventually killed him.

I have never forgotten Jimmy's collision with obscurity, and equally, as my career petered out, I discovered that many people who profess to love soccer find nothing sweeter than to revel in a former star's fall from grace.

One morning, while I was still on the books at Ayr United, I nipped into my local Safeway for a weekly shopping trip. As I was pushing the trolley round the aisles – there was over £70 worth of groceries in it – a packet of fillet steak slipped into one of the carrier bags at the back of the cart. After I had paid for the rest of the goods, I was stopped by one of the security staff. Ignoring my protestations of innocence he called the police, and the next few weeks became a waking nightmare. I was taken to the station in Ayr, and because it was a Sunday, they seemed unable to find somebody who could take my fingerprints, so I spent three hours in a prison cell. Nothing in my past existence had prepared me for that ordeal, and as I languished behind bars, I was petrified, shaking with trepidation. I had done nothing wrong, and yet I was aware that when the tabloids discovered what had happened, they would have a field day which would make the 1978 World Cup seem like a garden party. I felt sick to the pit of my stomach, and although I was released as soon as the police had completed their procedures and the business handed over to the Procurator Fiscal, the journey home was just the prelude to my being treated as a common criminal.

In a nutshell, I couldn't convince anybody that I wasn't a shoplifter, and the lurid newspaper headlines only exacerbated the situation. Journalists and photographers camped outside my house, and it was a rotten time for my family, who kept asking how I could have landed myself in such an unsavoury mess in the first place. For night after night, I could hardly sleep, and yet the whole affair was portrayed by the papers – and by Stuart Cosgrove, who, in my view, should have known better, in his subsequent book *Hampden Babylon* – as if it was one big joke. My simple response to Stuart's mirth is to ask him how he would feel if his loved ones were being pursued by gutter press photographers and pestered by idiots in the streets. Meanwhile I was being branded in the community as a thief who had squandered all his World Cup bonuses and had now resorted to stealing from supermarkets.

While my son Alan had to endure sustained abuse at school and Michelle was persistently faced with being called at home, usually by reporters in search of quotes, it is no exaggeration to state that my private life fell apart as the reverberations from the incident intensified.

Eventually, nearly a month after my arrest, I received a letter from the fiscal's office, which informed me that the police would not be pressing charges or pursuing the matter and the tone of the correspondence was apologetic. But the damage had already been done, and unfortunately Cosgrove's book, which relished poring over Scottish football's supposed scandals, has served to perpetuate the idea that I had been convicted of theft Not my cup of tea I must confess. The fact that I was never charged and I walked away without a stain on my character, was never followed up by any of the papers which had licked their lips in reporting my arrest in the first place. It was a sobering business; a clear case of being tried and condemned by the media, and I still remember the evenings when I would traipse downstairs, worried to death at the prospect of being jailed, and sitting alone, hollow-eyed in my kitchen.

Money was incredibly tight and I wasn't so much living on a shoestring budget as surviving on my name and what I had accumulated throughout my career. I pledged to be honest when I began this book, so I have to admit, however shame-faced I might feel, that I let it be known that I would be prepared to sell some of my caps to make ends meet. I was totally on my uppers, in an abyss of debt, and so I eventually sold three of them, plus my commemorative medal, awarded to mark my 50th appearance, to pay the electricity bill. When I look back, I wonder how I could have fallen so far. It was out of desperation – and I only received £300 for these items – but I was at rock bottom and it seemed that football had given me everything, but left me with nothing.

It was a black time, and if I imagined that I would soon bounce back, I couldn't have been more wrong. Instead my worries mounted as every month passed, my horizons narrowed and finally my marriage to Michelle ended after eighteen years. There were no shouting matches, nor messy divorce proceedings and the whole thing passed amicably enough. I still regard her as a friend and can understand why, despite her lack of interest in the game, the disintegration of my soccer career must have caused her such pain.

Now, here I was in 1990, shoulders slumped and reliant on the kindness of individuals such as Donald McCorquodale and Ally MacLeod. It seemed as though I might never escape from the mire. Thankfully, however, a new dawn loomed.

13

THE CUP THAT BOILETH OVER

Even from my adolescent days growing up in Glasgow I knew that football's appeal extended far beyond the Old Firm or Partick Thistle and Clyde. Often enough, on my journeys back from various schoolboy matches, I would hear people speaking about Pollok and Petershill in much the kind of animated tones which others used to conduct their arguments about Rangers and Celtic. While this talk of the Juniors meant little to me, it was obvious that there were thousands of fans and hundreds of clubs networked across the whole of Scotland who were engaged in their private turf wars, oblivious to the players, personalities and transfer sagas which proliferated in the newspapers.

Once I had concluded my moves from Hibs to Orlando, to Celtic, Hamilton Academical and finally Ayr United, the notion that I might quit football altogether, at least temporarily, flashed through my mind. I was too laid-back to indulge in screaming matches with adults, or punish miscreants for the deadly sin of breaking a curfew when I had done the same thing myself, so the prospect of advancing into management barely occurred to me. But then, suddenly, a telephone call from the wilds transformed my life and altered my perception of the esoteric phenomenon that is Scottish Junior football. The voice on the other end of the line buzzing and burbling with enthusiasm announced itself as John Timpany, and I was hooked. 'Hello there, I am on the committee of Glenafton Athletic, and we would like to meet with you to chat about your future.' As you might envisage, I was in the dark, and my knowledge of the Juniors could have been scribbled on the back of a postage stamp, but I reckoned there couldn't be any harm in forging new alliances. Thus it was I hooked up with John and Ian Bell, the Glenafton secretary, in the Carrick Lodge in Ayr.

Both men were upbeat and fizzing with ebullience. They had major plans for Glenafton and felt I could achieve great things for them. It was news to me. They told me of their ambition to transform the club into a match for Auchinleck Talbot and Cumnock Rangers, and the other giants of the circuit. They positively salivated at the thought of bringing silverware back to their trophy cupboard, and their optimism was so infectious that, within a hour, they had sold the notion to me. We shook hands and agreed that I would see what I could do for them during the next twelve months.

I was glowing by the climax of our meeting, but the sight of their park – heaven forbid I should slag off the volunteers who poured their heart and soul into Glenafton – came as the biggest psychological shock I have ever encountered, bigger even than stumbling into the grim environs of Hamilton. It was like climbing into a time machine and returning to the Victorian era. The amenities were sparse to the point of non-existent, and I was close to remarking that the place needed a coat of paint before the council would condemn it.

And yet there was something in the philosophy espoused by John and Ian which had appealed to me. Yes, this was football in the raw and there was no doubting that it was a different universe from what I had been accustomed to in the past, but I looked around me and concluded: 'I could stamp my mark on this, and by God, if I succeeded, it would be one hell of an achievement.' After all, what was wrong with getting my hands dirty? My parents hadn't been afraid of hard graft and I resolved there and then to knuckle down to the task, use my contacts, and, for the first time ever in my career, I merrily stumbled into the territory of *Field of Dreams*.

The first aspect of the Juniors which enthused me was that it commanded a humungous community involvement and a rapport with the supporters, beyond the wit of any senior clubs. Some of the latter might claim to be dedicated to nurturing a relationship with the grassroots, but at Glenafton everybody knew everybody, there was no standing on ceremony, the chap who painted the lines on the pitch was on first-name terms with the chairman, and anybody who dared to stick their nose in the air at anybody else was liable to earn a punch for his trouble. From the outset, I was in my element; I relished the fact that I was in charge. For years I'd had people such as John Collins cleaning my boots, but that had gone and now I bore a responsibility for the relationship between the club and the locals, which was all-pervasive: they trotted along in their hundreds every Saturday and, win, lose or draw, there was no lip service to the fans. On the contrary, I must have shaken a couple of thousand hands within a month of accepting the challenge and these were folk who cared deeply about Glenafton, and were prepared to dip into their own pockets to help finance the lofty aspirations of their committee.

If I had a fault it was my naivety. I picked up the reins and was quickly stitched up by a Sunday newspaper journalist – he knows who he is and loves publicity, so I won't mention his name – who phoned me with the line: 'This sounds like a really inspirational story and it should make for a nice, affectionate piece.' I duly invited him down to the club, where we seemed to get along well, only for him to produce a lengthy article about how I had allegedly fallen from a great height and hit the skids. (This was only a year after my wrongful arrest for alleged shop-lifting hit the headlines.) But, with hindsight, that was a valuable lesson for me, and it merely stiffened my resolve. The next time Glenafton and I attracted publicity, it would be for all the correct reasons.

In basic terms, that meant embarking on the trail of the OVD Scottish Junior Cup, one of the most gruelling, competitive events in any sport on the British beat. It is a marathon tournament in which 170 or 180 starters in the autumn are boiled down on merit every May into two finalists for a rambunctious, rowdy encounter. Whole villages and small towns flock en masse to the finale like children following the Pied Piper. It's the pinnacle of every player's career to secure a winner's medal in this visceral clash of bodies and souls, and I was fortunate enough to help steer Glenafton to an unprecedented sequence of success. We appeared in five consecutive semi-finals between 1991 and 1995, a successful streak which included a never-to-be-forgotten triumph over Tayport at Firhill on 23 May 1993. It was a wondrous time for everybody associated with the side, and while it might sound crazy to compare the Junior Cup to the World Cup, I was never involved in winning the latter, so why shouldn't I sound fanfares for the heroics which my lads delivered over the years?

From the outset it was clear that the Junior scene enjoyed the kind of support and revenue streams which were the envy of many SFL Second and Third Division clubs. One of our most notable sponsors came to be Tom Hunter – the same, inspirational individual who had established the Sports Division chain and who is now Scotland's richest man. One evening, John Timpany rang me and said: 'Alan, I have just discovered that Tom opened his first shop in New Cumnock, his father owned a business there, and he is apparently very proud of his roots, so I think that it would be worthwhile if we arranged a meeting with him.' It sounded like a decent shout, so John dashed away at his usual 150mph and almost immediately came back with the news that Tom had agreed to see us.

Hunter called us into his office and said: 'Right, I know why you are here, I have a meeting scheduled every fifteen minutes for the rest of the day, so spit out your case.' (Those were his precise words.) John then launched into this deluge of guff, some of which strayed into Never-Never Land, so Tom turned to me and asked what *I* wanted. I had been preparing for this so, after my colleague had finished wittering, I responded: 'We have identified several players, whose recruitment will enable us to compete with the Auchinlecks and Cumnocks of this world, but I reckon the first thing we need to do is smarten ourselves up. I am a firm believer that if your team looks smart off the pitch, they will be smart on it, and that if you turn up for matches in blazers and slacks and ties, and carrying professional-looking gear, our rivals will say: "Jesus, who is this we are playing?"'

Tom agreed with me immediately and, in the space of seventy-two hours, Glenafton had been supplied with a full set of top-notch equipment and kit. He backed us one hundred per cent thereafter, without ever asking for anything in return, such as his name on the jerseys or mentions in the programme. Nowadays, when I read about his commitment to tackling poverty in Africa and carrying out good works, it isn't anything other than what I would have anticipated. Tom cares about the balance sheet, but unusually, for a dynamo of business, he is as fixated with the concept of helping others, and we were indebted to him for the manner in which he came to our aid.

It was a measure of the man that when we reached our first Junior Cup final in 1992 – we had been beaten by Newtongrange Star in the semis in my debut season – he phoned me and asked: 'Right, Alan, what do you need for the lads?' And I answered, I guess a bit vaguely: 'Erm, well, nothing, we are just a Junior side.' But he wasn't to be swayed. 'Nonsense, if you are going to be professional in your preparation on the park, then you deserve to be supported behind the scenes,' said Tom. 'What about you and the boys staying at the Seamill Hydro for three days and I will pay for the lot?'

And he did. I had been there in the past with Scotland and Celtic and, suddenly, here I was on the road again with Glenafton and the guys were being pampered and treated like superstars. They loved it, of course they did, and despite their disappointment at being demolished 4-0 by Auchinleck, I like to think they were so inspired and thrilled that the great Tom Hunter had footed the bill for their party, it made them doubly determined to bring back the trophy to New Cumnock the following season.

That was one of the best aspects of the Junior circuit: namely, that these boys truly cared about their communities and you could count the number of mercenaries on one hand. It was a stark contrast from what was happening in Scottish professional football, as the 1990s took many clubs to the brink of bankruptcy on the back of signing foreigners whose sole priority lay in pocketing their monthly cheque, and scarpering to a bigger team if they could possibly engineer it.

By comparison, Glenafton, bolstered by Tom's largesse and the wiles of a canny committee, were in positively rude health as we entered the 1992-3 campaign. John Timpany was a terrific advert for the Juniors – you could almost hear the wheels whirring in his brain as he devised another money-making wheeze, and I recall him calling me at all hours with this or that notion. In one instance, he was raving about this lad who supplied custom-built strips, and John had dreamt up a new scheme whereby he could amass several different shirt sponsors, depending on where we happened to be playing. So I was hauled along to another meeting with the lad, who was beaming at the prospect of supplying us with a variety of jerseys. At first I couldn't figure out why he was quite so overwhelmed. Then John's mobile rang, and when he nipped outside to answer it, this boy, who operated from his home in Douglas, kept saying to me: 'I can't believe it, I really can't believe it, this is my big break, this is fantastic.' I wondered if he was a bit doolally as he seemed to think that all his Christmases had come at once: 'I have spoken to Mr Timpany and he has told me that he expects these replica strips to sell like hot cakes. In fact, he estimates a 10,000 sale in the first year – do you think that will happen, Mr Rough?' I did my best to keep a straight face, because this was fantasy stuff – most SPL clubs don't shift 10,000 strips a year. But that was the way the Juniors worked and, looking back, you have to admit it was a brilliant breeding-ground for bullshitters. And the young lad did profit from the situation as well, so there were no losers even if he never joined the Millionaire's Club!

The Juniors' scene also attracted some tough characters. The stereotypical descriptions of the Ayrshire Juniors being a hotbed of hooligans and head-cases weren't strictly true, but there were a few afternoons amongst the denizens of

Auchinleck and Cumnock when the atmosphere was closer to the Wild West than I might have wished. Some of the Talbot confrontations were scary, because they regarded themselves as being our superiors, and their ground became a bear-pit, especially if you had beaten them in the previous meeting. One afternoon 4,000 fans were packed into the arena, and our dug-out was surrounded by hundreds of their supporters calling us every expletive under the sun and we could hear every word. 'See you Rough, you are a f***ing c***, why don't you go and f*** yourself, you f***ing f***er,' was one of the more reasonable outbursts. It wasn't a theatre for the faint-hearted and the former referee, Willie Young, who knows what it is like to officiate at these type of contests, once commented memorably: 'Everybody was kicking lumps out of one another, there was blood and snotters everywhere, and red and yellow cards being waved like posies at a wedding, and we had been playing for ten minutes before someone noticed that we had forgotten to bring the ball out with us.' It's a priceless line, and often it wasn't that wide off the mark.

Anyway, in this particular clash with Auchinleck Talbot, we witnessed the best and worst of what the Juniors had to offer. We had this wee winger John Millar who could perform wonders with a ball at his feet. But he was also notorious for winding up opponents, and would walk away with this innocent expression on his face after getting involved with moments of trouble, which used to drive other teams mad. They knew that *he* knew exactly what he was doing. In this instance, Auchinleck had this stopper called Billy Mason who had been left clutching at straws and looking stupid by Millar on a number of occasions, and the red mist had descended. You could spot in his eyes the look which says: 'That's it, this wee bastard is getting a doing.' The next time they locked horns, Millar leapt up in the air as if he was auditioning for *Swan Lake* and I don't think Nureyev could have performed the routine any better. The referee produced a straight red card for Mason, and John was rolling around the pitch as if he had been shot . . . but there was nothing wrong with him. The incident provoked an orgy of niggle and acrimony, and when the game ended – in a draw – the players, the fans, the local press guys and even the committee worthies were arguing with one another, and I began to fear that there would be no escape from Auchinleck that evening. As we walked towards the dressing room I remarked to the referee: 'That was a bit of a battle, but I thought you handled it as decently as you could.' And the official turned and replied: 'Aye, well, I reckoned Johnny was hard at it, but the intent was there, so Mason had to go.'

What we hadn't counted on was the fact that Billy hadn't forgiven or forgotten, and when Millar walked past the Talbot dressing room, the door opened and Mason skelped him right in the face with a hay-maker of which Mike Tyson, in his prime, would have been proud. Cue, predictably, a mass brawl between all the guys and they weren't mucking about; this was a real-life version of a bar-room brawl in a John Wayne western, and it dragged on and on. By this point the ref and I had retreated to the edge of the tunnel, and I asked him: 'Now, are you going to go in there and sort it out?' He gazed at me and said: 'Are *you*?' Whereupon, we marched off to the bar and let them finish without us.

Sometimes, the malaise stretched to the committee members, with distressing results. After another tussle with Auchinleck, where we hadn't been anywhere near our best and deservedly lost 3-0 – albeit with a couple of debatable decisions from the referee – Ian Bell and I were in the Glenafton dressing room and he was going bonkers, screaming and howling that the whistler had been the worst he had ever seen. It was madness. I couldn't calm him down, he was ranting away: 'That guy was murder, he was pure diabolical, a f***ing disgrace,' and so on. Then the referee walked in and handed me his sheet which contained the details of the match, the bookings and so on, I said simply: 'Thanks' and handed the paper to Bell who scrunched it into a ball and hurled it at the ref's head. It pinged off him and I was about to grab Ian and lead him away, when the official twirled round, looked forlornly at me, and said: 'Dearie dear, I wouldn't have thought you would have resorted to that, Mr Rough!'

But while the Juniors often gain a negative press, we had a terrific support, our players responded in kind, and I generally think we did our community proud. You should have witnessed the scenes of joy among the citizenry when we brought the OVD Cup back with us from Firhill in 1993. This return to Partick after all those years had been an emotional experience for me and we couldn't have cared less that the match was not a classic.

Six minutes from the spectre of extra time, Ian Grey found Millar, who was prowling on the outskirts of the box, and he looked up and lobbed the ball towards the far corner. It was extremely audacious, and although the Tayport keeper sought to scramble over to the other side, he was never going to make it and Millar settled the game in our favour. The climactic scenes were as tear-stained as anything in my football career, and when we arrived back in New Cumnock that night, the community was collectively feeling no pain, a state of affairs shared by those of us on the open-top bus within a couple of hours. Yes, it is easy to knock the Juniors, but the cynics should have been with us and they may have appreciated that this Cup isn't about money or bonuses; it revolves around civic pride and, briefly, I was fast-tracked back to the Thistle celebrations in 1971.

In fact, there was more interaction between the Seniors and Juniors than you might imagine and it didn't always involve clapped-out old warriors heading off to Pollok or Whitburn or wherever. I remember Glenafton meeting Dalry one afternoon, and they boasted this smashing wee winger who gave his all and more to his team's cause, ignoring any scythes or lunges and mixing hard graft with conjuring tricks. I determined there and then that I would strive to sign him – his name was Tom Brown – and it was one of the brightest moves I ever made throughout my stint at Glenafton. Week in, week out, he was superb for us, his attitude was exemplary, and I wasn't unduly surprised when I received a call from the then-Kilmarnock manager, Tommy Burns, who inquired if he could request a trial for Brown.

From the outset I decided never to stand in the way of any of my players if they were offered the opportunity to graduate to a higher level, so off he went to Rugby Park where he performed excellently in three games, at which stage Burns phoned me again. 'Alan, this lad is great, how much do you want for him?' I replied that if it had been Auchinleck or Cumnock coming in with a bid for him, the fee would be £5,000, then he shocked me by responding: 'Oops, I don't think we can afford that at the moment.' I was gob-smacked, but then Burns said: 'What about if I give you it in instalments of £2,000, £2,000 and £1,000?' I told him: 'Fine, I don't want to stand in the wee lad's way.' I couldn't quite credit that Kilmarnock were so strapped for cash – I had heard they were toiling, but never envisaged they were in such dire straits.

Matters grew worse when Burns contacted me the following day, and declared: 'Look, I am really sorry, but we had a board meeting last night, and I am afraid that we can't stump up the first £2,000 payment.' I was annoyed by now, and barked at him: 'You are f***ing kidding me, aren't you!' But there was nothing else for it, they were skint, and it was up to me to be magnanimous. 'Fine, Tommy, just take the lad,' I concluded, 'and whenever you have cash again, you can repay it then. The main thing is that wee Brown has lived up to his part of the bargain. Kilmarnock had better do the same.'

When I passed this information on to Ian Bell, he was livid, and as we were motoring down to complete the paperwork his mind went into overdrive. 'You know, I think we should include a few clauses in Tommy Brown's contract,' he said. 'Why not, they have mucked us around in this matter, so why don't we put in a clause that they have to pay us £40,000 if he ever plays for Scotland?' I nearly skidded off the road in disbelief and replied: 'Oh, for heaven's sake, don't be so f***ing stupid, they will laugh us out of the room if we walk in there like two guys from Wall Street.' But, in retrospect, Ian's scheme wasn't so daft, because Brown was an instant hit when he joined Kilmarnock (we did receive the full £5,000 by the way) and, at the beginning of the following season was called up into the Scotland B ranks, and he was worth the shout. Another indication that business really wasn't my strongest suit.

But, regardless of that, I was pleased for the player, who subsequently became a cult hero at Kilmarnock, and not in the slightest surprised when he subsequently collected a Scottish Cup winner's medal with the Rugby Park club in 1997. Essentially, he possessed the qualities which comprise the best Junior exponents: a lion-sized heart, a surfeit of commitment and esprit de corps, allied to no shortage of skill, and the confidence to beat a man at close quarters.

For the most part, he was more professional than the others in my squad, but even when he wasn't, he had sufficient talent to compensate. I learned that from one episode when Brown approached me at a Wednesday night training session and said: 'Alan, I am sorry, I know that we have a Scottish Cup tie against Bathgate on Saturday, but my brother is getting married on Friday and I have to be at the wedding. Don't worry, though, I will not be drinking.' My first reaction was to laugh inwardly, but the boy had served us well and I took him at his word. Anyway, Archie Halley, our very own supersub, who was usually sent on for the last twenty minutes, and who scarcely ever started a match, was watching the situation closely and when the clock struck two on Saturday and there was no sign of Tommy, he piped up: 'I knew it, you won't see him today. He has got pished at the wedding reception and he is sobering up somewhere.' I told him to hang on a bit, but half an hour later, when I read out the Glenafton team sheet, which still included Tom, big Archie was incandescent. 'This is a f***ing joke. He's not even here and I still cannae make it into the first eleven,' he wailed, as if it was a national disaster.

Finally, at 2.40pm, Brown climbed out of a pal's car, white as a sheet and quaking in his boots. 'I am sorry, I have let you down, I have let the whole team down. But I was persuaded to have a few beers, then . . . well, I have been spewing my load for most of the night.' Despite his dishevelled state, he begged me: 'C'mon gaffer, give me twenty minutes. I'll do you a turn for that period, I promise you I will. It's the least I can offer after all the hassle that I have put you and the rest of the lads through.'

At 2.50pm I launched into my team talk, and had barely started before Tommy, as white as a Milky Bar, asked if he could go to the toilet. So I started again, and pointed out that we had to be careful with Bathgate's wingers, and that they weren't a great side, but . . . I was interrupted by the sound of somebody retching their guts in the cubicle. I paused, then continued with the instruction that we also had to beware Bathgate's central defence, because . . . but it was no good, my voice was drowned out by this almighty boaking sound. Archie could stand it no longer. 'This is just f***ing unbelievable, we have a man dying in the lavvy, and I am being forced to sit on the bench.' It was a surreal experience, I have to admit, and I harboured some sympathy for Halley. But you have to give credit to Brown: he lasted twenty-five minutes, scored a hat-trick, and then stuck his hand up to be replaced, and dashed straight off to the bathroom.

That incident encapsulates why so many Scottish football aficionados flock to the Juniors. Stay away if you are seeking sophistication or style over substance, but if you are searching for rugged, tough-as-teak action, then the likes of Glenafton and Largs, unglamorous or not, are unbeatable. And just once in a while the football gets confused with boxing, as happened in the 1994 Junior Cup final – one of the most coruscating, controversial, protracted spats in the tournament's history. I will not attempt to condone the kicks and the head-butting which led to the dismissal of four players – two from each side, including the aforementioned Halley – and I can understand why the SJFA has grown wearily accustomed to announcing: 'There will be an enquiry', following the latest act of bampottery from members of their battalion. But, ultimately, and irrespective of what some of the drawing-room columnists who never come near a Junior game would have you believe, the vast majority of those who participate on the circuit are in thrall to the sport. If they can become local heroes once or twice in their careers, is that really so reprehensible? A little less piety from the Fourth Estate might do the trick, given the stories I have heard of journalists brawling at their own functions. These tend to go unreported, a form of hypocrisy which explains why so many people distrust the press. Personally, I felt privileged to be involved with Glenafton, and it marked the dawning of the realisation that I had to worry about other people besides myself.

REALLY SAYING SOMETHING

Even now, in 2006, when I walk the streets of Glasgow or Airdrie, Falkirk or Ayr and people approach me and ask how the 'radio superstar' is faring, I invariably do a double take: it's me they are speaking to! Certainly, a decade ago, I would have laughed if somebody had predicted that I would be chatting on air every night to a massive audience across the country, discussing the burning topics in the rumbustious world of Scottish football, but I suppose that nothing much surprises me any more. Rock groups and politicians, fashion trends and celebrities, may come and go, but soccer remains one of the constants which binds the nation together, even as it occasionally threatens to tear it apart. And, being honest, when you have progressed from being acclaimed by your international manager, Ally MacLeod, as 'the best goalkeeper in the world', to hearing rival supporters on the Junior circuit deliver the chant, to the tune of *My Darling Clementine*: 'Where's the mince beef, where's the mince beef, where's the mince beef, Alan Rough, it's in your pocket, it's in your pocket, it's in your pocket, Alan Rough,' you can cope with anything.

Nonetheless, my emergence as a radio rival to a host of other pundits on the talk-show circuit happened as much by accident as design. Indeed, the notion came together amidst a drunken evening with Jay Crawford, who was then the controller of Scot FM, following a charity golf tournament at Turnberry. As the clock ticked past midnight we were sitting in the lounge exchanging anecdotes and indulging in heated debate on the state of football in Scotland, as the prelude to sloping off to our rooms. As far as I was concerned, it was a pleasant occasion, and thought nothing more about it. But soon afterwards in 2000, I received a call from Jay who shocked me by asking: 'I've been thinking about our recent conversation, and wondered if you might fancy doing a phone-in show on my station.' I was in the dark until Crawford explained the format to me, and while I was initially dubious – I mean, I didn't know one end of a microphone from the other – he reassured me I would be assisted by a professional DJ, who would teach me the ropes. All he was interested in was finding somebody who could entertain listeners, without talking down to them, and he was convinced, on the basis of our Turnberry chat, that I was the man.

I was still sceptical and inquired what night he intended airing this programme. 'Every evening for ninety minutes,' he replied, nonchalantly, as if was the simplest proposal in the world. Then his tone changed and he said insistently: 'Trust me, this will work.' I wasn't sure, as I was still involved with Glenafton at that stage, and the prospect of having to drive to and from Edinburgh five times a week was hardly appealing, so I was on the verge of saying 'Naw'. But there was something about his confidence and his commitment to the concept which had gripped me and, oblivious to what I was letting myself in for, I accepted his offer. He told me I wouldn't regret it, and by God, he was right. However, it did mean a parting of the ways with Glenafton because not even a man of my ability could present a show in Edinburgh and coach a team in Ayrshire at the same time, so I had to say farewell to the Juniors. I was sorry about that, and I kept in contact with Glenafton, because they had been good to me. I still look for their result every Saturday evening, and I helped broker the deal which recently saw Gerry Collins, who used to be John Lambie's number two at Thistle, take on the Glenafton job. And so it was on to the radio.

When I made my first faltering steps as the Frasier Crane of football psychoanalysis, Scot FM hadn't yet been bought over by Real Radio. I had formed an immediate partnership with Steve Jack; he was a consummate professional and a decent guy to boot, and he didn't mind an amateur joining him in the studio or cramping his style. I remain grateful to him, because there were plenty of times in the opening weeks when we might as well have been broadcasting to Uranus for all the feedback we received. It actually reminded me of an early episode of *Frasier* when he chastises his producer Roz Doyle for letting a nutcase on to the show. 'I thought that you were meant to be screening these calls,' he says pompously. 'Yes I am,' she responds, 'but you just have to become a little less choosy when there is only one person waiting on the line.' Trust me, I have been there, and survived it, though not without spouting some of the most long-winded shite in the history of radio. On my debut, for instance, we attracted a mere five callers in the space of an hour and a half, and that meant prattling on a grand scale. I was convinced I wasn't repeating myself, but it must have sounded like a continuous loop. At the end I was downcast, and was certain that I faced the axe. But Jay, a mercurial pillar of strength in adversity, put on a brave face, declared that matters would improve, and was gradually vindicated as we began to draw a cult following.

There was no doubt I was inexperienced in these days, but

Steve told me that I had to react to the caller as if I was speaking to an enthusiast in the pub – minus the expletives, of course – and as the months passed I settled into the job, relaxed in the chair, cracked a few gags to lighten the mood and wasn't frightened of stirring up controversy if it was required. We never shied away from tackling thorny issues, and have always been ahead of the BBC in that regard.

When we were taken over by the Guardian Media Group, owner of Real Radio, I agreed with their decision to move us from Edinburgh to Glasgow, even if it was regrettable that they split up my burgeoning partnership with Steve. My next companion was Bill Young, but unfortunately he fell foul of the new company. My subsequent pairing with Ewen Cameron has seen our programme's popularity surge at an unprecedented rate.

Ewen has his detractors, and has incurred the wrath of several high-profile organisations, including the Old Firm and the SFA. This, in Scotland, is usually guaranteed to spell trouble for any football reporter. But, once again, he was Jay Crawford's appointment, he brings a spark of danger to the party, and I can guarantee you that he will argue his case until he is blue, green, red or maroon in the face. Ewen has an opinion on everything. Indeed, there have been many times when he has become embroiled in a battle of wills with a caller, and their debate has carried on relentlessly to the stage where I have wandered off to the canteen for a coffee and a glance at a newspaper. The pair of them will still have been arguing the toss when I returned to the studio. In these circumstances, Ewen often turns to me and pleads: 'C'mon big man, help me out here.' But I always offer the same reply: 'Sorry wee man, but I don't know what you are talking about, I haven't been listening.' That tends to drive him nuts, but there are times when you have to tune him out, and the truth of the matter is that Ewen frequently doesn't realise when he is rubbing people up the wrong way and, in certain respects, that is a strength. It means, for instance, that when he goes along to a Celtic press conference, and the other football guys are obsessed with asking Gordon Strachan whether he is intending to deploy a 4-4-2 or a 4-5-1 formation, Cameron blithely ignores their treading on eggshells and isn't afraid to pipe up: 'Now Gordon, can you tell us: is Neil Lennon's girlfriend really pregnant?'

Understandably, this approach goes down in some places like a cup of cold sick, but he simply calls it as he sees it and he is impervious to criticism. On many occasions I have sat down with him and said: 'Look, Ewen, you have been banned by the SFA, by Rangers and Celtic, and the referees hate you, where is it all going to end?' But he views these banning orders as a badge of honour and claims he is merely putting the questions to the likes of Strachan, Walter Smith and Alex McLeish which the man and woman in the street would like to ask. He will follow that up by arguing – and, to be fair, our show's audience figures seem to suggest that his standpoint is shared by an awful lot of Scots – that the public is entitled to more than bland plat-itudes from Park Gardens or Ibrox. After all, it is the supporters who are ultimately paying the wages of the employees at these clubs – and I am with him in that.

In any case, despite the criticism heaped on Ewen by some of his snootier rivals and sections of the blazerati, we work on the basis that our programme has no agenda; that it is up to the listeners to decide what they want to concentrate on – there is no priority lent to the callers or attempts at censorship. If Billy from Pollok wishes to discuss the failings of the Rangers defence, then Davie from

Larkhall pops up next with his belief that Barry Ferguson has not been the same player since returning from Blackburn, we don't feel obliged to cut in and make sure that the next call is from Paddy in Croy. That would be self-defeating and it runs counter to our conviction that you have to go with the flow, even if it steers you down some bizarre avenues or into cul-de-sacs of lunacy, and create a rapport with the folk on the other end of the line.

Of course, there are the usual idiots who try to swear on air, under the delusion that it is hugely amusing to insert an f-word into the middle of their opening sentence. But they are in the minority, and although I have been hauled into some fairly belligerent spats down the years, I am pretty laid-back. As long as the chat keeps away from racist nonsense, or bigoted abuse, then I am happy to fight my corner, and tolerate being called a 'numpty' or an 'eejit' by the occasional caller. After all, when football fans argue in the pub, they don't pepper their conversation with garden-party bon mots, so I don't expect that on the show. And if we are being honest, ingrained passion, loyalty and devotion to the cause are the reasons why football remains a pivotal feature of Scottish life, because it definitely isn't down to results on the pitch for the last five years. During the tenure of Berti Vogts I was concerned that we might be in trouble against Iceland, but I feared the worst if we ever met Asda, Tesco and Morrison's . . .

On some evenings, of course, the format works better than others. Let's face it, there are only so many different opinions that one can express about a disputed penalty decision. They range from 'the referee got it right,' to 'naw he didnae, he's a Mason and I've seen him in the back of the Rangers supporters' bus.' One can at such times lose the will to live. In the course of one infamous night we managed to spend two hours with one caller after another obsessing over a spot kick, and my brain was frazzled by the climax. That, however, is the risk Ewen and I have chosen to take and, for the most part, the programme works. We never patronise the respondents or fall into the trap of thinking they are there for us to mock. On the contrary, we realise that we wouldn't be in a job without the phones ringing, and that knowledge keeps us honest.

It has also fostered a sense of trust with the callers, and although we occasionally find ourselves in off-the-wall situations, the formula has worked because there *isn't* a formula. Sometimes the most bizarre experiences occur in the company of gentlemen who sound if they have just left the House of Lords. One such fellow – a plummy-voiced lad you could picture wearing a bow tie and a pinstripe suit – phoned in to remonstrate with us for the amount of time devoted to the Old Firm. 'Frankly, my good chaps, I have been listening to your programme for a month and I am disgusted, quite disgusted, at the fact it is always Rangers this Celtic that every night.' So I asked him: 'What team do you support?' He replied 'Motherwell.' And I told him that we were delighted to be speaking to him and he was now being allowed a platform to share his thoughts on affairs at Fir Park with a quarter of a million listeners. There was a pause: 'Oh, you misunderstand my position. I have nothing to say about Motherwell. Thank you and goodbye.' And he hung up.

One similarly well-spoken caller was chatting away merrily about his feelings on Gordon Strachan's managerial qualities, and we were relaxed in the studio, because he was articulate and inoffensive. Suddenly, in the midst of his argument, he inquired: 'Incidentally, chaps, this Stilian Petrov intrigue – what the f*** is all that about?' and we were forced to cut in quickly. I believe that element of unpredictability is one of the most satisfying factors behind our programme's success. So, too, is the manner in which we have our regulars, who phone in once a week and start the conversation: 'Hi, Roughy, it's Willie here from Easterhouse,' and they treat me as one of their mates.

It is almost as if the same camaraderie which I shared with many of the Partick Thistle fans thirty years ago has been transplanted to the airwaves. Don't get me wrong, not everybody is amiable – there have been some X-certificate exchanges down the years – but the best times are when callers crack jokes or unconsciously make chumps of themselves by saying something contradictory in the space of two sentences. Meanwhile Ewen and I will be corpsing, hyper-ventilating in our seats. Overall there is generally a humour and spontaneity to the proceedings which proves that most listeners recognise football isn't a matter of life and death.

For instance one of our callers, Stevie, is blind, and has a dog called Oscar. At first I was puzzled as to how he managed to work out what was happening on the pitch if he couldn't see the action. However, he explained: 'I go with my mates, and they are all blind as well, but we carry horns and we honk them to indicate what is going on.' I must admit I was still struggling to understand this concept, and pressed him on the system they had devised. But he just replied: 'Ach, I don't really care about that. We know when a goal has been scored, but, for the rest of the time, I am just happy honking with my friends.' I was speechless.

Mind you, that doesn't happen very often, because if I have learned anything from the likes of Jay Crawford and Steve Jack, it is that controversy attracts an audience and that the worst thing you can do as a pundit is pull your punches. We have had a variety of big-name guests on the show, including Andy Goram, Richard Gough and Charlie

Nicholas, and they have been shocked at the vitriol and personal abuse which pours forth from some of the callers, but it is like water off a duck's back to me. After all, Ewen and I have been handed our own personal soapbox by Real Radio and the worst thing we could do is to start imposing rules and regulations on our listeners.

Indeed, the best part of the job for me is the appreciation that there are so many intelligent, passionate fans out there prepared to engage in all kinds of debates from the serious to the light-hearted. Whether we are exploring sectarianism or discussing which SPL club has the worst pies for sale, the lines will invariably be buzzing. This makes a mockery of those who dismiss Scottish football supporters as a group of meat-heads with low IQs. It is incredible that after being allowed to do something I loved for twenty years – by being a professional footballer – that I have been handed a chance to progress into an extension of my former trade where I am actually paid money to talk about the game. Understandably, most days I drive to Baillieston with a big grin on my face.

As we move into the future, at least there are signs that the SPL has finally begun to face reality. A decade ago I was convinced that many clubs were descending into madness, spending money they didn't possess, hiring foreigners and ignoring their indigenous talent, and generally juddering to hell in a handcart. One Saturday afternoon I recall glancing down the team sheets, and there were comfortably more overseas players in the ranks than Scots. If they had all been of the calibre of Thierry Henry or Henrik Larsson, even that wouldn't have justified a policy which has been extremely detrimental to the interests of the national team. I can now sympathise with Walter Smith, because, having inherited a shambles from Berti Vogts, he is still confronted with an almighty task to transform his side's fortunes to the point where he can contemplate qualifying for major finals again on any kind of consistent basis.

However, there are green shoots of recovery – there is no reason why the likes of Shaun Maloney, Andy Webster, Craig Gordon, Kris Boyd, Garry O'Connor, Derek Riordan, Ross Wallace, Kevin McNaughton and Darren Fletcher, alongside more experienced campaigners such as Paul Hartley, Barry Ferguson, Steven Pressley, Gary Naysmith and Kenny Miller, shouldn't provide stern opposition for most of the leading European sides. But we shouldn't be deluded over the fashion in which the well of talent has dried up. The only people who are making a genuine impression in England these days are managers.

With that in mind, and without wandering unduly into politics, we really need to start encouraging the Scottish Executive to acknowledge the link between obesity and the dearth of competitive sport in my country. With so many children who sit for hours in front of computers and PlayStations, and who tend to react to sunshine and fresh air much as Dracula did, it's not surprising we are called the sick man of Europe. When I was at school, we used to have ten hours of PE on the curriculum every week and, while that might be excessive in the present climate, it didn't do me any harm. By all means, if kids aren't interested in sport, let's not force them into activities they detest. The link between health and fitness is well established, and maybe the politicians should cease faffing around on the touchline and acknowledge how far we are languishing behind our counterparts in Europe and the rest of the world.

In Australia, for example, the sports minister's job is one of the most important in the cabinet, and the country boasts some of the best athletes on the planet, so there is nothing pie-in-the-sky about the concept of nurturing athletic children. What *is* stupid is pretending that we can solve the problem with a sticking plaster here, and a bandage there. And yet in Scotland we still appear to have limited vision when it comes to creating facilities which our children might actually wish to use. Ultimately, it's like anything else – you get what you pay for.

If that sounds negative, my attitude to sectarianism is probably even more downbeat. I know that there has been a raft of initiatives launched by the Executive, while groups such as Bhoys Against Bigotry and Nil By Mouth have striven to tackle the blot on the landscape. But I have met the people singing the songs about being up to their knees in Fenian blood and the problem is primarily Rangers' to solve in my opinion. These bigots come from all over Scotland. It is a fallacy to pretend that the malaise is restricted to Glasgow; these attitudes are ingrained. They won't change, they don't recognise they are offending others, and while we have to do our best to minimise sectarianism, we are never going to eradicate it completely. The extremists need somebody to hate, and that isn't going to change, irrespective of any number of directives and political bills.

I discussed this with Ewen on one of the most inflammatory programmes we ever broadcast, and his argument was that we should start shutting down stands at Ibrox, and if that meant 10,000 supporters being denied access to the ground, then so be it. But I told him: 'You are punishing the wrong people. You are punishing the 9,500 people who got up with their families on the day of the match, paid top dollar for their tickets, and who are only interested in cheering on their team, and if their language is a bit ripe at times, well we would have to close down every pub in Scotland if we objected to folk effing and blinding.'

What we have to do, I argued, is focus on the reprobates who are bringing Rangers into disrepute. I know that a few Celtic fans seem to think it is all right to chant pro-IRA slogans at away matches, which is unacceptable, but they are a tiny minority. I can't believe that today's sophisticated CCTV technology can't be used to catch the worst offenders. I have been inside police control rooms at football matches, and some of their equipment looks as if it was rented from NASA. If you can press a button and zoom in on ten people chanting 'F*** the Pope', why can't you get security to whisk them out of the ground? If these so-called fans have any complaints, they can argue their case with the police, and attempt to dispute that it isn't them in the CCTV images. The majority, however, would be bang to rights and it would then be up to Rangers to ensure that they weren't allowed back into Ibrox.

But we shouldn't kid ourselves that exorcising sectarianism will happen in a year, or a decade, or even a generation. I went to a do not that long ago, outside Glasgow, at the request of a friend, who had told me: 'Alan, I know you are an ex-Celtic player, but we would like you to speak at a dinner we are organising.' I should probably have asked for more details, but he said there was a comedian, plus a former Rangers player and myself on the bill, so I didn't envisage any problems. I soon realised it was a Rangers rally for their supporters in that area, and as I glanced around the hall and discerned the Red Hand and FTP tattoos, I was close to shitting myself. A significant part of my speech featured Billy McNeill, Frank McAvennie and Roy Aitken, and I just sat there, picking away at my fingernails, and thinking: 'I'll get murdered if I mention anything to do with Celtic Park or even mention the word "green".'

The Rangers player got up first and participated in a Q & A session and, soon enough, he was asked: 'In the present day, which of the current Celtic team would you most like to have a kick at?' And he responded: 'I would never get tired of kicking Neil Lennon.' Well, the whole place rose to acclaim him as if he had just delivered the Gettysburg Address, and that was scary, because the mood was utterly entrenched: these Rangers acolytes were proud of their culture, their heritage, and they were not going to be silenced by any politically correct MSPs or pressure groups. Needless to say, I kept my speech short and pithy – and never mentioned the 'C' word.

This story illustrates why I think this problem may never be solved. I don't care that the drawing-room pundits consistently argue that things are improving. If they genuinely want to discover the mood amongst the die-hards, they should go out into the wilds of Lanarkshire and Ayrshire and West Lothian on Old Firm match days and discover the manner in which the shit hits the fan with a vengeance. Nor is it confined to violence and hooliganism and the occasional murder: there is also the more insidious, pernicious phenomenon of parents refusing to allow their children to wear anything green or to write with a green pencil, or have any connection with the colour. Taken to its logical conclusion – if there was any degree of logic involved in the whole wretched business – it would surely mean that grass was off-limits.

I have no truck, either, with those callers to Real Radio, who profess: 'Ach Roughy, I am only a ninety-minute bigot.' To which I usually respond: 'OK, so when you walk out of the stadium, having sung *The Sash* and *The Billy*

Boys and sworn abuse at the Pope for the previous two hours, you suddenly change into a different person, a pillar of civilised behaviour and calmness, who would root for Celtic if they reached a European final?' I'm not actually saying that they should follow that policy – nobody should be forced to back a team they don't support – but the bigots always rise to the bait and strive to argue that these trips to Ibrox offer them a safety valve.

I have never bought that argument, and never will, on the grounds it doesn't make any sense. In its simplest form, it is seeking to justify the unjustifiable and I know plenty of Rangers fans who cheer on their heroes, grow passionate in the heat of battle, and slag off the referee, without feeling obliged to introduce religious hatred to the equation. Why can't the rest behave like that?

But as I have said, there is no quick fix to this blight and I speak as somebody who has watched otherwise intelligent, hard-nosed businessmen, with Catholics amongst their friends, change completely once the drink starts flowing and tongues grow loose. On one instance, at the Albany Hotel in Glasgow, I could hear several of the other guests muttering: 'What the f*** is he doing here?' as they gestured in my direction, and this was all down to me having committed the cardinal sin of turning out for Celtic in seven matches. Yet the longer that evening progressed, the worse the atmosphere became – and we are referring here to some of the biggest names in Scottish commercial life. By the time the waitresses were serving the desserts, a group of these guys had climbed on to a table and were giving *The Sash* laldy. I just thought: 'I shouldn't be here, but, on the other hand, do these people have any idea exactly how ridiculous they look?'

*   *   *

This is one of the reasons why, on the radio programme, I am curious about asking Catholic callers whether they are offended by the lyrics of the more inflammatory Rangers anthems. And, from experience, I know that many of them aren't really bothered. The majority of the more sensible fans would prefer not to have to listen to *The Sash*, just as they would be happier if a minority of Celtic's following didn't disgrace their club by chanting pro-IRA slogans. But ultimately, I suppose I am hard-nosed in my approach to sectarianism and bigotry. Whether we are dealing with the scenes which plague most Old Firm encounters, or the casual racism and stadium violence which is rife across Italy and Eastern Europe, anybody who cares about football has to put pressure on UEFA and FIFA to address their responsibilities. Governing bodies should not continually pass the buck on to the politicians.

Some of the comments heard at Ibrox are uttered by people so stupid that they wouldn't even be able to spell 'sectarianism', but that is no excuse in this day and age, and especially considering that there are often more Catholics in the Rangers than Celtic ranks on any given Saturday. One Rangers director used to tell the story of how Lorenzo Amoruso approached Barry Ferguson and asked him: 'Barry, Barry, what are these songs that our fans are singing? What do they mean?' And the Scot replied: 'They mean £25,000 a week for you and me, so just keep singing them!' OK, that is tongue in cheek, and I would hate to think that Scottish supporters might ever be frightened to open their mouths for fear of offending anybody, but there is a difference between cheering on your team, winding up your opponents and indulging in religious or racist discrimination. I like to think that most of us can make the distinction between the two. As to ridding Scotland of this problem – well I am fifty-five now and I do not think that any amount of legislation will have completely silenced the idiots if I live to be ninety-five.

Passion, mind you, is a significant part of football's attraction and one of the reasons why Ewen and I have found ourselves in such demand. Whatever happens in the sport, whether it be a player demanding a transfer, some London-based official striving to resurrect the notion of an all-British team, or an off-the-field incident splashed on the front page of the *Daily Record* or the *Sun*, there will be twenty different theories springing into life within hours as the Internet spreads conspiracies to every corner of the globe. If I had a pound for every instance I have been told, in solemn fashion, by some of the more extreme members of the world wide web, that x was gay, y was a child molester or z was into wacky baccy, I would be a rich man. And yet the plotlines of *Footballers' Wives* have had to grow more ridiculous because of the surreal stories which keep occurring in the real-life game. Who, for instance, would have dared write a script which covered Hearts' season in 2005-6?

For those of us with a devotion to the weird and the downright crazy, Scotland remains a glorious melting pot, serving up a regular diet of tales of the unexpected from Gretna's emergence from the depths of poverty to qualifying for Europe, to Clyde's surprising, but thoroughly merited Scottish Cup victory over Celtic last season, or Roy Keane's arrival at Parkhead. I know that almost anything is possible in this business.

Much water has passed under the bridge since Partick Thistle's stunning success in the 1971 League Cup final – good grief, as I write this, I am thinking: can it really be thirty-five years ago? – and I have still retained a near-boyish enthusiasm for everything to do with football. Even in 1990, when I was on my uppers and wondering if I deserved any more strokes of misfortune, I recall switching on the television and watching Scotland tackle Costa Rica at the World Cup and quietly wondering if we could finally make an impression in the event.

For the next ninety minutes, life elsewhere ceased to matter, as I travelled through the whole gamut of emotions from hope and expectation to anger and frustration as another ignominious result was chalked up on the nation's debit sheet. But, by the death, I could understand why hardened adults, welders, miners and ship-builders cried in the street when we steered them to the brink of glory with Archie Gemmill's famous goal against Holland in 1978. It mattered, it genuinely mattered, and cold logic doesn't come into it: instead, there is something deep in our psyche which stirs to life whenever Scots come together in a common pursuit and although I have never harboured any illusions about my ability, neither do I believe that I ever offered less than one hundred per cent whether with Scotland, Partick, Hibs or Celtic. If I have regrets, they are easily out-numbered by the occasions when I have been kissed by Lady Luck.

So, as they say, here's to the future, and to heaven knows how many more telephone exchanges with the diverse assortment of characters who ignore Scotland's descent down the FIFA rankings and stay true to the notion that football is one of the few common languages, even if the message is sometimes obscured in the delivery. No doubt Ewen Cameron will have ruffled half a dozen people's feathers in the time it has taken you to read this, but while he may be many things, he is never dull, and that applies to Scottish football. As for myself, I will carry on stressing the positive, but not ignoring the negative, relishing each fresh chapter in our soccer history. But above all, I will be striving to adhere to the guiding principle of my professional career, whether in the box or on the radio: to keep it honest.

Away from the microphone, I am equally blessed. Following the break-up of my marriage to Michelle, I was desolate for a long time. At least it was amicable and there were no disputes over the house or alimony or maintenance. That miserable period in the early 1990s demonstrates how quickly things can go horribly wrong and I have never been remotely complacent ever since. However, I thank my lucky stars that in 1994, when I was at the press club ball as the guest of Donald McCorquodale, I was introduced by Alex Ferguson, a man with a contacts book to rival anyone on Scotland, to a lady called Maggie Barry, who was at the Tennent Caledonian table. She didn't know who I was, beyond having a vague recollection that I had played for Scotland, but the spark was immediate. Maggie, a journalist by profession, and I established an instant rapport, and I finished the night by saying 'I'll phone you and perhaps we can arrange to meet up for lunch together?' She responded 'I've a better idea, why don't I call you and we can link up tomorrow?' and we have been together ever since.

It might seem strange to some people that I should have fallen in love with a member of the press, given that I have been on the receiving end of hostile treatment from sections of the media throughout my life. But she is a news reporter, whose values were forged on the basis of honesty, integrity and decency. I have grown to accept that journalism is like anything else and you shouldn't damn an entire profession because of a few rotten apples at the bottom of the barrel.

When I first met her, Maggie had a nine-month-old child, Lucy, and an older daughter, Sarah, who are now thirteen and nineteen, and together with my son, Alan, who is twenty-five, we are as happy as any family has a right to be and part of that springs from the fact we are both doing jobs which we love. Lest this sound syrupy, I know I have been a fortunate individual, and that there have been many pivotal moments in my career – from the doctor who recommended amputating my arm, for instance, to the chain of coincidences which led Jimmy Dickie to watch me on that ash park at Anniesland. Things might have happened differently, and prevented me from fulfilling my ambitions, but on the storm-tossed voyage, I couldn't have asked for a better crew.

Football, of course, is still very important to me, but I'm passionate about it, not obsessed with it, and it helps that the rest of my family have other interests which allow me an escape from the goldfish bowl. My son, Alan, and brother, Gordon, have neither been especially interested in the game, whilst Maggie and the girls are more keen on horses and equestrianism and this has become a new enthusiasm in my life. Often, at the slightest opportunity, we will venture off to the countryside, and Lucy and Sarah are both actively involved in show-jumping, so we go along and support them and, believe me, I get every bit as carried away as when I am watching Scotland's football team but I couldn't possibly comment.

More importantly, perhaps, although I am in my mid-fifties, Maggie and the girls keep me young and many's the time when I have been in Glasgow and received a text message from one of the teenagers, asking if I can meet them at Debenham's or W H Smith. I know, of course, that it's going to cost me my right arm, but what the hell, I am just delighted I have a right arm.

Which is where we came in.

CAREER STATISTICS

Alan Roderick Rough, born 25 November 1971, served under four Scotland managers:

Willie Ormond: 14 February 1973 – 27 April 1977
Ally MacLeod: 28 May 1977 – 20 September 1978
Jock Stein: 25 October 1978 – 10 September 1985
Alex Ferguson: 16 October 1985 – 13 June 1986

Rough was awarded 53 international caps, 51 while at Partick Thistle and two at Hibs. He made his Scotland senior debut against Switzerland at Hampden on 7 April 1976, in a match which the hosts won 1-0, and his swansong was against England at Wembley on 23 April 1986, when the visitors lost 2-1. He came on as a substitute for Jim Leighton at Ninian Park in Cardiff, on 10 September 1985, in a World Cup qualifying match, which finished 1-1, but will forever be remembered as the night Jock Stein collapsed and died towards the end of the proceedings.

SCOTLAND MATCHES

1976
(1) April 7. Friendly. Scotland 1 (Pettigrew, 2), Switzerland 0.
Scotland: Rough, McGrain, F Gray, Forsyth, Blackley, Craig, Dalglish (D Bremner, 64), Pettigrew (McKean, 46), A Gray, MacDonald, Johnstone.
Switzerland: Burgener, Guyot, Stohler, Bizzini, Fischbach, Hasler

(Andrey, 53), Botteron, Risi, Elsener (Schnyder, 64), Muller, Jeandupeux.

Referee: Patridge (England).

(2) May 6. Home International Championship. Scotland 3 (Pettigrew 38, Rioch 44, E Gray, 69), Wales 1 (Griffiths, 61, pen).

Scotland: Rough, McGrain, Donachie, Forsyth, Jackson, Rioch, Pettigrew, Masson, Jordan, Gemmill, E Gray.

Wales: Lloyd, D Jones, J Jones, D Roberts, J Roberts, Harris (Cartwright, 46), Yorath, Griffiths, Curtis, O'Sullivan, James.

Ref: Wright (N Ireland).

(3) May 8. Home International Championship. Scotland 3 (Gemmill 23, Masson 47, Dalglish, 52), Northern Ireland 0.

Scotland: Rough, McGrain, Donachie, Forsyth, Jackson, Rioch (Hartford, 56), Masson, Gemmill, Pettigrew (Johnstone, 66), Jordan, Dalglish.

Northern Ireland: Jennings, Rice, Scott, Nicholl, Hunter, Finney, Hamilton, Sharkey (McCreery, 61), Cassidy, McIlroy, Morgan (Spence, 85).

Ref: Reynolds (Wales).

(4) May 15. Home International Championship. Scotland 2 (Masson 18, Dalglish, 49), England 1 (Channon, 11).

Scotland: Rough, McGrain, Donachie, Forsyth, Jackson, Rioch, Masson, Gemmill, Dalglish, Jordan, E Gray (Johnstone, 79).

England: Clemence, Todd, Mills, Thompson, McFarland (Doyle, 70), Kennedy, Keegan, Francis, Taylor, Channon, Pearson (Cherry, 46).

Ref: Polatai (Hungary).

(5) September 8. Friendly. Scotland 6 (Rioch, 7, Masson, pen, 16, Dalglish, 23, A Gray, 44, 80, E Gray, 68), Finland 0.

Scotland: Rough, McGrain, Donachie, Rioch, Forsyth, Buchan, Dalglish, Gemmill, A Gray, Masson, E Gray.

Finland: Alaja (Enckelman, 46), Heikinnen (Ahonen, 75), Vihtala, Makynen, Ranta, Jantunen, Suomalainen, Toivola, Russanen, Dahllund, Paatelainen (Nieminen, 39).

Ref: Kew (England).

(6) October 13. World Cup Qualifier. Czechoslovakia 2 (Panenka, 46, Petras, 48), Scotland 0.

Scotland: Rough, McGrain, Donachie, Buchan, McQueen, Rioch, Dalglish (Burns, 56), Masson (Hartford, 68), Jordan, A Gray, Gemmill.

Czechoslovakia: Vencel, Biros, Capkovic (Jurkemic, 68), Ondrus, Gogh (Kozak, 13), Pollak, Dobias, Panenka, Masny, Nehoda, Petras.

Ref: Michelotti (Italy).

(7) November 17. World Cup Qualifier. Scotland 1 (Evans og, 15), Wales 0.

Scotland: Rough, McGrain, Donachie, Blackley, McQueen, Gemmill, Burns, Rioch (Hartford, 67), E Gray (Pettigrew, 84), Dalglish, Jordan.

Wales: Davis, Page, J Jones, Phillips, Evans, Griffiths, Yorath, Flynn, Thomas, Toshack, James (Curtis, 74).

Ref: Biwersi (W Germany).

1977

(8) April 27. Friendly. Scotland 3 (Hellstrom, og, 30, Dalglish 56, Craig, 79), Sweden 1 (Wendt, 51).

Scotland: Rough, McGrain, Donachie, Glavin (Jardine, 58), Forsyth, Blackley (Narey, 76), Dalglish, Hartford, Burns (Craig, 76), Pettigrew, Johnston.

Sweden: Hellstrom, M Andersson, B Andersson, Nordqvist, R Andersson, Larsson, Turstensson (Borg, 55), Borjesson (Ljunberg, 65), Johansson (Nordin, 71), Wendt, Sjoberg.

Ref: Taylor (England).

(9) May 28. Home International Championship. Wales 0, Scotland 0.

Scotland: Rough, McGrain, Donachie, Rioch (Johnston, 65), McQueen, Forsyth, Masson, Gemmill, Parlane (Burns, 74), Dalglish, Hartford.

Wales: Davies, R Thomas, J Jones, Philips, Evans, Sayer, Mahoney, Yorath, Flynn, Deacy, James (M Thomas, 67).

Ref: Moffatt (N Ireland).

(10) June 1. Home International Championship. Scotland 3
(Dalglish, 31, 79, McQueen, 61), Northern Ireland 0.
Scotland: Rough, McGrain, Donachie, Forsyth, McQueen, Rioch,
Masson, Hartford, Jordan (Macari, 69), Dalglish, Johnston
(Gemmill, 86).
N Ireland: Jennings, Nicholl, Rice, Jackson, Hunter, Hamilton,
McCreery, McGrath, McIlroy, O'Neill, Anderson (Spence, 56).
Ref: Gow (Wales).

(11) June 4. Home International Championship. England 1
(Channon, pen, 87), Scotland 2 (McQueen, 43, Dalglish, 61).
Scotland: Rough, McGrain, Donachie, Forsyth, McQueen, Rioch,
Masson (Gemmill, 83), Dalglish, Jordan (Macari, 43), Hartford,
Johnston.
England: Clemence, Neal, Mills, Hughes, Watson, Greenhoff (Cherry,
77), Kennedy (Tueart, 67), Talbot, Channon, Francis, Pearson.
Ref: Palotai (Hungary).

(12) June 15. Friendly. Chile 2 (Crisosto, 49, 72), Scotland 4
(Dalglish, 19, Macari, 30, 57, Hartford, 37).
Scotland: Rough (Stewart, 45), McGrain, Donachie, Buchan, Forsyth,
Rioch (Gemmill, 45), Masson, Dalglish, Macari, Hartford (Jardine,
80), Johnston.
Chile: Nef, Machuca, Escobar, Figueroa, Quintano, Quiroz, Inostroba,
Soto (Crisosto, 37), Veliz (Moscoso, 79), Farias, Pinto.
Ref: Silvagno (Chile).

(13) June 18. Friendly. Argentina 1 (Passarella, pen, 81), Scotland
1 (Masson, pen, 77).
Scotland: Rough, McGrain, Donachie, Gemmill, Forsyth, Buchan,
Masson, Dalglish, Macari, Hartford, Johnston.
Argentina: Baley, Pernia, Killer, Passarella, Carrascosa, Ardiles, Gallego,
Larrosa (Trossero, 70), Gonzalez (Tarantini, 59), Luque, Houseman.
Ref: Filho (Brazil).

(14) June 23. Friendly. Brazil 2 (Zico, 70, Cerezo, 75), Scotland 0.
Scotland: Rough, McGrain, Donachie, Rioch, Forsyth, Buchan,
Masson, Gemmill, Dalglish, Hartford, Johnston (Jardine, 61).

Brazil: Leao, Ze Maria, Marinho, Pereira, Edinho, Paulo Isidoro, Cerezo, Rivelino, Paulo Cesar, Gil (Zico, 45), Reinaldo.
Ref: Saltaro (Brazil).

(15) September 21. World Cup Qualifier. Scotland 3 (Jordan, 19, Hartford, 35, Dalglish, 54), Czechoslovakia 1 (Gajdusek, 80).
Scotland: Rough, Jardine, McGrain, Forsyth, McQueen, Rioch, Dalglish, Masson, Jordan, Hartford, Johnston.
Czechoslovakia: Michalik, Paurik, Capkovic, Dvorak, Gogh, Dobias (Gallis, 69), Pollak, Moder (Knapp, 45), Gajdusek, Masny, Nehoda.
Ref: Rion (Belgium).

(16) October 12. World Cup Qualifier. Wales 0, Scotland 2 (Masson, pen, 79, Dalglish, 87).
Scotland: Rough, Jardine (Buchan, 57), Donachie, Masson, McQueen, Forsyth, Dalglish, Hartford, Jordan, Macari, Johnston.
Wales: Davies, Thomas, J Jones, Phillips, D Jones, Sayer (Deacy, 75), Mahoney, Yorath, Flynn, Thomas, Toshack.
Ref: Wurtz (France).

1978

(17) May 13. Home International Championship. Scotland 1 (Johnstone, 36), Northern Ireland 1 (O'Neill, 26).
Scotland: Rough, Jardine, Buchan (Burns, 37), Forsyth, McQueen, Rioch, Masson, Gemmill, Jordan (Dalglish, 45), Johnstone, Robertson.
N Ireland: Platt, J Nicholl, Scott, B Hamilton, C Nicholl, McCreery, McIlroy, O'Neill, McGrath (W Hamilton 63), Anderson (Cochrane, 77), Armstrong.
Ref: Gow (Wales).

(18) May 20. Home International Championship. Scotland 0, England 1 (Coppell, 83).
Scotland: Rough, Kennedy, Donachie, Burns, Forsyth, Rioch (Souness, 74), Masson (Gemmill, 74), Hartford, Dalglish, Jordan, Johnston.
England: Clemence, Neal, Mills, Hughes (Greenhoff, 73), Watson, Coppell, Currie, Wilkins, Barnes, Mariner (Brooking, 76), Francis.
Ref: Konrath (France).

(19) June 3. World Cup. Scotland 1 (Jordan, 15), Peru 3 (Cueto, 43, Cubillas, 70, 76).

Scotland: Rough, Burns, Kennedy, Forsyth, Buchan, Rioch (Macari, 70), Masson (Gemmill, 70), Hartford, Dalglish, Jordan, Johnston.

Peru: Quiroga, Duarte, Manzo, Chumpitaz, Diaz, Munante, Velasquez, Cueto (Rojaz, 82), Oblitas, Cubillas, La Rosa (Sotil, 62).

Ref: Eriksson (Sweden).

(20) June 7. World Cup. Scotland 1 (Eskandarian, og, 43), Iran 1 (Danaifar, 60).

Scotland: Rough, Buchan (Forsyth, 57), Donachie, Jardine, Burns, Macari, Gemmill, Hartford, Jordan, Dalglish (Harper, 73), Robertson.

Iran: Hejazi, Nazari, Kazerani, Abdollahi, Eskandarian, Parvin, Ghasempour, Sadeghi, Danaifar (Naybagha, 89), Faraki (Roshan, 83), Djahani.

Ref: Ndiaye (Senegal).

(21) June 11. World Cup Match. Scotland 3 (Dalglish, 44, Gemmill, 46, pen, 68), Holland 2 (Rensenbrink, pen, 34, Rep, 72).

Scotland: Rough, Donachie, Kennedy, Buchan, Forsyth, Rioch, Hartford, Gemmill, Souness, Dalglish, Jordan.

Holland: Jongbloed, Suurbier, Rijsbergen (Wildschut, 44), Poortvliet, Krol, Jansen, Neeskens (Boskamp, 10), R Van de Kerkhof, Rensenbrink, W Van de Kerkhof, Rep.

Ref: Linemayr (Austria).

(22) September 20. European Championship Qualifier. Austria 3 (Pezzey, 27, Schachner, 48, Gemmill, og, 64), Scotland 2 (McQueen, 65, A Gray, 77).

Scotland: Rough, Kennedy, Donachie, Gemmill, McQueen, Buchan, Dalglish, Hartford, Jordan (Graham, 61), A Gray, Souness.

Austria: Fuchsbichler, Sara, Obermayer, Strasser, Pezzey, Weber, Jara, Prohaska (Oberarcher, 87), Schachner, Kreuz, Krankl.

Ref: Michelotti (Italy).

(23) November 23. European Championship Qualifier. Portugal 1 (Alberto, 29), Scotland 0.

Scotland: Rough, Kennedy, F Gray (Donachie, 65), Narey, McQueen, Buchan, Dalglish, Hartford, Jordan (Wallace, 78), Gemmill, Robertson.

Portugal: Bento, Artur, Coelho, Alhinho, Alberto, Pietra, Oliveira (Eurico, 82), Alves, Costa (Sheu, 45), Nene, Gomes.

Ref: Dolflinger (Switzerland).

1979

(24) May 19. Home International Championship. Wales 3 (Toshack, 28, 35, 75), Scotland 0.

Scotland: Rough, Burley, F Gray, Wark, Hegarty, Hansen, Dalglish, Hartford, Wallace (Jordan, 55), Souness, Graham.

Wales: Davies, Stevenson, J Jones, Phillips, Dwyer, James, Mahoney, Yorath (Nicholas, 89), Flynn, Curtis, Toshack.

Ref: Partridge (England).

(25) June 2. Friendly. Scotland 1 (Graham, 85), Argentina 3 (Luque, 33, 60, Maradona, 70).

Scotland: Rough (Wood, 45), Burley, Munro, Narey, Hegarty, Hansen, McGarvey, Wark, Dalglish, Hartford (F Gray, 70), Graham.

Argentina: Fillol, Olguin, Tarantini, Villaverde (Trossero, 21), Passarella, Barbas, Gallego, Maradona, Valencia, Houseman (Outes, 56), Luque.

Ref: Partridge (England).

This was Diego Maradona's first international goal for his country. As Alan Rough recalls: 'He had so much time on the ball you could tell he was going to be one of the greats. Even though the Scotland supporters were disappointed with the result, there was no real disgrace in losing to the reigning world champions and the Tartan Army cheered the little man off the pitch at the end.'

(26) June 7. European Championship Qualifier. Norway 0, Scotland 4 (Jordan, 32, Dalglish, 39, Robertson, 43, McQueen, 55).

Scotland: Rough, Burley (Hegarty, 45) (Wark, 70), Munro, Burns, McQueen, Gemmill, Graham, Dalglish, Jordan, Hartford, Robertson.

Norway: Jacobsen, Pedersen (Hansen, 67), Karlsen, Grondalen, Aas,

Kordahl, Albertsen, Thunberg (Svendsen, 75), Mathisen, Larsen-Okland, Thoresen.
Ref: Nielsen (Denmark).

(27) September 12. Friendly. Scotland 1 (Hartford, 4), Peru 1 (Leguia, 85).
Scotland: Rough, Jardine, Munro, Souness, McQueen, Burns, Cooper (Graham, 65), Wark (Cooper, 70), Dalglish, Hartford, Robertson.
Peru: Acasuzo, Gastulo, Olaechea, Chumpitaz, Diaz, Mosquera, Velasquez, Cueto, Leguia, Labarthe (Ravello, 46), La Rosa.
Ref: Courtney (England).

(28) October 17. European Championship Qualifier. Scotland 1 (Gemmill, 75), Austria 1 (Krankl, 40).
Scotland: Rough, Jardine, Munro, Souness, McQueen, Burns, Wark, Gemmill, Dalglish, Graham (Cooper, 61), Robertson.
Austria: Koncilia, Sara, Mirnegg, Hattenberger, Pezzey, Weber, Jara, Prohaska, Schachner (Steinkogler, 80), Kreuz, Krankl (Hintermaier, 89).
Ref: Palotai (Hungary).

(29) November 21. European Championship Qualifier. Belgium 2 (Van der Elst, 7, Voordeckers, 46), Scotland 0.
Scotland: Rough, Jardine, Munro (F Gray, 61), Hansen, Miller, Wark, Souness, Hartford, Robertson, Dalglish, Jordan (Provan, 61).
Belgium: Custers, Gerets, Millecamps, Meeuws, Renquin, Cools, Van Moer (Verheyen, 66), Vandereycken, Van der Elst, Ceulemans, Voordeckers.
Ref: Zade (Soviet Union).

(30) December 19. European Championship Qualifier. Scotland 1 (Robertson, 55), Belgium 3 (Vandenberg, 18, Van der Elst, 23, 29).
Scotland: Rough, Jardine, McGrain, Wark, McQueen, Burns, Dalglish, Aitken, Johnstone, Bannon (Provan, 45), Robertson.
Belgium: Custers, Gerets, Millecamps, Meeuws, Martens, Cools, Van Moer (Plessers, 49), Vandereycken, Van der Elst, Ceulemans, Vandenbergh (Dardenne, 73).
Ref: Aldinger (W Germany).

1980

(31) March 26. European Championship Qualifier. Scotland 4 (Dalglish, 6, A Gray, 26, Archibald, 68, Gemmill, pen, 84), Portugal 1 (Gomes, 74).

Scotland: Rough, Burley, McGrain, Narey, McLeish, Hansen, Dalglish (Archibald, 48), Souness, A Gray, Gemmill, Robertson (Provan, 75).

Portugal: Bento, Teixeira, Coelho, Simoes, Alberto, Frasco (Manuel, 77), Eurico (Sheu, 35), Nene, Costa, Jordao, Gomes.

Ref: Wurtz (France).

(32) May 21. Home International Championship. Scotland 1 (Miller, 26), Wales 0.

Scotland: Rough, McGrain, Munro, Hegarty, McLeish, Miller, Strachan, Gemmill, Dalglish, Jordan, Weir (Aitken, 84).

Wales: Davies, Price, J Jones, Yorath, Pontin (Phillips, 45), Nicholas, Giles, Flynn, Thomas, James, Walsh (Rush, 15).

Ref: Wilson (N Ireland).

(33) May 24. Home International Championship. Scotland 0, England 2 (Brooking, 8, Coppell, 75).

Scotland: Rough, McGrain, Munro (Burley, 62), Hegarty, McLeish, Miller, Strachan, Aitken (A Gray, 53), Dalglish, Jordan, Gemmill.

England: Clemence, Cherry, Sansom, Thompson, Watson, Wilkins, Brooking, McDermott, Coppell, Johnston, Mariner (Hughes, 71).

Ref: Garrido (Portugal).

(34) May 28. Friendly. Poland 1 (Boniek), Scotland 0.

Scotland: Rough, Burley (Dawson, 80), McGrain, Narey, McLeish, Miller, Strachan, Aitken, Dalglish (Weir, 56), Archibald, Jordan (Brazil, 45).

Poland: Mowlik, Dziuba (Ciolek, 69), Barczak, Zmuda, Janas, Nawalka, Palasz (Terlecki, 45), Kmiecik, Lipka, Lato, Boniek.

Ref: Josifov (Bulgaria).

(35) May 31. Friendly. Hungary 3 (Torocsik, 4, 65, Kereki, 69), Scotland 1 (Archibald, 67).

Scotland: Rough, McGrain, Dawson, Narey, McLeish, Miller, Brazil (Strachan, 45), Archibald, Dalglish, Gemmill, Weir.

Hungary: Meszaros, Paroczai (63), Balint, Garaba, Toth, Pasztor, Kereki, Nyilasi, Csongradi, Kiss (Esterhazy, 68), Torocsik.
Ref: Baumann (Switzerland).

(36) September 10. World Cup Qualifier. Sweden 0, Scotland 1 (Strachan, 72).
Scotland: Rough, McGrain, F Gray, Miller, McLeish, Hansen, Dalglish (Archibald, 80), Strachan, A Gray, Gemmill, Robertson.
Sweden: Hellstrom, Gustavsson, Borg, Bild, Arvidsson, Ramberg, Erlandsson (P Nilsson 80), Nordgren, Ohlsson, T Nilsson, Sjoberg.
Ref: Wohrer (Austria).

(37) October 15. World Cup Qualifier. Scotland 0, Portugal 0.
Scotland: Rough, McGrain, F Gray, Souness, Hansen, Miller, Strachan, Dalglish, A Gray, Gemmill, Robertson.
Portugal: Bento, Gabriel, Laranjeira, Simoes, Pietra, Eurico, Manuel, Chalana (Sheu, 60), Costa, Jordao (Nene, 60), Fernandes.
Ref: Redelfs (W Germany).

1981
(38) February 25. World Cup Qualifier. Israel 0, Scotland 1 (Dalglish, 54).
Scotland: Rough, McGrain, F Gray, Souness, McLeish, Burns, Wark (Miller, 46), Dalglish (A Gray, 69), Archibald, Gemmill, Robertson.
Israel: Mitzrahi, Machines, A Cohen, Y Cohen, Bar, Shum, Ekhoiz, Sinai, N Cohen, Tabak, Damti.
Ref: Andreco (Romania).

(39) March 25. World Cup Qualifier. Scotland 1 (Wark, 75), Northern Ireland 1 (Hamilton, 70).
Scotland: Rough (Thomson, 80), McGrain, F Gray, Burns (Hartford, 77), McLeish, Miller, Wark, Archibald, A Gray, Gemmill, Robertson.
N Ireland: Jennings, J Nicholl, Nelson, O'Neill, C Nicholl, Cochrane, McClelland, McCreery, McIlroy, Hamilton (Spence, 78), Armstrong.
Ref: Scheurell (W Germany).

(40) April 28. World Cup Qualifier. Scotland 3 (Robertson, 21, pen, 30, pen, Provan, 53), Israel 1 (Sinai, 58).
Scotland: Rough, McGrain, Gray, Hansen, McLeish, Souness, Provan, Archibald, Jordan, Hartford, Robertson.
Israel: Mitzrahi, Machines, A Cohen, Y Cohen, Bar, Shum, Ekhoiz, Sinai, Zeituni, Tabak, Damti.
Ref: Haroldsson (Iceland).

(41) May 16. Home International Championship. Wales 2 (Walsh, 17, 20), Scotland 0.
Scotland: Rough, Stewart, Gray (McGrain, 45), Burns, McQueen, Miller, Hartford, Narey, Jordan, Provan, Graham (Sturrock, 85).
Wales: Davies, Price, J Jones (Boyle, 71), Phillips, Ratcliffe, Harris, Nicholas, Flynn, Thomas, James, Walsh (Charles, 76).
Ref: Donnelly (N Ireland).

(42) May 23. Home International Championship. England 0, Scotland 1 (Robertson, 64, pen).
Scotland: Rough, Stewart, Gray, McGrain, McLeish, Miller, Provan (Sturrock, 80), Archibald, Jordan, Hartford (Narey, 72), Robertson.
England: Corrigan, Anderson, Sansom, Wilkins, Watson (Martin, 45), Coppell, Robson, Hoddle, Rix, With, Woodcock (Francis, 45).
Ref: Wurtz (France).

(43) September 9. World Cup Qualifier. Scotland 2 (Jordan, 20, Robertson, 83, pen), Sweden 0.
Scotland: Rough, McGrain, F Gray, Wark, McLeish, Hansen, Provan, Hartford, Dalglish (A Gray, 70), Jordan, Robertson.
Sweden: T Ravelli, A Ravelli, Borg, Fredriksson (Hallen, 45), Hysen, Erlandsson, Bjorklund, Borjesson, Svensson, Larsson, Sjoberg.
Ref: Daina (Switzerland).

(44) October 14. World Cup Qualifier. Northern Ireland 0, Scotland 0.
Scotland: Rough, Stewart, F Gray, Souness, Hansen, Miller, Strachan (A Gray, 76), Hartford, Dalglish, Archibald, Robertson.
N Ireland: Jennings, J Nicholl, Donaghy, J O'Neill, C Nicholl, McCreery, Brotherston, M O'Neill, McIlroy, Hamilton, Armstrong.
Ref: Butenko (Soviet Union).

1982

(45) February 24. Friendly. Spain 3 (Munoz, 26, Castro, 83, pen, Gallego, 86)), Scotland 0.

Scotland: Rough, McGrain, F Gray, Souness, McLeish, Hansen, Strachan (Archibald, 54), Wark, Brazil, Dalglish, Hartford.

Spain: Arconada, Camacho, Gordillo, Alesanco, Tendillo, Sanchez, Alonso, Munoz (Gallego, 54), Lopez, Saura, Satrustegui (Castro, 45).

Ref: Thomas (Holland).

(46) March 23. Friendly. Scotland 2 (F Gray, 13, pen, Dalglish, 21), Holland 1 (Kieft, 30).

Scotland: Rough, McGrain, F Gray, Narey, Evans, Miller, Dalglish (Brazil, 45), Archibald (T Burns, 45), Jordan (Strachan, 62), Bett, Wark.

Holland: Van Breukelen, Van der Korput, Spelbos, Metgod, Krol, Hovenkamp, Peters, Rukaard, Muhren, Tahamata, Kieft.

Ref: Hunting (England).

As Alan Rough recalls: 'This was a notable game, as much for the size of the crowd as anything else. Although it was only a friendly, staged in the middle of the football season, the attendance at Hampden Park was an incredible 71,848. Obviously, the Tartan Army were gearing up for another World Cup trip abroad.'

(47) May 24. Home International Championship. Scotland 1 (Hartford, 7), Wales 0.

Scotland: Rough, Stewart (Burley, 72), Gray, Souness, Hansen, Narey, Dalglish, Brazil, Jordan (Sturrock, 72), T Burns, Hartford.

Wales: Davies, B Stevenson, J Jones, Marustik, N Stevenson, R James, Nicholas, Flynn (Thomas, 75), Curtis (Walsh, 75), L James, Rush.

Ref: McKnight (N Ireland).

(48) May 29. Home International Championship. Scotland 0, England 1 (Mariner, 13).

Scotland: Rough, Burley, McGrain, Hansen, Evans, Narey, Dalglish, Souness, Jordan (Sturrock, 63), Hartford (Robertson, 45), Brazil.

England: Shilton, Mills, Sansom, Thompson, Butcher, Coppell, Wilkins, Robson, Brooking, Keegan (McDermott, 56), Mariner (Francis, 45).

Ref: Redelfs (W Germany).

(49) June 15. World Cup. Scotland 5 (Dalglish, 18, Wark, 29, 32, Robertson, 73, Archibald, 80), New Zealand 2 (Sumner, 55, Wooddin, 65).
Scotland: Rough, McGrain, Gray, Hansen, Evans, Souness, Strachan (Narey, 83), Dalglish , Wark, Brazil (Archibald, 53), Robertson.
New Zealand: Van Hattum, Hill, Malcolmson (Cole, 77), Almond (Herbert, 66), Elrick, Mackay, Cresswell, Boath, Rufer, Sumner, Wooddin.
Ref: Socha (United States).

(50) June 18. World Cup. Scotland 1 (Narey, 18), Brazil 4 (Zico, 33, Eder, 48, Oscar, 64, Falcao, 86).
Scotland: Rough, Narey, Gray, Souness, Hansen, Miller, Strachan (Dalglish, 65), Hartford (McLeish, 69), Archibald, Wark, Robertson.
Brazil: Waldir Peres, Leandro, Oscar, Luisinho, Junior, Cerezo, Falcao, Socrates, Eder, Zico, Serginho (Paolo Isidoro, 82).
Ref: Calderon (Costa Rica).
This was Alan Rough's 50th cap and, as he recalls: 'I couldn't have asked for anything more than to celebrate that achievement against the mighty Brazil, who were simply wonderful footballers, in love with the game. The atmosphere inside the Estadio Benito Villamarin was fantastic, and although there were only 47,000 supporters, it sounded like 100,000, especially when David Narey broke the deadlock with his famous goal and the Tartan Army, however briefly, began to dream of miracles.'

(51) June 22. World Cup. Scotland 2 (Jordan,15, Souness, 87), Russia 2 (Chivadze, 60, Shengelia, 84).
Scotland: Rough, Narey, F Gray, Souness, Hansen, Miller, Strachan (McGrain, 71), Archibald, Jordan (Brazil, 71), Wark, Robertson.
Russia: Dasaev, Sulakvelidze, Bessonov, Chivadze, Demianenko, Borovsky, Baltacha, Bal, Blochin, Gavrilov, Shengelia (Andreev, 89).
Ref: Rainea (Romania).

1985

(52) September 10. World Cup Qualifier. Wales 1 (Hughes, 13), Scotland 1 (Cooper, 81, pen).

Scotland: Leighton (Rough, 45), Gough, Malpas, Aitken, McLeish, Miller, Nicol, Strachan (Cooper, 61), Sharp, Bett, Speedie.

Wales: Southall, J Jones, Van der Hauwe, Phillips, Ratcliffe, R James (Lovell, 80), Jackett, Nicholas, Thomas (Blackmore, 83), Rush, Hughes.

Ref: Keizer (Holland).

This booked Scotland's passage to the play-offs for the 1986 World Cup, but that fact was completely overshadowed by the death of Jock Stein. As Alan Rough recollects: 'The whole circumstances were too ghastly to contemplate and the expressions on the faces of the Scottish fans later on in the evening, as the news began to sink in, reflected the fact that, for once, football really had been a matter of life and death. The colour drained from all our faces and it was one of the worst experiences of our lives.'

1986

(53) April 23. Rous Cup. England 2 (Butcher, 27, Hoddle, 39), Scotland 1 (Souness, 57, pen).

Scotland: Rough, Gough, Malpas, Souness, McLeish, Miller, Nicol, Aitken, Bannon, Nicholas (Nevin, 58), Speedie.

England: Shilton, Stevens, Sansom, Butcher, Watson, Hodge (Steven, 60), Wilkins (Reid, 45), Hoddle, Waddle, Francis, Hateley.

Ref: Vautrot (France).

This was the final fling for Rough on Scotland duty and although he enjoyed significant success against England during his career, this wasn't the swansong he had envisaged. 'They were developing into a very good team and what strikes me about looking at the line-up is the number of players who finished up at Rangers – you have Gary Stevens, Terry Butcher, Trevor Steven, Ray Wilkins and Mark Hateley in there, and it reflected the ambition of Graeme Souness to mould a European-class side. Mind you, he was assisted by the fact that English clubs were banned from Europe, following the disaster at the Heysel stadium in 1985.'

Substitutions

v Chile (Santiago) 2–4, 15 June 1977, replaced by Jim Stewart (Kilmarnock) at half-time. Friendly.

v Argentina (Hampden) 1–3, 2 June 1979, replaced by George Wood (Everton) at half-time. Friendly.

v Northern Ireland (Hampden), 1–1, 25 March 1981, replaced after 80 minutes by Billy Thomson (St Mirren). Home International Championship.

v Wales (Ninian Park), 1–1, 10 September 1985, came on for Jim Leighton at half-time. World Cup qualifier.

CLUB RECORD

(1) Signed for Partick Thistle on 20 October 1969 and made 624 appearances for the Maryhill-based club. The highlight was his part in the 1971 League Cup victory over Celtic at Hampden Park.

Partick's day of Hampden glory

23 October 1971: Partick Thistle 4 (Rae, Lawrie, McQuade, Bone), Celtic 1 (Dalglish).

Partick: Rough, J Hansen, Forsyth, Glavin (Gibson), Campbell, Strachan, McQuade, Coulston, Bone, Rae, Lawrie.

Celtic: Williams, Hay, Gemmell, Murdoch, Connelly, Brogan, Johnstone (Craig), Dalglish, Hood, Callaghan, Macari.

(2) Signed for Hibernian on 26 October 1982, for a £60,000 fee and made 175 appearances, including gaining a loser's medal in the 1985 League Cup final against Aberdeen, who won 3–0. Alan was freed by the Edinburgh club, after an acrimonious relationship with Alex Miller, on 19 April 1988.

(3) Signed up with the Orlando Lions and played in America for four months.

(4) Signed for Celtic on 9 August 1988, as understudy/back-up to Pat Bonner and Ian Andrews. He made seven appearances, five

in the league, one in the League Cup and one on the European Cup against Honved (the only European opposition who Alan faced in his 20-year career).

(5) Signed for Hamilton Academical on 23 December 1988. Freed 12 May 1989.

(6) Signed for Ayr United on 26 September 1989. Freed 15 May 1990.

(7) Joined Glenafton Athletic as player-coach on 18 July 1990. Alan became manager on 27 September 1990. Quite apart from his team's successes in the OVD Junior Cup, he once came on as an outfield substitute for Glenafton in January 1992, whereupon he missed a penalty, before scoring with a header from a corner kick. The following year, his side won the Junior Cup by beating Tayport at Firhill.

Glanafton's Junior Cup final triumph

23 May 1993: Glenafton Athletic 1 (Millar), Tayport 0. Firhill. Glenafton, coached by Alan Rough, had already beaten Islavale 4–0 in a replay (the first game finished 2–2), Camelon (1–0), Neilston (1–0), Cambuslang Rangers (1–0), Dundee St Joseph (0–5), Lesmahagow (2–1) en route to the final. Their team: Kelly, Lowe, Gray, Rennie, Kennedy, McFarlane, Walker, Archer, Brown, Montgomery, Millar.

(Information supplied by the SFA Football Museum)

INDEX

Aberdeen 124–5, 134, 165, 171–3
  European Cup-Winners' Cup final vs Real Madrid 168
Airdrie 50–1
Airs, Gordon 111–12
Aitken, Roy 195, 222, 225, 264
Albiston, Arthur 197
alcohol 52–5, 58–60, 95–6, 143–4
All-Stars team 215
Allan, Thomson 43
Allofs, Klaus 195
Ally's Tartan Army 93, 97, 143
Alta Gracia 99–101, 117–19
Amoruso, Lorenzo 267
Andrews, Ian 208, 215, 219, 221, 223–4, 226, 227–8
Archer, Ian 120
Archibald, Steve 136, 148, 191, 226
Arnesen, Frank 190
Arok, Frank 185
Arrol, John 43
Auchinleck Talbot 238, 242–4, 245–6
Auld, Bertie
  curfew 39–40
  Partick Thistle 33–43
  pie throwing 35
  rule by fear 34–5
  training 72–3, 161
  volatile 124
Australia and sport 262–3
Avon Glen XI 9
Ayr United 19–20, 231–2

Ayrshire Juniors 243

Baillie, Rodger 120
Barry, Lucy 270–1
Barry, Maggie 270–1
Barry, Sarah 270–1
Batista, Jose 198
Battiston, Patrick 156
Baxter, Jim 49, 59–60, 127, 199
Beedie, Stuart 201
Bell, Ian 238, 245–6, 248
Benitez, Rafael 208
Bento, Manuel 136
Berggreen, Klaus 190
Best, George 199, 215–17
Bett, Jim 176
Bhoys Against Bigotry 263
Bingham, Billy 192
Black, Eric 172, 173
Blackley, John 62, 169–70, 200, 203
Blyth, Jim 117
Bone, Jimmy 23,-4, 27
Bonner, Pat 215, 219, 227
Boys' Brigade XI 8–9, 13, 21
Brattbakk, Harald 220
Bremner, Billy 57–9
Bremner, Dan 57
Brooking, Trevor 77
Brown, Craig 183
Brown, Sandy 12
Brown, Tom 247–50
Buchan, Martin 90, 114
Burns, Kenny 96, 135
Burns, Tommy 222, 247
bus parades 26, 96–7, 246
Butcher, Terry 50, 193–4, 202, 222

Callaghan, Ralph 165
Cameron, Andy 93, 104
Cameron, Ewen 256–70
Campbell, David 129
Campbell, Jackie 26, 41
Celtic 264, 267
  benefit from Rangers spending 194
  European Cup final 1967 vs Inter Milan 17
  European Cup vs Honved 223–4, 226–7
  joining 215–16, 219
  leaving 228
  6000th league goal 45
  supporters on bus 22
Cerezo 86
Channon, Mick 69–71, 77, 79
Chisholm, Gordon 170
Chivadze, Aleksandr 155
Clemence, Ray 64, 69, 71, 77
Clyde 268
Collins, Gerry 255
Collins, John 171, 206, 239
Conn, Alfie 52
Connery, Sean 146
Cooke, Charlie 56, 61
Cooper, Davie 141, 179–80, 184
'Copenhagen Five' 57–9
Coppell, Steve 94
Cormack, Peter 162–3, 209
Cosgrove, Stuart 234
Coulston, Frank 16, 23
Coventry City 35

Cowan, Steve 170
Cowell, Simon 45
Coyne, Tommy 225
Craig, Tommy 62, 74, 169, 200, 203, 215, 224–5, 226–7
Crawford, Jay 253–5, 256
Cubillas, Teofilo 102–4
Cueto, Cesar 103
Cumnock Rangers 238

Daily Record 111–12
Dalglish, Kenny 6, 21, 25, 42, 52, 56–7, 63, 69–71, 73–4, 76–9, 82, 86–7, 90, 99, 108–9, 136, 137, 140, 148, 150, 157
Dalry 247
Danaifar, Iraj 107
Deans, Dixie 45
Delaney, Mike 201
Dempsey, Jim 228–30
Dickie, Jimmy 9, 11, 28, 51, 271
Dillon, Mark 210–14
Donald, Dick 168
Drinkell, Kevin 221
Duffy, Neil 12, 16
Dundee 50
Durie, Gordon 170, 203
Durrant, Ian 222

East Fife 167
Eder 153
Elkjaer-Larsen, Preben 190
England, Mike 177, 181
Eskandarian, Andaranik 107
Evans, Gareth 226
Evans, Ian 73

Falcao 153
Falkirk 20–1
Fencamfamin 105
Ferguson, Alex 10, 53, 124, 134, 168, 174, 175, 178–81, 183–8, 192, 270
Ferguson, Barry 267
Ferguson, Ian 222
Ferguson, Taylor 92
Fitzsimmons, John 105–6
Flo, Tore Andre 220
Flower of Scotland 97, 109
football
    African nations 12

arguing with referees 89–90
Bosman ruling 46
contract system 38
myth of employment for old players 232–3
player's wages 40–1
post-playing careers 46–7, 232–3
see also Scottish football
'football perm' 92–3
Forsyth, Alex 27, 33
Forsyth, Tam 69, 71
Fraser, Cammy 194
Fricker, Werner 217
Fulton, Mark 202

Gajdusek, Miroslav 87
Gemmell, Tommy 21
Gemmill, Archie 69, 70, 84, 86, 98, 99, 103, 109–10, 129, 136
    goal for Scotland vs Holland 109, 269
Giggs, Ryan 199
Gilfinnan, John 5
Glavin, Ronnie 20, 23, 27, 33
Glenafton Athletic 238–51, 254–5
Goal Post, The [public house] 127–9
goalkeepers
    aggressive forwards 19–20
    Bento, Manuel 136
    blaming others 13–14
    challenge of role 4–5
    defending corners 65
    free kicks 64–5
    school games 4–5
    Schumacher, Harald 156
    Scottish international 67–8
    short 13
    unbeatable feeling 136
    Wembley graveyard for Scottish goalkeepers 76–7
Goram, Andy 172, 190, 208, 260–1
Gough, Richard 190, 222, 260–1
Graham, Arthur 57–9, 131
Graham, Jimmy 30

Grandstand 186–7
Gray, Andy 72, 94, 136, 140, 149, 174
Gray, Frank 62, 63
Greig, John 164–5
Gretna 268
Grey, Ian 246
Guardian Media Group 256

Haffey, Frank 51–2, 76
Halley, Archie 249–50
Hamilton Academicals 228–30
Hamilton, Willie 138–9
Hampden Babylon 234
Hansen, Alan 45–6, 63, 134, 150, 154–5, 171, 200
Hansen, John 20, 27
Harkness, Willie 99–100
Harper, Joe 57–9, 95–6, 100, 114–15, 125
Hartford, Asa 6, 42, 52, 74, 82, 87, 150
Harvey, David 43, 55, 62–3
Hay, Davie 23
Hearts 268
Hepburn, Ray 120
Hewitt, John 173
Hibernian
    decline in standard 202–3
    finances 51
    leaving 210–11
    management 165
    Miller, Alex 203, 205–11
    Premier League 1986 vs Rangers 200–2
    Scottish League Cup final vs Aberdeen 171–3
    testimonial 209
    training 166–7
    transfer from Partick Thistle 161–5
Higgins, Tony 37–8
high scoring matches
    5–1 Celtic vs Partick Thistle 45
    5–1 England vs Scotland 1975 69
    5–1 League Cup 1970–71 Partick Thistle vs St Johnstone 20

5–1 Rangers vs Celtic 221
5–2 Scotland vs New Zealand 1982 147–9
5–5 Rangers reserve XI vs Partick Thistle reserve XI 10
6–6 Scotland vs Northern Ireland friendly 192–3
7–0 Celtic vs Partick Thistle 45
7–2 Aberdeen vs Patrick Thistle 28
9–3 England vs Scotland 52
10–0 at half-time Boy's Brigade match 13
12–0 Celtic reserve XI vs Partick Thistle reserve XI 10
Hill, Jimmy 78
Holmes, David 193
Holton, Jim 56
homosexuality 84
Honved 31–2, 223–4, 226–7
Houston, Bobby 34, 126
Hughes, Emlyn 77
Hughes, Mark 177, 179, 199
Hull City 28, 161
Hunter, Tom 241–2

I Have a Dream 143–4
Ingram, Dixie 19–20

Jack, Steve 255–6, 260
Jardine, Sandy 90
Johnston, Mo 188, 191–2
Johnston, Willie 83, 89, 104–7, 121
Johnstone, Derek 54, 92, 95–6, 100, 114–15, 126
Johnstone, Jimmy 21, 23, 49, 59–60, 78, 134, 184, 199, 232–3
Jones, David 89
Jordan, Joe 42, 52, 54, 69, 77, 87, 89, 103, 106–7, 109, 111, 139, 141, 149, 154

Kane, Paul 206, 229
Kean, Sammy 16
Keane, Roy 268
Keegan, Kevin 69, 71, 77

Keizer, Jan 180
Kennedy, Stewart 55, 76
Kennedy, Stuart 104, 108
Kilmarnock 247–8
Kirkwood, Billy 201
Knightswood Secondary School 3, 8
Knox, Archie 183

Lambie, John 255
Larsson, Henrik 50, 220
Laudrup, Brian 50, 220
Laudrup, Michael 190
Law, Denis 49
Lawrie, Bobby 23–4
Leicester City 208
Leighton, Jim 171–2, 174–9, 187, 190
Lennon, Neil 265
Lennox, Bobby 21, 45
Lerby, Soren 190
Lincoln Avenue team 5–6, 8–9
Livingstone 50
Lorimer, Peter 44

Macari, Lou 21, 25, 82, 99, 103–4, 113, 121
MacDonald, Alex 62
MacLeod, Ally
    attacks on home and family 108
    Ayr United 231–2, 235
    McDonald, Trevor 106–7
    optimist 75
    reaction to World Cup 1978: 112–13, 118–19
    replaced 130
    training methods 101–2
    World Cup enthusiam 90, 91–2
MacLeod, Faye 91, 92
Maradona, Diego 130–1
Martin, Fred 76
Mason, Billy 244–5
Masson, Don 70, 77, 83, 90, 94, 96, 98, 99, 103, 105, 108, 121, 200
McAdam, Tom 194
McAvennie, Frank 184, 188, 191–2, 221, 225, 227, 264
McCarthy, Mick 222
McCloy, Peter 126

McCluskey, George 201–2
McCluskey, Pat 54, 57–9
McCoist, Ally 136, 171, 208, 221–2
McCorquodale, Donald 232, 235, 270
McCulloch, Eddie 51, 161
McDonald, Trevor 106–7
McGrain, Danny 69, 92, 94, 148
McLean, Tommy 126
McLeish, Alex 134, 168, 172
McNamara, Jackie 165, 206
McNeill, Billy 23, 78, 127, 215–16, 219–21, 226, 227–8, 264
McParland, Dave 15–16, 19–20, 23–4, 27, 33, 161
McPherson, Davie 208
McQuade, Denis 20–1, 23–4, 27, 36
McQueen, Gordon 42, 62, 73–4, 76–8, 84, 94, 112, 149
McStay, Paul 197, 222
Menotti, Cesar 84
Middlesborough 161
Millar, John 244–5, 246
Miller, Alex 203, 205–10, 225, 230
Miller, Willie 134–5, 154–5, 168, 172, 190, 197, 200
Miss United Kingdom 47
Miss World 47
Molby, Jan 190
Motherwell 51
Munante, Juan 103
Munro, Iain 131
Munro, Ian 52
Murdoch, Bobby 45
Murray, David 219

Narey, David 135, 148, 151
Neal, John 161
Neill, Terry 28, 161
New Cumnock 241, 246
Newtongrange Star 242
Nicholas, Charlie 190, 260–1
Nicol, Steve 196, 198
Nil By Mouth 263
Nisbet, Scott 222

Niven, George 12
Northern Ireland terrorist organisations 141–2

O'Rourke, Jimmy 165–7, 169
Oakbank Hospital 1–8, 5
Oakbank school 3
Oblitas, Juan Carlos 103
Old Anniesland 9
Oldham Athletic 208
Ole Ola 143
Olsen, Jesper 190
Ondrus, Anton 72
Orlando Lions 210–16, 229
Ormond, Willie 44, 55–6, 60–3, 69–71, 74–5
Oscar 153
OVD Scottish Junior Cup 240, 246–7, 250

Panenka, Antonin 72
Parlane, Derek 52
Partick Thistle
  Auld, Bertie 33–43, 72–3, 124, 161
  break up of successful team 27, 33
  camaraderie 12
  cherished institution 17
  League Cup 1971 campaign 18–28
  League Cup 1971 final vs Celtic 18, 21–8
  leaving and transfer to Hibernian 161–2
  Malaysia and Indonesia tour 29–30
  McCulloch, Eddie 11–12
  OVD Scottish Junior Cup Final 246
  players representing Scotland 27
  reserve team 9–10
  Scottish Cup 1978: 124–5
  Scottish Cup 1979: 126
  scouting 9
  Sighthill Amateurs 11–12, 14, 18, 51
  supporters' repartee 125–6
  'team that kicks together sticks together' 20

testimonial season 129
UEFA Cup 1971–72 vs Honved 30–2
under-16 XI 11
'Pass the chicken' 213
Passarella, Daniel 83, 85, 87
Paterson, Craig 194
Pernia, Vicente 83–4
Petras, Ladislav 72
Petrov, Stilian 259
Pettigrew, Willie 62
Phipps, Colin 214
Provan, Davie 141
Puerto Banus 157
Purdie, David 231
Puskás., Ferenc 31

Rae, Alex 23–4, 26
Rae, Gordon 173, 209–10, 226
Rangers 50, 126, 164–5, 193–4, 219
  European Cup-Winners' Cup final 1967 vs Bayern Munich 18
  supporters 263–7
Real Radio 13, 120, 255–70
Rensenbrink, Rob 108
Rep, Johnny 108, 110
Rioch, Bruce 69, 70, 94, 98, 103
Riseth, Vidar 220
Rivelino 86
Robertson, B A 143
Robertson, John 137, 139–41, 144, 148, 149
Rough [AR grandfather] 1
Rough, Alan
  ability at part-time club queried 72–3
  amputation possibility 1–8, 271
  Auld curfew 39–40
  best Scotland player on South American tour 86
  Celtic contract 220–1
  challenged by Argentine police 100
  childhood 1–9
  corners training 149
  debut for Celtic vs Dundee 225

debut for Hibernian vs Celtic 167
debut for Orlando Lions vs Miami 212
debut for Partick Thistle vs Morton 19
debut for Scotland as substitute vs Romania 55–7
debut for Scotland vs Switzerland 62–4
debut on radio 255
'fashion icon' 92–3
50th international 151–2
final international as substitute 194–6
final international match 158
financial affairs 15, 129, 229, 233–5
first involvement with radio 253–4
'football perm' 92–3
hairstyle 92–3
Hibernian contract 207, 209
illnesses 85
injuries and accidents 1–8, 85, 138–9, 142, 167–8, 222–3
international career summary 200
'man with the perm' 92–3
never considered self world-class 51
no fear of failure 22–3
only player not booked for Hibernian vs Rangers fighting 201
Partick Thistle contract 38, 42, 45–6, 124, 126
playing strengths 64
playing weaknesses 64
public house 'The Goal Post' 127–9
recall for Scotland 173–5
retirement from football considered 237
retirement not anticipated 158–9
retirement planning 173

saved by supporters
from scandal 58
Scotland vs Wales
1976: 73–4
shoplifting accusation
233–4
sports shop 229
sunburn 29–30, 146,
186
United States of
America 211–18,
229
white socks 137–8
World Cup after-
thoughts 199–200
World Cup poor
memories 117–18
Rough, Alan [AR son] 210,
234, 271
Rough, Jean [AR mother]
7, 21, 67, 101
Rough, Michelle [AR wife]
93, 210, 215, 223,
234–5, 270
Rough, Robert [AR father]
1, 7, 14–15, 31, 67
Roxburgh, Andy 183
Rush, Ian 179

St Johnstone 20
Sash, The 265, 266, 267
Schumacher, Harald 156
Scot FM 254–5
Scotland
international standard
49
magical mystery tour 75
media relationship 120
politics and social life
123
under-18s 52–3
under-23s 42, 54, 57,
63
vs Argentine 80, 83–4,
130–1
vs Australia 183–7
vs Austria 129
vs Brazil 80, 85–6
vs Chile 80–3
vs Czechoslovakia
72–3, 87
vs England 69–71,
76–80, 140–1
vs Iceland 174–6
vs Israel 136–8, 139–40
vs Northern Ireland
138–9, 141–2

vs Northern Ireland
friendly,
Albuquerque 192
vs Portugal 135–6, 142
vs Sweden 135, 141
vs Wales 88–90, 176–81
World Cup 'kings of
wishful thinking'
156
World Cup inevitability
of disappointment
43–4
Scotland – Home
International
Championships
1976–77: 67–71
1976: 73–4
1977–78: 94
1977: 75–80
1979 129–30
1985: 174–6
Scotland the Brave 97
Scotland World Cup –
1974 West Germany
42–4
vs Brazil 44
vs Yugoslavia 44
vs Zaire 44
Scotland World Cup –
1978 Argentine
Johnston, Willie 104–7
pre-season South
America tour 80–6
preparations 91–102
qualifying matches
72–5, 87–90, 86–90
reception on return
114–16
1000th goal scored in
World Cup 108
vs Holland 108–11
vs Iran 107, 119, 200
vs Peru 102–4, 200
Scotland World Cup –
1982 Spain
corners training 149
Germany vs France 156
Italy vs Brazil 156
Portugal acclimatisa-
tion 145
preparations 131,
134–42
qualifying matches
135–42
vs Brazil 149–54
vs New Zealand 147–9
vs Russia 154–6, 200

Scotland World Cup –
1986 Mexico
afterthoughts 198–200
qualifying matches
183–7
telephone call restric-
tions 189, 192, 196
vs Denmark 190, 195
vs Germany 194–6
vs Uruguay 197–8
Scott, Brian 120
Scottish Executive 262–3
Scottish FA
accommodation for
team 99
bonus payments for
World Cup
successes 94–5,
99–101
'Copenhagen Five' 57–9
life bans 57–9
pre-World Cup parade
96–7
reaction to World Cup
1978: 121
telephone call restric-
tions 101, 189, 192,
196
Scottish football
alcohol 52–5, 58–60,
95–6, 143–4
anything possible
268–9
competitive edge 12–13
foreign players 49–51
impact on Scottish life
75
obesity 262
Old Firm pressure 220
optimism 1970s 61–2
sectarianism 261,
263–7
Scottish Junior football
238–51
Scoular, Archie 5, 9
Seamill Hydro 242
sectarianism 261, 263–7
Serginho 153
Sharp, Graeme 174, 185–7,
191–2, 195–7
Sheffield Wednesday 35
Shengelia, Ramaz 155–6
Shilton, Peter 64
Sighthill Amateurs 11–12,
14, 18, 51
Sinclair, John Gordon
143–4

sleeping pills 85, 105–6
Small, Roy 52–3
Smith, Bobby 165
Smith, Charlie 40–1
Smith, Walter 127, 183, 185–7, 261–2
Sneddon, Alan 225
Socrates 152
Sotogrande 145, 157
Souness, Graeme 42, 50, 52, 54, 63, 77, 108–9, 118, 135, 154, 156–7, 188–9, 191, 193–4, 196–7, 200–2, 219
Speedie, David 178, 85–7
sports administrators failings 82–3
stadiums
    Hampden Park 69, 171–3
    Maracana 85–6
    Wembley 77–80
Stallon, Molly 162
Stanton, Pat 163, 165–7, 168–9
Stark, Billy 172, 173, 227
Stavin, Mary 47
Steele, Jimmy 137, 175
Stein, Jean 174
Stein, Jock
    alcohol 53–5
    core values 181–2
    death 180–1
    disciplined approach 158
    gamesmanship dislike 140
    master planner 131, 138
    meticulous preparation 144–7
    punishment system 132–4
    recall of AR for Scotland 173–5
    Scotland manager 130–1, 134–42, 173–81
Scotland vs Wales 178–9
Scottish Cup final vs Partick Thistle 25
    tributes 184–5
Steven, Trevor 50, 193
Stevie [blind caller] 260
Stewart, George 165, 167, 169
Stewart, Jim 43, 82
Stewart, Rod 191
Strachan, Gordon 134, 135, 147–8, 150, 154, 168, 195, 198–9, 259
Strachan, Hugh 26, 41
Stringer, Madeleine 47
Sturrock, Paul 197
Sumner, Steve 148
Sunday Mail 165
Sunderland 35
'Super Caley Go Ballistic, Celtic Are Atrocious' 18
supporters
    anti-English 68
    confidence 62
    enjoyment 91, 93–4
    gallows humour 120
    mood swings 116
    reaction in Argentine 104
    saved Rough from scandal 58
    Scotland vs England 1977: 78–80
    sectarianism 263–7
    World Cup 1978 91, 93–4, 97
    World Cup enthusiam 87, 88
Symon, Scot 15

Tabak, Beni 139
Tartan Army *see* supporters

Tartan Army [gang] 2
Tayport 240
Thomas, Mickey 179
Thompson, Arthur 127–8
Thomson, Billy 139, 142
Thordarsson, Teitur 176
Thornton, Willie 10, 15
Timpany, John 238, 241, 243
Top of the Pops 143
Toshack, John 73–4, 89, 129

United States of America 211–18

Vance, Billy 10
Venglos, Josef 73
Vogts, Berti 258, 261–2
Voller, Rudi 195
Vossen, Peter van 220

Walker, Andy 222, 227
Walker, Ernie 99–100, 137
Walters, Mark 221–2
Wark, John 130, 139, 148
Waugh, Kenny 162–4, 207
We're On the March with Ally's Army 87
Weir, Mickey 202, 206
Wilkins, Ray 221–2
Williams, Evan 23
Wilson, Bob 76–7, 187
Wohrer, Franz 135
Wood, George 130, 132, 157–8
Wooddin, Steve 148
Woods, Chris 50, 193–4
Wurtz, Robert 89–90

Young, Bill 256
Young, Willie 52, 54, 57–9, 244

Zico 86, 87, 152–3, 211